Contemporary Diplomacy in Action

Contemporary Diplomacy in Action

New Perspectives on Diplomacy

Edited by
Professor Jack Spence, Dr Claire Yorke and
Dr Alastair Masser

I.B. TAURIS

I.B. TAURIS
Bloomsbury Publishing Plc
50 Bedford Square, London, WC1B 3DP, UK
1385 Broadway, New York, NY 10018, USA
29 Earlsfort Terrace, Dublin 2, Ireland

BLOOMSBURY, I.B. TAURIS and the I.B. Tauris logo are
trademarks of Bloomsbury Publishing Plc

First published in Great Britain 2021

Copyright © Jack Spence, Claire Yorke and Alastair Masser, 2021

Jack Spence, Claire Yorke and Alastair Masser have asserted their right under the
Copyright, Designs and Patents Act, 1988, to be identified as Editors of this work.

For legal purposes the Acknowledgements on p. xvi constitute
an extension of this copyright page.

Cover design: ianrossdesigner.com
Cover image © [top] Tomohiro Ohsumi/Getty Images; [middle]
SAUL LOEB/AFP/Getty Images; [bottom] Eze Amos/Getty Images

All rights reserved. No part of this publication may be reproduced or transmitted
in any form or by any means, electronic or mechanical, including photocopying,
recording, or any information storage or retrieval system, without prior
permission in writing from the publishers.

Bloomsbury Publishing Plc does not have any control over, or responsibility for,
any third-party websites referred to or in this book. All internet addresses given in
this book were correct at the time of going to press. The author and publisher
regret any inconvenience caused if addresses have changed or sites have
ceased to exist, but can accept no responsibility for any such changes.

A catalogue record for this book is available from the British Library.

A catalog record for this book is available from the Library of Congress.

ISBN: HB: 978-1-8386-0462-2
PB: 978-1-8386-0461-5
ePDF: 978-1-8386-0464-6
eBook: 978-1-8386-0463-9

Typeset by Integra Software Services Pvt. Ltd.

To find out more about our authors and books visit www.bloomsbury.com
and sign up for our newsletters.

Contents

List of contributors	vi
Preface *Professor Jack Spence OBE*	x
Foreword *Professor Myles Wickstead CBE*	xiii
Acknowledgements	xvi
List of abbreviations	xviii

Introduction: Contemporary diplomacy in action
Professor Jack Spence, Dr Claire Yorke and Dr Alastair Masser 1

1 The globalization of insecurity and the new imperative for cooperation *Dr Alastair Masser* 11

2 Engaging with proxy groups and indirect state influence in Ukraine and Syria *Dr Samir Puri* 29

3 Approaches to strategic resets in diplomacy: The case of the Fifth Marquess of Lansdowne *Dr Andrew Ehrhardt* 53

4 The Middle East and North Africa in the twenty-first century: An analysis of social media impact and corresponding diplomatic trends *Negah Angha and Inga Kristina Trauthig* 77

5 Defining environmental interest: Identity, discourse and American engagement with global environmental frameworks *Dr Harris Kuemmerle* 99

6 Diplomacy and domestic populations *Dr Thomas Colley* 121

7 'Information War' – The Russian strategy that blends diplomacy and war *Dr Ofer Fridman* 143

8 Social movements, diplomacy and relationships of trust *Dr Francesca Granelli* 165

9 Embody, empower and relate: Emotions in international leadership *Dr Philippe Beauregard* 187

10 Gender and diversity in diplomacy *Ambassador Dr Bonnie Jenkins* 209

Conclusion *Professor Jack Spence, Dr Claire Yorke and Dr Alastair Masser* 219

Select bibliography 224
Index 232

Contributors

Negah Angha is a PhD Candidate in the Department of War Studies at King's College London. Her research interests include the role of religion, conflict and peacebuilding in the Middle East and North Africa, as well as ethical practices and local conflict resolution techniques in Sufi communities in the diaspora and MENA region. Negah is currently on a sabbatical from the US Department of State where she represented the United States on complex bilateral and multilateral negotiations; advised on issues related to the UN, peacekeeping, sanctions, counter-terrorism, and anti-corruption, and coordinated international donor and assistance efforts in MENA and South Asia.

Dr Philippe Beauregard has a PhD from Laval University and is now a postdoctoral researcher at the Otto Suhr Institute for Political Science, part of Freie Universität Berlin. He has received a 2019 Postdoctoral Fellowship of the Social Sciences and Humanities Council of Canada. His work focuses on international cooperation and leadership, the role emotion and cognition in international politics, and international security, especially on the transatlantic community responding to internationalized intrastate conflicts.

Dr Thomas Colley is a Teaching Fellow in the Department of War Studies at King's College London, and a Fellow in the King's Centre for Strategic Communications. His research interests include propaganda, strategic communication and their historical and contemporary use in war. His first book, *Always at War*, investigates the similarities in how British citizens construct stories about war. His current research interests are diverse, encompassing the use of narratives in military strategy, the societal impact of disinformation, contemporary insurgency and the utility of social media data. In 2017, Dr Colley was awarded KCL's 'Rising Star' Teaching Excellence Award.

Dr Andrew Ehrhardt is a postdoctoral fellow with the Centre for Grand Strategy at King's College London. His doctoral thesis focused on the role of the British Foreign Office in the creation of the United Nations. A native of New Orleans, Louisiana, Andrew is a graduate of King's College London and the University of Texas at Austin.

Dr Ofer Fridman is Lecturer in War Studies at King's College London and the Director of Operations at the King's Centre for Strategic Communications (KCSC). His main research interests include: strategic communications, military strategy and transformation, civilian casualties in armed conflicts, Russian military culture and strategy. His recent publications are *Enemy Civilian Casualties: Politics, Culture, and Technology* (Lexington Books, 2019); *Russian 'Hybrid Warfare': Resurgence and Politicisation* (Oxford University Press, 2018); and *Hybrid Conflicts and Information Warfare: New Titles, Old Politics* co-edited with Vitaly Kabernik and James C. Pearce (Lynne Rienner, 2018). Before embarking on an academic career, Ofer served for fifteen years in the Israeli Defence Forces.

Dr Francesca Granelli is a Teaching Fellow in the War Studies Department at King's College London and a member of the King's Centre for Strategic Communications. Her research interests span trust, language, strategic communications, community cohesion, conflict and revolution. Francesca's book, *Trust, Politics, and Revolution: A European History* (I.B. Tauris, 2019), is the first full length study of the relationship of trust and revolution. Her research disputes the conventional interpretation of revolution as a power struggle between conflicting social forces. She holds a BA (Hons) in Geography and Psychology from the University of Manchester, alongside her MA in International Relations and PhD in War Studies from King's College London. She is a Fellow of the RGS-IBG and the RSA.

Ambassador Dr Bonnie Jenkins is the founder and president of Women of Color Advancing Peace, Security and Conflict Transformation, a non-resident senior fellow at the Brookings Institution, and Chairperson of the Committee on Radioactive Sources, National Academy of Sciences. She previously served as coordinator for threat reduction programs at the Bureau of International Security and Nonproliferation at the US Department of State with the rank of Ambassador, and represented the United States at four Nuclear Security Summits between 2010 and 2016. In January 2021, she was appointed Under Secretary of State for Arms Control and International Security Affairs in the Biden Administration.

Dr Harris Kuemmerle is a researcher specializing in the intersection of climate and environment, political philosophy, and science in society. He completed his PhD in the War Studies and Geography departments from King's College London, with a thesis entitled *The Scalar Hydropolitics of the Indus Basin*, which examined the multi-scalar discursive and ideational considerations embedded within Pakistani international hydropolitics over the Indus River. Currently, he is developing a major project to further interrogate the political and ideational nuances of state participation in, and implementation of, global environmental frameworks across a range of scales and cases.

Dr Alastair Masser is Director of Global Programmes at the Legatum Institute in London. Prior to joining the institute, he spent almost a decade in politics serving latterly as a Special Adviser in two posts under David Cameron. He holds a PhD in War Studies from King's College London, examining UK-Nigerian development and security cooperation during the coalition government. Alastair is an alumnus of the US State Department's International Visitor Leadership Programme (IVLP) and has taught at the Ministry of Defence's Joint Services Command Staff College (JSCSC) at Shrivenham.

Dr Samir Puri is Adjunct Professor at the Johns Hopkins School of Advanced International Studies, and Visiting Lecturer in War Studies at King's College London. His advisory work has included being embedded in the Ministry of Defence's think tank to work on 'global strategic trends', and drafting the Commonwealth Secretariat's 'countering violent extremism' strategy. He previously taught as a full-time lecturer at King's (2015–18). Prior to this he worked at the Foreign Office (2009–15) and began his career at RAND (2006–9). In 2020, his latest book, *The Great Imperial Hangover: How Empires Have Shaped the World*, is published by Atlantic.

Professor Jack Spence OBE retired from the Department of War Studies in 2020 after more than twenty years. He held a variety of senior posts throughout his distinguished long career, including serving as Pro-Vice Chancellor at the University of Leicester, Director of Studies at Chatham House and Academic Adviser to the Royal College of Defence Studies. He served on the Goldstone Commission which investigated political violence as part of South Africa's transition from Apartheid and has lectured widely throughout his career, including at the UK's Joint Services Command and Staff College, the US Defence Intelligence Agency and State Department and South Africa's Department of Foreign Affairs. He was awarded an OBE in 2002 for teaching services to the UK Ministry of Defence.

Inga Kristina Trauthig is a PhD Candidate at the War Studies Department and Research Fellow at the International Centre for the Study of Radicalisation (ICSR) at King's College London. She holds an MLitt in Middle East, Caucasus and Central Asian Security Studies from the University of St Andrews and attended the University of Würzburg and the University of Texas at Austin for her undergraduate studies.

Myles Wickstead CBE is Visiting Professor (International Relations) at King's College London. He has held senior positions in the FCO and DFID, including representing the UK on the Board of the World Bank and as British Ambassador to Ethiopia and the African Union.

Dr Claire Yorke is a writer, researcher and academic. Between 2018 and 2020, she was a Henry A. Kissinger Postdoctoral Fellow and Lecturer at International Security Studies and the Jackson Institute for Global Affairs at Yale University. Her writing and research explore the role and limitations of empathy and emotions in international affairs, diplomacy, leadership and policymaking. She completed her PhD in International Relations in 2018 at the Department of War Studies, King's College London. In 2014, she was a member of the NATO and Atlantic Council Young Leaders Working Group, reporting to the NATO Secretary General. Prior to academia she worked at the Royal Institute of International Affairs and in the UK Parliament.

Preface
Professor Jack Spence OBE

As a key concept in the theory and practice of international relations, diplomacy has a long and impressive history. For Hedley Bull, diplomacy comprised one of the six key institutions essential for the maintenance of what he termed a 'society of states', and an integral part of the international order.[1] The effective conduct of diplomacy has long been based on identifying where the interests of states within that society overlap, and where agreement might be found. It therefore requires a demonstration of certain key values: restraint, civility, patience, empathy and the skilful use of what Sir Ernest Satow characterized as 'tact and intelligence'.[2]

Diplomacy as an institution has always been in a state of near constant evolution as change occurs in the international system, exemplified by Woodrow Wilson's 'open covenants' which laid the groundwork for a new diplomacy in the aftermath of the First World War. An enduring task of diplomacy has been to provide the 'oil' for maintaining and enhancing the machinery of international cooperation at a variety of levels. Diplomats resident in a country – whether ally or adversary – play a key role in assessing the capabilities and intentions of their hosts. They have a broad range of responsibilities, from providing informed and salient commentary on political issues such as leadership changes and forthcoming elections, to identifying potential opportunities for increased cooperation, to resolving disagreements between nations. This combination of virtues emphasizes the civilized nature of the diplomatic enterprise and the sheer intellectual capacity required to make diplomatic activity meaningful and productive while adding significantly to a country's reputation at home and abroad.

The contemporary theory and practice of diplomacy is no different. Nations, their institutions and representatives continue to interact with each other at different times and in different places to assist in the promotion of what is often only a precarious degree of international order. Painstaking diplomacy is vital to such success as might arise; indeed, it might be described as the 'master' institution insofar as it makes possible that depth and range of a multitude of agreements. Such agreements are achievable only if the interests of the parties, though different, overlap. The art of the diplomat, therefore, is to determine this synergy of interests and 'between reason and persuasion to bring the parties to it'.[3]

The fruits of diplomatic activity are omnipresent, and too often taken for granted. Painstaking negotiations have played a decisive role in making the world more interconnected, enabling us to communicate and to travel with relative ease. It is easy to forget that every time we post a letter abroad or board an aeroplane, we are taking advantage of international agreements that have been the result of painstaking negotiation.

This question of the value placed on diplomatic activity has taken on a new significance in the face of sustained public criticism of foreign policymakers of a kind that contrasts sharply with the considerable latitude enjoyed by their predecessors for much of the twentieth century. It also reflects the increasing erosion of the traditional distinction between domestic and foreign policy issues. We see this, for example, in the impact of domestic terrorism on national and social media and the necessary pressure on governments to take action to deter and prevent future attacks.

Nevertheless, it is hard to argue that diplomacy remains anything but essential to modern international relations. Most recently – and most dramatically – it has been the COVID-19 pandemic that has illustrated the fundamental need for effective international cooperation and the importance of diplomacy to our shared security and prosperity. As the scholar Jared Diamond has rightly remarked, 'until the unprecedented danger posed by COVID-19 there has never been a struggle which united all peoples of the world against a widely acknowledged common enemy … COVID-19 is at last providing world citizens with a shared enemy, an unequivocal quick killer, a threat to the inhabitants of every nation'.[4]

These are some of the many new features of diplomacy that require new perspectives. This collection of papers is the product of many years of reflection with students and colleagues in the Department of War Studies at King's College London. I am profoundly grateful to each of the contributors and especially to my two co-editors, Dr Claire Yorke and Dr Alastair Masser, for their efficiency and commitment to bringing this project to life. The two volumes will, I hope, prove a thought-provoking text for students and practitioners of diplomacy, as well as the general reader with an abiding interest in contemporary international studies. It is my belief that diplomacy will need to continue to evolve to meet current and future challenges of the international order, and to sustain the values that underpin it.

Notes

1 Hedley Bull, *The Anarchical Society – A Study of Order in World Politics*, 4th ed. (Basingstoke: Red Globe Press, 2012).
2 Sir Ernest Satow, *A Guide to Diplomatic Practice* (London: Longmans, 1997), 3.
3 Hedley Bull, ibid., 164.
4 Jared Diamond, 'After the Storm', *Financial Times*, 30/31 May 2020, 2.

Foreword
Professor Myles Wickstead CBE

Some elements of diplomacy do not change. The purpose of diplomacy is always to influence, to persuade others to your point of view. 'Your' in this context is traditionally the nation state. How that diplomacy is exercised is very much a matter of perspective; a large, powerful country is able to back its diplomatic efforts with the promise, or threat, of its military capability and the exercise of its 'soft power', which can be economic or cultural. Smaller, weaker countries do not have that luxury, and have to spend more effort building alliances and partnerships with countries in a similar position – or persuading larger countries that they have something to offer which makes them a useful ally.

The nature and practice of diplomacy must necessarily reflect the world in which it takes place. The world order has changed significantly over the past seventy-five years. The end of the Second World War saw the establishment of a new set of global political and economic bodies – the United Nations and the Bretton Woods Institutions – designed to play a key role in developing a more peaceful, stable, prosperous and fairer world. The preamble to the UN Charter refers to the determination of the peoples of the UN 'to promote social progress and better standards of life in larger freedom' and is complemented by the Universal Declaration of Human Rights in 1948.

The international context shifted dramatically with the fall of the Berlin Wall in 1989. It seemed as if the ideological battle had been won and lost forever, and the next quarter of a century did indeed see unprecedented economic growth and political stability. Governance, democratization and human rights took centre-stage, and the key task of diplomacy became to encourage those trends, both in bilateral (country to country) relationships and within the multilateral system. The world came together in the 1990s in fora such as the Jomtien 'Education for All' Conference and the Rio 'Earth Summit' to think about how to address a range of global challenges. The development of information technology and the growth in international trade meant that the world was joined up as never before; globalization had arrived.

Not all aspects of globalization were positive. The attack on the twin towers in New York in September 2001 was an only too vivid illustration of the dangers posed by sophisticated groups operating outside the framework of the nation state; and while there was a significant decrease in conflicts between states, conflicts within states remained a serious and continuing problem – not least as citizens demanded their rights from Governments which often seemed unwilling to concede them. One of the key challenges of diplomacy is whether and how to intervene in such conflicts and ideological struggles (such as the Arab Spring) in which there may be limited strategic interests but where universal media coverage reveals the full horror of repression and humanitarian suffering which is often the consequence of such internal division.

The financial crash of 2008 was another example of the potential downside of globalization, as the serious economic downturn which followed saw ripples across the world – though for many countries not fully connected to that system, notably China and India but many other countries in Asia and Africa too, this was a period of unprecedented growth and increasing prosperity, with hundreds of millions of people being pulled out of poverty. At the same time, economic growth in much of the developed world stagnated. Just as the East/West dynamic of international diplomacy had changed irrevocably in 1989, so the North/South dynamic shifted following 2008. Power leaked from the G7/G8 to the G20, and the emerging economies increasingly flexed their muscles.

What had appeared to be an inexorable advance towards an emerging global liberal international order has come to an abrupt halt over the past five years. The United States has elected a president whose motto is 'America First', and who is pushing the US system of democratic checks and balances to its very limit. Russia seems increasingly keen to return to its pre-1989 status as a global power, and China is determined to be seen as a leading player on the world stage – as indeed it is. Populist leaders elsewhere, such as in Brazil and Hungary, are halting and reversing the trend towards more open, democratic societies. Multilateralism is under serious threat, at a time when internationalism has arguably never been more important.

It has historically been the practice of dictators to conjure up an external threat to their countries in an effort to promote national unity. But we face real and present threats, genuine global challenges, which political leaders must recognize and address, and collaborate with others where this is necessary. In some cases, indeed, it is essential. As we know only too well from the coronavirus pandemic, diseases (like terrorism and threats to the environment) have no respect for national boundaries; putting up shutters or building walls will not keep them out. There is an increasing recognition that climate change represents an existential threat to the world – everyone on it and everything in it. None of us can address these threats alone; we need to work together, and refresh and reinvigorate our international institutions.

We do have a framework within which to address these issues as a global community – the Sustainable Development Goals (SDGs), agreed at the UN in September 2015, grouped around the five P's of People, Prosperity, Planet, Peace and Partnerships (recognizing that civil society and the private sector have important roles to play alongside Governments). It is crucial that we do not turn inwards in these challenging times and look only at our narrow self-interest; we must recognize that working together is the only way in which we will be able to address successfully the global challenges that threaten us and the world in which we live.

So, let us come back to the key focus of this Foreword – which is about the nature and practice of diplomacy. The key objective remains to influence, to persuade others to 'your' point of view. Except that the definition of 'your' has changed. Given the global challenges we all face, it now means the same as 'our'. Not all politicians recognize that, of course – and diplomats have a job to do internally as well as externally. Alongside its traditional roles of building bilateral and multilateral political, security, economic and commercial alliances, contemporary diplomacy must also persuade politicians and citizens in their own countries that internationalism and multilateralism are crucial – and then use all the skills at its disposal help to implement this new global framework for action.

Myles Wickstead CBE is Visiting Professor (International Relations) at King's College London. He has held senior positions in the FCO and DFID, including representing the UK on the Board of the World Bank and as British Ambassador to Ethiopia and the African Union.

Acknowledgements

A co-edited series such as this is a collective effort. These volumes have been many years in the making, and over that time we have benefitted from the kind support and generosity of so many.

Firstly, we owe a huge thank you to all of our brilliant contributors. They have shared their expertise and research in these pages to create a vision of diplomacy that is both eclectic and rich. We would like to offer a special thanks to Professor Sir Lawrence Freedman and Professor Myles Wickstead who brought their experience and expertise to the Forewords, and have been a wonderful source of encouragement throughout this project.

The Department of War Studies at King's College London has been our shared intellectual home. We owe a genuine thank you to all our colleagues in the department for supporting this project, and for cultivating an environment where academics and practitioners can come together to research and understand the intersection of international relations, diplomacy and conflict. The breadth and quality of expertise within the department makes for a unique interdisciplinary environment that combines academic rigour with policy relevance. As part of this, we want to acknowledge the many students in the department whose curiosity, insights and new perspectives on the world continually shape and inform our own work.

Bloomsbury and I.B. Tauris have offered invaluable support and encouragement throughout this process. Special thanks are due to Lester Crook who started us on this journey, as well as to Jo Godfrey, Olivia Dellow and Tomasz Hoskins for all their advice and support. We also wish to thank the reviewers of both volumes, and all those who have offered comments on the various drafts. Their constructive feedback makes our work stronger, although we acknowledge all errors are our own. Sincere thanks are also due to the many practitioners of diplomacy whose candid insights have improved our understanding of the political context in which diplomacy takes place, and which have helped shape the analysis of this book.

Claire and Alastair would like to thank friends and colleagues at the International Security Studies and the Jackson Institute of Global Affairs at Yale University, and at the Legatum Institute respectively who have offered a productive and rewarding environment to complete these books.

They also wish to record a final, and particularly special acknowledgement. Professor Jack Spence has been a doctoral supervisor, mentor, champion and friend to us throughout our academic careers. Yet the unwavering support he has offered us is by no means unique. Many of the contributors have their own stories of his generosity and his mentorship, and he is a beloved figure in the Department of War Studies. His desire to help others is not limited to doctoral students and staff. Jack is known to give out his phone number to undergraduates so they can reach him for help and guidance, and he will collect newspaper clippings and articles to send to those who share their research interests with him. His enthusiasm and love for this topic, as well as his extensive expertise and experience, infuse the whole volume. We are so grateful for his help and for championing and leading this project.

Abbreviations

AFC	Asian Financial Crisis
AFRICOM	Africa Command (US)
ANA	Afghan National Army
AQ	Al Qaeda
AQAP	Al Qaeda in the Arabian Peninsula
ASF	African Standby Force
ATO	Anti-Terrorist Operation
AU	African Union
BBC	British Broadcasting Company
CEO	Chief Executive Officer
CIA	Central Intelligence Agency (US)
CNI	Critical National Infrastructure
COVID-19	Corona Virus 2019
DOS	Department of State (US)
DPR	Donetsk 'People's Republics' (Ukraine)
EU	European Union
FGM	Female Genital Mutilation
GAO	Government Accountability Office (US)
G20	Group of Twenty
G7	Group of Seven
G8	Group of Eight
GDP	Gross Domestic Product
HIV/AIDS	Human Immunodeficiency Virus/Acquired Immunodeficiency Syndrome
HNC	The High Negotiating Committee (Syria)
IAEA	International Atomic Energy Agency
IR	International Relations
ISAF	International Security Assistance Force
ISIL	Islamic State in Iraq and the Levant
ISIS	Islamic State in Iraq and Syria
ISSG	International Syria Support Group

JCCC	Joint Centre for Control and Coordination (Ukraine)
JCPA	Joint Comprehensive Plan of Action
KGB	Komitet Gosudarstvennoy Bezopasnosti (Russian Committee for State Security)
LGBTQ+	Lesbian, Gay, Bisexual, Transgender, Queer, +
LPR	Luhansk 'People's Republics' (Ukraine)
MARPOL	International Convention for the Prevention of Pollution from Ships
MENA	Middle East and North Africa
MI5	The UK Security Service
MP	Member of Parliament
MPLA	The Movimento Popular de Libertação de Angola
NAP	National Action Plan (US)
NATO	North Atlantic Treaty Organisation
NGO	Non-Governmental Organisation
NSA	National Security Agency
NSC	National Security Council (UK)
OAU	Organization of African Unity
OSCE	Organisation for Security and Cooperation in Europe
OWS	Occupy Wall Street
PMSC	Private Military Security Company
PSYOP	Psychological Operation
R2P	Responsibility to Protect
RSSS-I	Reconstruction Security Support Services Iraq
SDGs	Sustainable Development Goals
SF	Special Forces
SIT	Social Identity Theory
SMM	Special Monitoring Mission
SOI	Subject of Interest
TL;DR	Too Long; Didn't Read
SSR	Security Sector Reform
UK	United Kingdom
UN	United Nations
UNICEF	United Nations International Children's Emergency Fund
UNSC	United Nations Security Council
UNSCR	United Nations Security Council Resolution
US	United States

USAID	US Agency for International Development
USSR	Union of Soviet Socialist Republics
WHO	World Health Organisation
WMD	Weapons of Mass Destruction
XR	Extinction Rebellion

Introduction: Contemporary diplomacy in action

Professor Jack Spence, Dr Claire Yorke and Dr Alastair Masser

It is easy to underestimate the extent to which the world has been transformed in the three decades since the end of the Cold War. The advent of America's 'unipolar moment' seemingly cemented the primacy of a Western-dominated international order.[1] Many in the West thus viewed the end of the Cold War as the righteous – and inevitable – triumph of a liberal world order, founded on the twin pillars of democracy and capitalism, and maintained through American military strength and global leadership.[2] This belief fuelled the widespread expectation that such an order would eventually extend to 'encompass all regions of the globe' and that 'shared values and goals would render conditions within states more humane and conflicts between states less likely'.[3]

These expectations proved to be misplaced. The optimism which characterized the end of the Cold War swiftly gave way to uncertainty, as the United States proved itself to be something of an 'ambivalent superpower'.[4] Consequently, American global leadership has been a far from consistent feature of the post-Cold War order, as the United States encountered the 'paradox' of American power, proving itself unwilling or unable to shape international relations unilaterally.[5] Although the number of conventional conflicts between states has decreased, the 1990s witnessed a litany of atrocities resulting from intra-state violence, including genocides in Rwanda in 1994 and Bosnia in 1995. The following two decades were dominated by the threat posed by transnational terrorism, illustrated to devastating effect by the attacks of 9/11. Meanwhile, economic progress was far from universal, and interspersed by major economic shocks, from the Asian Financial Crisis (AFC) after 1997 to the so-called Great Recession which followed the global crisis of 2007–8.

These events served to demonstrate both the inherent interconnectivity and unpredictability of contemporary international relations. The era of American primacy coincided with the era of globalization, which, in the broadest sense, fast became the defining feature of the economic and political relationships between states. Interactions between nation states and their populations, once limited and largely formalized, are now anything but. The era of globalization has served to create an international order more interconnected than ever before, ensuring both opportunities and threats are able to cross national borders with ease. It has also prompted intense debate over the perceived and actual benefits of such interconnectivity, with the anticipated growth in universal prosperity proving elusive for too many. The emergence of populism, exemplified by the unanticipated election outcomes in the United States and UK in 2016, is viewed by many as the inevitable reaction to the inequity of globalization.

These trends have given populations in nations around the world more information, agency and influence in international affairs – technology really has become one of the 'governing concepts of our age'.[6] The impact of the so-called digital revolution has been profound. By 2017, around 50 per cent of the global population had internet access, while two-thirds own a mobile device. An estimated 500 million tweets are sent each and every day via the social media platform Twitter – with President Trump responsible for an average of twenty-six of these – resulting in an unprecedented and unpredictable degree of influence for a company only founded in 2006. Similarly, Facebook, a company launched the same year, today has an estimated value greater than 164 of the 193 members of the United Nations.

For those born during this era of US hegemony, Facebook is arguably a more valuable entity than the UN. Many continue to question the relevance and legitimacy of the international institutions, partnerships and alliances that underpinned much of the post-1945 order. The UN has been subject to a near-endless series of reform, with critics both inside and out acknowledging concerns over its funding, neutrality and ability to deliver on the 'lofty goals' of its founders.[7] President Trump's hostile posture towards NATO has fostered speculation about America's continued commitment to an alliance widely viewed as the cornerstone international security throughout the five decades of the Cold War. Likewise, the European Union, seeming on an inexorable trajectory of inclusion, has been rocked by the departure of Britain.

Today, the international order is undergoing a seismic shift every bit as fundamental as that which followed the Cold War. It is, in short, in flux. The period of US hegemony which characterized the three decades since the end of the Cold War is under increasing challenge from an array of emergent nations eager to assert their economic, military and political power. American pre-eminence is fading, and fast. New, emerging powers are reshaping international relations in the twenty-first century. It is clear we are entering a new era of multipolarity. We are witnessing a major geopolitical shift, one that promises to transform the world as we know it. The fragmenting of this Western-dominated, liberal international order is undoubtedly underway.

The effects of this fragmentation are already being felt. Many of the key normative assumptions underpinning international relations are under challenge, as distinctions which once appeared clear – and inviolable – are diminished; between war and peace, between state and non-state actors, between formal and informal dialogue, between values and interests. This poses significant challenges for governments and those that represent them, as notions of power and legitimacy are no longer limited to those acting in official capacities. Furthermore, though an unprecedented degree of cooperation is required to address a growing array of international challenges, strategic rivalries abound in what some characterize as an increasingly 'zero sum world'.[8]

The changing nature of today's order and the growth in the number of influences upon it poses fundamental questions which lie at the heart of both volumes of *New Perspectives on Diplomacy*: namely how are these profound changes altering the nature of diplomacy, and do they make it more or less relevant to contemporary international relations? Throughout the period since the end of the Cold War, diplomats have been an omnipresent feature of international relations. They have played a leading role in shaping some the most seminal events of the past thirty years, from expediting the release of Nelson Mandela in 1990 to prosecuting the so-called War on Terror which followed the terrorist attacks of 9/11 to engineering the global response to COVID-19 in 2020. The centrality of diplomacy and the diplomats that choreograph it appears to indicate that diplomacy is as indispensable today as ever.

However, the profound geopolitical, technological and demographic changes reshaping international relations will inevitably impact diplomacy, which, as Geoffrey Berridge rightly acknowledges, 'both reflects and reinforces the balance of power'.[9] These changes, which are examined in detail through the analysis contained within both volumes, have ensured that states – and those that represent them – are confronted with a dizzying array of responsibilities. The list of core tasks that now falls under the purview of embassies and consulates has increased exponentially; political work, long seen as the principal function of diplomats, now extends well beyond interaction with host governments to incorporate sustained engagement with their host population. Similarly, economic and commercial diplomacy, once limited to episodic negotiations of bilateral and multilateral trade deals, now requires diplomatic representatives to engage in a near incessant campaign of trade promotion on behalf of their private sectors.

The new and often competing demands upon diplomats are symptomatic of what Ronald Barston describes as the 'widening content' of diplomacy.[10] Today there are more diplomatic actors than ever before, as nations, corporations and peoples vie for influence and attention, while states have more tools at their disposal with which to conduct foreign policy. This widening aperture of influence has given rise to a litany of new sub-disciplines, from oil diplomacy, to sports diplomacy, to digital diplomacy. Yet it is important to acknowledge that these have joined – rather than replaced – the pantheon of diplomatic responsibilities. Longstanding challenges remain. Although the threat of nuclear confrontation was significantly diminished by the collapse of the Soviet Union, the risk of proliferation has increased, with Pakistan and North Korea joining the rank of nuclear powers since the Cold War, and with coercive diplomacy leading efforts to obstruct Iranian efforts to develop nuclear weapons.

The international nature of many of the challenges confronting today's diplomats – from nuclear proliferation to climate change to pandemics, suggests the need for a greater degree of multilateralism. However, despite this apparent imperative for cooperation – and the unique ability of the United States to spearhead it – much of the world has instead regressed into a form of neo-isolationist populism. There has been a concerted shift from statesmen to strongmen, as national interests increasingly trump international concerns. In the United States, the ambivalence highlighted by Henry Kissinger has arguably given way to antipathy, sparking intense debate over America's willingness and ability to continue it leadership of the liberal order.

In the United States as elsewhere, funding for diplomatic activity is declining, despite the mounting importance of diplomacy to our collective prosperity and security. The United States Congress rejected sizeable budget cuts to the US State Department in both 2018 and 2019, totalling 33 per cent and 29 per cent respectively.[11] For some like Ronan Farrow, diplomatic negotiation has been subordinated to a new militarism in what he characterizes as the 'war on peace'.[12] The threats confronting diplomats have been literal rather than metaphorical. Being a diplomat has become more dangerous, with embassies increasingly viewed as targets, along with their staff. This fact was brought home by the death of Christopher Stevens, the US Ambassador to Libya, who was among those killed in the 2012 attack by the Islamist group Ansar al-Sharia on America's consulate in Benghazi.

Stevens's murder illustrated the growing public profile of diplomats in the twenty-first century, something arguably considered a pre-requisite for success. Far from serving quietly as state functionaries, many diplomats enjoy celebrity status as proven 'fixers', exemplified by the role played by George Mitchell in bringing peace to Northern Ireland and by Richard Holbrooke's role as US Special Envoy to Afghanistan and Pakistan between 2009 and 2010. Elsewhere, organizations have sought to recruit celebrities to advocate on behalf of humanitarian causes, using their popularity to help raise the public profile of issues from refugees to climate change, in an effort to galvanize public opinion and pressure governments to act. The profile of diplomats has also evolved to become more reflective of the societies they represent, with women in particular taking on more frontline roles. In the United States, no woman had ever served as the country's leading diplomat prior to the appointment of Madeline Albright as Secretary of State in 1997. Of her six successors, two – Condoleezza Rice and Hillary Clinton – were women, with Rice serving previously as National Security Advisor, and Clinton going on to become the Democratic nominee for president in 2016.

Incidents during both Clinton's tenure at State and her later presidential run exemplified the extent to which the digital revolution has transformed both diplomacy and international relations. The 2010 publication by Wikileaks of over 250,000 classified State Department cables from over 250 of its embassies and consulates around the world amounted to the largest and most damaging leak of correspondence in diplomatic history. Similarly, Clinton's campaign for the presidency was subject to widespread interference from the Russian Federation. The 2020 report from the US Senate Intelligence Committee reported that 'Russian operatives ... used social media to conduct an information warfare campaign ... designed to spread disinformation part of a foreign government's covert support of Russia's favoured candidate in the US presidential election'.[13]

Readers will be able to detect these recurring themes throughout this volume and its counterpart. Specifically, the role of technology as an enabler and multiplier of diplomatic dialogue, the corresponding growth in the influence of non-state actors, as well as the growing influence of public opinion upon the foreign policies of nations. Similarly, the nature of partnerships is evolving towards a more informal, transient and transactional format based as much upon the interests as the values of nations states. Likewise, as the world recalibrates towards a new Sino-American superpower rivalry, we can already detect the increasingly assertive use of diplomacy, namely Washington's emphasis upon 'competitive diplomacy' and Beijing's 'wolf warrior diplomacy'.

Many of the fundamental hallmarks of diplomatic practice remain unchanged; diplomacy can still be characterized by the familiar adage of getting the right people around the table, and the right issues on it. However, contemporary diplomacy is arguably less about shaping events, and more about reacting to them. In this current era of multipolarity and reluctant multilateralism, that is a daunting task. Nowhere is this more apparent in the international response to the coronavirus pandemic. As at 1 February 2021, there have been 102,399,513 confirmed cases of COVID-19, including 2,217,005 deaths, reported to the World Health Organisation (WHO). The only countries yet to report cases are a handful of isolated Pacific archipelagos, from Nauru and Palau.[14]

This project has been motivated by the need to make sense of these changes, and to understand the implications for the conduct of international relations in a new era. To do this we have brought together staff and alumni from King's College London's Department of War Studies which, for over half a century, has been at the forefront of the study of contemporary international relations and the implications for peace and security. We have drawn on the department's network of expertise, from theorists to practitioners, to contribute their insights to this book. It is this breadth of expertise, the range of methodological approaches and differing styles of analysis, which we feel provides a unique contribution to the study of diplomacy at a crucial juncture.

We argue throughout both volumes that diplomatic practice has, inevitably, been altered by this new age. To illustrate how, we have sought to examine some of the many trends, phenomena and events reshaping the diplomatic landscape; from the influences of gender and empathy to the changes in the collection and utilization of intelligence, from the growing influence of small states and non-state actors to the role of ethical considerations in foreign policymaking, from the challenge posed to existing diplomatic norms by malign powers to the role of populism, from the tension between the individual and the state to how we can reapply the lessons of history to today's diplomatic challenges.

This volume, together with its counterpart, provides an assessment of the implications of today's fluid world order on the contemporary practice – and study – of diplomacy. However, both volumes do not seek simply to examine foreign policy and the practice of statecraft but to instead provide insights into the concept of diplomacy and its fundamental role within this changing international order, and the policy and political debates that shape it. It is intended to serve as a continuation of the debates contained in Volume One, illustrating how they are being manifested in the practice of contemporary diplomacy, and highlighting the innumerable array of actors influencing modern diplomacy, from ISIS to Extinction Rebellion (XR). Like its counterpart, it benefits from a broad range of perspectives, including from many contributors with experience of working either in or with governments, as well as a varied number of methodological approaches, from practice theory to comparative analysis.

This volume comprises ten distinct chapters. Individually, they illustrate some of the many trends reshaping today's diplomatic landscape, from how technological innovation has revolutionized diplomatic practice to the impact of the significant growth in the number and influence of non-state actors. Collectively, they provide an insight into the challenges confronting professional diplomats and foreign policymakers seeking to manage the varied and complex relations between states that characterize today's shifting international order.

In Chapter 1, Alastair Masser assesses the rapid evolution of security cooperation, as states are forced to confront an increasingly complex strategic threat environment. He argues that the globalization of insecurity has made collaboration between nation states not only desirable but essential, as recent crises from transnational terrorism, to the global financial crisis, to coronavirus, have demonstrated the irrelevance of notions of statehood to challenges which pay little or no respect to international borders. He suggests that this new threat environment has also upended many of the fundamental normative assumptions that defined concepts of national security, and the international institutions which underpin them.

In Chapter 2, Samir Puri analyses the impact of what he characterizes as the 'twilight of US unipolarity' on the role played by proxy groups in conflict. Using examples from both Ukraine and Syria, he examines how American ambivalence has altered the strategic calculus of proxy actors, as well as the implications for multilateral efforts at conflict resolution. He argues that in both theatres the United States has been effectively sidelined, and that unless Washington is willing and able to impose its will in such complex – and competitive – proxy war scenarios, the end of its unipolarity will be hastened, with profound implications for global stability.

In Chapter 3, Andrew Ehrhardt explores the central role of statesmen in managing pivotal moments of strategic reset. Adopting an applied history approach, he assesses the role played by the Fifth Marquess of Lansdowne in mitigating the innumerable risks to British strategic interests at the turn of the twentieth century. He evaluates Lansdowne's remarkable transformation of British grand strategy, specifically his determination to mollify longstanding antagonists and to forge new alliances to shore up British vulnerabilities, and what lessons this offers to the United States as a global hegemon tasked with managing the inevitability of its own relative decline.

In Chapter 4, Negah Angha and Inga Trauthig explore the impact of the communications revolution, which has outpaced the ability of governments and their diplomatic representatives to react to events. They examine the transformative impact of 'techplomacy' in catalysing popular protests across the Middle East, from the 2009 Iranian uprisings to the 2011 Arab Spring, and the new onus now placed on diplomats to become more effective users of social media. In light of the greater informality and accessibility provided by social media, they ask how traditional diplomatic practice must respond if policymakers are to shape rather than react to events.

In Chapter 5, Harris Kuemmerle analyses the extent to which climate change has come to shape the international diplomatic agenda, through an analysis of the US role in underpinning and undermining the Kyoto and Paris Climate Change Agreements. He discusses the implications for diplomacy of competing environmental identities, as well as divergent understandings of what constitutes national environmental interest. While this issue arguably epitomizes the necessity of effective multilateralism, he suggests that this lack of national and international consensus is hindering efforts to address this fundamental challenge, despite the considerable influence wielded by established political actors such as President Trump or new groups like XR.

In Chapter 6, Thomas Colley assesses public perceptions of diplomacy, and the extent to which these have been democratized by the digital revolution. He adopts a novel approach to this dynamic, exploring the public's understanding of diplomacy in an age where public opinion is playing an increasingly influential role in shaping foreign policy. Using the example of Britain's 2016 referendum on its membership of the European Union, he examines lingering perceptions of the elitism of diplomatic practice, and how the referendum campaign was shaped by narratives of British diplomatic superiority. He argues that such perceptions played a significant role in the outcome, convincing many voters that Britain would be able to secure favourable post-Brexit terms with relative ease.

In Chapter 7, Ofer Fridman assesses Russia's deliberate subversion of diplomatic norms, and how the Kremlin has used misinformation effectively to further its strategic ends. He explores the roots of the Russian approach to war and diplomacy and how 'Information War' has fast become the preferred method by which to achieve desired political goals through a combination of both military and non-military means. Using Russia's seemingly unrelated programme of counter-sanctions and its intervention in the Syrian conflict in

2015 as illustrations, he suggests that both instead exemplify Russia's increasingly strategic conduct of international relations, one that that blends war and diplomacy together to great effect.

In Chapter 8, Francesca Granelli examines the growing importance of contemporary social movements, and the role trust, technology and society play in shaping the international order. She illustrates how these social movements are often better placed to shape public perceptions and, indeed, shift the discourse on single issues from LGBTQ+ rights, to climate justice and conservation. She argues that the growing prominence of social movements has diminished several key distinctions, specifically those between notions of public and private, domestic and foreign, citizen and state. As such, social movements are playing an increasingly influential role in the evolution of diplomacy from traditional and club diplomacy towards public and network diplomacy.

In Chapter 9, Philippe Beauregard examines how the use of emotive language and rhetoric has come to shape the way in which leaders articulate foreign policy to their populations, allies and adversaries. He argues for a more processual conception of cooperation where the role of emotions in shaping notions of power is given greater prominence. Using the example of President Obama's characterization of the ISIS takeover of the Iraqi city of Mosul in 2013, he outlines the necessity for leaders to harness the persuasive power of emotive rhetoric, demonstrating their *representativeness* of their respective populations, their acknowledgement of emotions as a force amplifier, as well as their own morality and humanity.

Finally, in Chapter 10, Bonnie Jenkins examines the extent to which issues of gender and diversity have come to play an increasingly prominent role in the practice of diplomacy. She argues that diplomats must be reflective of the diversity of the societies which they serve if they are to be considered truly representative. She notes, however, that achieving this is about more than simply making a compelling argument for change. Instead, states like the United States must acknowledge the barriers to entry to a career in diplomacy for too many of their citizens, especially women of colour.

Notes

1 C. Krauthammer, 'The Unipolar Moment', *Foreign Affairs*, Vol. 70, No. 1 (1990), 23–33.
2 F. Fukuyama, *The End of History and the Last Man* (New York: Free Press, 1992).

3   H. Kissinger, *World Order* (London: Penguin, 2014), 362.
4   H. Kissinger, *World Order* (London: Penguin, 2014).
5   J. S. Nye, *The Paradox of American Power* (Oxford: Oxford University Press, 2002).
6   H. Kissinger, *World Order* (London: Penguin, 2014), 330.
7   P. Kennedy and B. Russett, 'Reforming the United Nations', *Foreign Affairs*, Vol. 74, No. 5 (September/October 1995), 56–71.
8   G. Rachman, *Zero Sum World* (London: Atlantic, 2010).
9   G. R. Berridge, *Diplomacy: Theory and Practice*, 5th ed. (Basingstoke: Palgrave Macmillan, 2015), 1.
10 R. P. Barston, *Modern Diplomacy*, 5th ed. (New York: Routledge, 2019), 1.
11 'Despite Pompeo's Call for "Swagger," Trump Slashes Diplomatic Budget', *Foreign Policy*, 11 March 2019.
12 R. Farrow, *The War on Peace: The End of Diplomacy and the Decline of American Influence* (New York: W. W. Norton, 2018).
13 United States Senate Committee on Intelligence (2020), *Report of Russian Active Measures, Campaigns and Interference in the 2016 US Election: Volume 2: Russia's Use of Social Media*, 116th Congress, 1st Session, 3.
14 'Which Countries Have Not Reported Any Coronavirus Cases?', *Al Jazeera*, 30 March 2020.

1

The globalization of insecurity and the new imperative for cooperation

Dr Alastair Masser

Today, states face an unprecedented number of threats to their national security. The latter half of the twentieth century witnessed a rapid evolution of the strategic threat environment, and the emergence of a litany of new challenges, many of them unimaginable to the previous generation of policymakers. In the three decades since the fall of the Berlin Wall, this environment has changed – fundamentally. In addition to the threat posed by 'traditional adversaries', the 2019 US *National Intelligence Strategy* lists a dizzying array of 'evolving threats', from the proliferation of weapons of mass destruction (WMD) and cyberattack to transnational terrorism, global pandemics, organized crime and mass migration.[1]

As well as being more diffuse, such threats are arguably now more dispersed. As the number and nature of such threats have increased, so has the ease with which they can be transported across national borders. In many respects, the same advances in technology, transportation and communication that have enabled the globalization of the international economy have also transformed international security. The interconnected nature of the contemporary international order has rendered states increasingly vulnerable to malign actors. Insecurity has, in essence, become *globalized*.

However, there has been a persistent reluctance to examine the implications of this 'obverse side' of globalization.[2] The evolution of the strategic threat environment it has catalysed has challenged many of the state-centric normative assumptions underpinning security policymaking and scholarship. First, it has eroded the fundamental distinction between *national* and *international* security and highlighted the inherent interconnectedness of the contemporary international order. Second, it has rendered cooperation between security actors not only desirable, but essential. Third, as the demands of providing security increase, it has prompted a re-evaluation of the appropriate balance of responsibility between the public and private sector in this *'age of choice'*.[3]

These emerging – and accelerating – trends have exposed the increasingly outmoded nature of the key institutions which underpin today's order, the majority of which reflect the post-war or Cold War balance of power, and the state-based nature of the principal threats to national security. This reality poses fundamental questions about the role of diplomacy in providing stability. Specifically, it remains unclear the extent to which diplomats have adapted to this new environment, and the role they can – and must – play in fostering a greater degree of security cooperation between nations.

This chapter examines this new imperative for security cooperation. First, it examines the foundations of contemporary security cooperation, and describes the cooperation orthodoxy that has historically been a key feature in mounting or deterring aggression within the international order. Second, it analyses how globalization has transformed that orthodoxy, as the interconnected nature of today's order ensures that responsibility for security is increasingly an international, rather than national, concern. Third, it assesses the implications of this *globalization of insecurity* upon the international order, specifically its impact upon the relevance of established notions of 'hard' power, as well as the state's monopoly on the provision of national security. Finally, it explores how this shifting dynamic has created a new imperative for effective – and agile – security cooperation between nation states, as well as between public and private actors.

The foundations of security cooperation

Security cooperation is by no means a new phenomenon. Historically, it has principally taken the form of cooperation between two or more states and has been viewed as a feature of the balance of power, with the principal objective of mounting or deterring aggression within the international order. As such, the concept has been used as a somewhat crude, blanket term to describe various forms of collaboration between nations, and is frequently used interchangeably with a multitude of others, including *coalitions, security communities* and *strategic partnerships*.[4] Such cooperation, often formalized by alliance or entente, was long predicated on a largely rational – if not predictable – concert of nations;

instances of such formal alliances abound, from the Hellenic Alliance of Greek states against the Persian Empire in the fifth century BC, to the creation of the North Atlantic Treaty Organisation (NATO) in 1949.

At their heart, such forms of security cooperation exhibited two common features: first, they were predominantly deterrent in nature; second, they were chiefly in response to state-based, symmetric threats. They can thus be characterized as *deterrent symmetric* forms of security cooperation. NATO, rightly lauded as the 'cornerstone' of international security for its thirty member states, was a key example of a *deterrent symmetric* security alliance.[5] During his 1949 testimony to the US Senate Committee on Foreign Relations shortly after the formalization of the North Atlantic Treaty, former US Secretary of State Dean Acheson was at pains to concur with the statement that 'unless a nation ... contemplates, meditates, or makes plans looking toward aggression or armed attack on another nation, it has no cause to fear this treaty'.[6] However, key features of the Alliance, notably Article 5, were arguably features of collective defence rather than of security cooperation – its advent was predicated on the notion of strategic deterrence of Soviet aggression, rather than as a means of improving the coordination of Alliance nations against it.

Despite their deterrent nature, participation in such forms of security cooperation has posed risks for member states, to both their national sovereignty and their national security. The implications are two-fold: first, nations risk exploitation at the hands of a more powerful partner; second, they risk falling victim to the security dilemma, becoming unintentionally embroiled in a large-scale international conflict as a direct result of their participation in an alliance system designed to deter aggression.[7] Undoubtedly the most infamous example, the entente-alliance system was widely credited with providing a major structural contribution to the outbreak of the First World War. This reality placed an onus on leaders to calculate the risk and reward associated with participation in such forms of deterrent symmetric cooperation.

Inevitably, the states-based foundation of this cooperation orthodoxy placed considerable emphasis on executive agency. The temperament and experience of national leaders, as well as the strengths of relationships between them, all formed a key feature of the security calculus; leaders viewed by allies and adversaries alike as predictable and rational helped uphold the deterrence framework that characterized Cold War-era international relations. Meanwhile, unpredictable and irrational leaders imperilled it, with potentially catastrophic consequences.

The implications of the globalization of insecurity

Definitions of *globalization* vary considerably across both geographic region and academic discipline. The phenomenon has been defined 'in a variety of ways' ranging from liberalization to Westernization, to supra-territorialization.[8] In practice, the term is used to describe the phenomenon by which national economies have become integrated into a global economic system, and the increases in trade, growth and productivity it has catalysed. The results have been transformative, and created a world – and a world order – more interconnected and inter-reliant than ever before. Today, around a quarter of all goods produced worldwide are exported, while services, ideas and innovation now cross international borders swiftly, and with relative ease.[9]

So too can insecurity. Today's globalized world order has dramatically altered the international security landscape. The same logistical, infrastructural and communications platforms that have enabled the rapid growth of international trade can also be exploited by terrorist and organized crime networks, facilitate the spread of pandemics or improve the capabilities of malign state actors. This is perhaps best illustrated by the globalization of the international drugs trade, the value of which has grown exponentially to between $350–500 billion annually, the approximate value of the global oil and gas sector.[10]

Globalization challenges many of the normative assumptions underpinning the notion of security cooperation. While *formal* military alliances such as NATO are still of fundamental importance to international security, examples of more *informal* security cooperation are commonplace, and witnessed across an inexhaustible list including intelligence sharing, border security, counter WMD, counterterrorism, counter narcotics, counterinsurgency, stabilization, cyber, disaster relief, maritime security, airport security, training, personnel exchanges and capability assessments.[11]

Similarly, the distinction between *defence* and *security* has also diminished. This shift has been evident in political discourse, not least in the UK, where 'national security' has seemingly replaced 'defence' as 'the first duty of Government'. More so than ever, discharging this duty requires leaders to assemble the agile suite of capabilities required to protect civilians from security threats at home, rather than harbouring military assets for deployment abroad. In response, the turn of the twenty-first century has witnessed a declining emphasis upon conventional, *hard power* defence capabilities designed to counter such traditional, state-based threats. This has been replaced by a greater balance between 'hard' and 'soft' security capabilities, designed to give nations the requisite flexibility to respond to increasingly opaque and unpredictable threats to national security.

This shift has prompted a greater reliance upon non-military assets such as the police and intelligence services, a development which has, in turn, had an impact on the nature of civil-military relations. The military – notably Special Forces (SF) – now regularly complement civilian security structures, rather than *vice versa*. Furthermore, a greater number of non-state actors are today essential though reluctant providers of national security, from airport security personnel to those responsible for operating elements of nations' Critical National Infrastructure (CNI).

The globalization of insecurity has arguably also served to diminish the significance of economic strength to national security. Historically, economic strength has enabled states to develop and maintain extensive militaries as the most effective means of aggression or deterrence. In today's international order, however, nations are able to compensate for smaller defence budgets by exploiting the interconnected nature of our globalized world. In many respects, the application of 'smart' power can compensate for a lack of 'hard' power, or a reluctance to utilize it.[12] Nowhere has this been more evident than in China's web-enabled industrial espionage against American defence contractors, which has enabled it to close significantly the military-technology gap with the United States.[13]

Globalization has given a new coterie of nations a greater degree of agency in debates on international security, diminishing the distinction between *core* and *peripheral* states. The experiences of African nations in particular are beginning to generate greater interest from policymakers and academics alike, as localized empirical examples of African insecurity such as coups and civil wars are joined by transnational ones, including failed states, terrorism, migratory pressures and the global narcotics trade. Consequently, the days when the debate over African security involved solely Western deliberations over humanitarian intervention are long gone.

Instead, African cooperation in international security is more urgent than ever. Since the cessation of the Cold War, much of the debate surrounding African security focused upon human security; most notably the issues of HIV AIDS and the merits and demerits of the so-called responsibility to protect (R2P) in the face of civil war, famine and genocide. Yet today, African states are an increasingly important partner in confronting transnational security threats. The continent still accounts for a disproportionate number of deaths from political violence and is home to fourteen of the world's twenty most fragile states, while an estimated two-thirds of all cocaine destined for Europe from South America is believed to pass through West African states. In the realm of security as elsewhere, the changing international order means that Africa is no longer a recipient of solutions proffered by international diplomacy, but increasingly a partner in their creation.

The challenges for today's policymakers and diplomats

The question of how best to address and mitigate this complex strategic threat environment preoccupies policymakers around the world. Globalization has inexorably altered the diplomatic landscape and the role of the diplomat within it. Greater integration has thrown up significant risks and opportunities which require effective management, principally at the international level between states themselves.[14] The impact of globalization on the relationships between states has raised the question of whether the tenets of established diplomatic practice remain as effective as in the past and, indeed, whether the concept of diplomacy has itself been re-defined.

The boundaries of diplomacy are 'more porous' than ever before, resulting from a greater number of actors and a consequential weakening of more established state-to-state diplomacy. Indeed, some assert that this increase in the number of diplomatic participants has resulted in the fragmentation of traditional state-to-state diplomacy and its ultimate 'mutation'.[15] Such assertions suggest that the practice of diplomacy is, if not necessarily less relevant to international security, certainly more constrained in terms of its effectiveness.

Yet in practice, diplomats remain the principal representative agents of their governments, placing them at the forefront of this changing security landscape. As such, they are required to negotiate this evolving dynamic, and the challenges it presents. Specifically, how best to identify and manage threats, to rely increasingly on a cohort of unappealing or unreliable partner nations, to manage public expectations of absolute invulnerability, and to do so using institutional structures for cooperation designed for a different strategic environment.

The myriad threats confronting nations pose an obvious challenge for their governments – namely how best to identify and manage threat as they emerge. This has placed a predictable emphasis on the role of intelligence agencies, which have seen their budgets and resources increase. Combined intelligence spending in the UK delivered through the Single Intelligence Account has increased steadily since 2000, while the 2015 Strategic Defence and Security Review committed the government to recruit and additional 1,900 security and intelligence staff across the agencies to 'respond to, and deter those behind, the increasing international terrorist, cyber and other global threats'.[16]

However, the number, severity and nature of these threats are subject to near constant change. In October 2019, the Commissioner of the Metropolitan Police, Cressida Dick, stated that some twenty-four terror plots had been disrupted since April 2017. While sixteen of these were Islamist in nature, eight had been engineered by right-wing groups, with the number of arrests of such extremists rising to its highest recorded level. Similarly, the threat from Northern Ireland-related extremism, long thought to be in decline following the 1998 Good Friday Agreement, has fluctuated, with attacks increasing by almost 80 per cent in a single year between 2009 and 2010.[17] These British experiences of change are reflected around the world.

In response, governments have sought to improve their ability to manage multiple unforeseen threats, by increasing the coordination of the greater number of departments, agencies and personnel now contributing to national security. In the UK for example, this has led to a string of welcome initiatives, from the creation of the National Security Council (NSC) in 2010 to the introduction of a new Fusion Doctrine in 2018, designed, in the words of then Prime Minister Theresa May, to 'ensure that in defending our national security we make better use of all of our capabilities: from economic levers, through cutting-edge military resources to our wider diplomatic and cultural influence on the world's stage'.[18] Although such structures have improved governments' ability to identify and manage threats, the fluctuating nature of today's strategic threat environment inevitably hinders effective long-term prioritization of one over others.

It also requires nations to adopt a more flexible posture towards their security partners. Security cooperation has become increasingly transactional in nature, as nations form and dissolve informal mechanisms to address such unforeseen priorities. This has become a hallmark of the counter-terrorism cooperation that has evolved since 9/11, with all nations around the world required to adhere to new security standards, not least the enhanced screening of air passengers and international maritime cargo.

This more inclusive dynamic has given states less agency in choosing optimum partners. Instead, they are increasingly compelled to cooperate with an array of often less than desirable state actors – partners of necessity, as opposed to partners of choice. Such partners of necessity are typically less preferable for two reasons. First, they are often unreliable, and thus require significant support. Second, they are frequently unpalatable, often in the form of autocratic regimes with questionable human rights records.

The unreliability of such partners presents a host of challenges. Efforts to improve the capability of weaker partners have involved initiatives that acknowledge and address the systemic causes of some forms of insecurity in emanating from poorer nations through a greater emphasis on development. However, the link between poverty and insecurity is somewhat opaque, and the contribution of development assistance to national security unquantifiable. This has led – somewhat confusingly – to concurrent debates over the 'securitization of development' and the 'developmentization of security'.[19]

Nevertheless, the spread of Islamist terrorism across numerous developing nations has made them as much partners in the 'War on Terror' as in the 'War on Poverty'. This was ably illustrated by the rise of the Nigerian terrorist group Boko Haram, who in 2014 overtook ISIS as the world's most deadly terrorist organization, forming the House of Commons Foreign Affairs Committee characterized as 'a new frontline of violent extremism'.[20] While such developments have brought developing nations previously considered peripheral to international security 'in from the margins', it has placed the onus for improving their security capability squarely with others.[21]

This has prompted a strategic reassessment of the deployment of military and security assets. This is demonstrated by the US Department of Defense's establishment of a new regional strategic command, Africa Command (AFRICOM), in February 2007. It has also necessitated a concerted programme of support for national, regional and continental capacity-building initiatives, with examples ranging from the African Standby Force (ASF) to the Afghan National Army (ANA). Such initiatives have catalysed widespread interest in the concept of Security Sector Reform (SSR), designed to improve the capability and management of nation's security apparatus, thus reducing the requirement for external intervention.[22]

Unpalatable partners present nations with altogether different challenges. The cultivation of bilateral relationships with autocratic regimes based on shared security interests is suggestive of an intensely pragmatic approach to foreign policy. Such forms of cooperation therefore undermine notions of a values-led foreign policy promulgated by such regimes' democratic partners. For these nations, such partnerships pose a further political challenge, as the dividends of such collaboration tend to be necessarily secret, while the excesses of their autocratic counterpart are frequently all too public.

Nowhere is this more evident than in Saudi Arabia's controversial status as a 'vital partner' for many nations, including the United States and UK.[23] Security cooperation has fast replaced energy interests as the foundation of such partnerships with Riyadh in the post-war era, intensifying in the period since the 9/11 attacks, despite the revelation that fifteen of the nineteen hijackers were Saudi nationals. Indeed, for the security communities both in Washington and London, Saudi has become an indispensable source of intelligence. In October 2010, Saudi authorities uncovered a plot by al Qaeda in the Arabian Peninsula (AQAP) to detonate two bombs concealed in printer cartridges aboard flight from Yemen to the United States.[24] Such considerations have shaped nations' political dynamic with Saudi Arabia, placing security interests above humanitarian ones. This was exemplified by former UK Prime Minister David Cameron's refusal to condemn Riyadh's decision to execute seventeen-year old Ali Mohammed al-Nimr for his alleged participation in pro-democracy protests during the Arab Spring.[25] Similarly, despite the international condemnation that resulted from the assassination of Jamal Khashoggi in Turkey in October 2018, US President Donald Trump and Secretary of State Mike Pompeo did not raise the issue in their first meeting with Saudi Crown Prince Mohammed bin Salman since the killing the following June.[26]

The public opprobrium generated by such seemingly unpalatable security partnerships reveals another challenge facing today's policymakers and diplomats – namely how to manage public expectations about the degree of security the state is able to provide, and the economic, political and reputational trade-offs involved in providing it. While governments around the world have succeeded in reducing the growing number of threats to national security, they are unable, inevitably, to make such threats obsolete. However, there appears to be little correlation between the public's concern over distinct security threats and their prevalence. Such concerns have disproportionately shaped policymaking in nations like the United States where a 2018 survey indicated that Americans ranked tackling terrorism as the top priority for the Administration and Congress, despite estimates that the actual likelihood of a person living in the United States dying in a terrorist attack over the course of his or her lifetime is 1 in 75,000.[27]

Nevertheless, when such threats materialize, especially those of a terrorist nature, governments are criticized. Despite its instrumental role in foiling seventeen terrorist attacks in almost as many months prior to August 2018, the UK's Security Service (MI5) was heavily criticized for its apparent failure to maintain its surveillance of the ringleader of the London Bridge terror attack on 3 June 2017, in which eight people were killed.[28] Khruam Butt was the listed as a 'subject of interest' (SOI) by MI5 and had been under active investigation from mid-2015 until the time of the attack. However, the operation was twice suspended due to 'resourcing constraints brought on by a large number of P1 [priority] investigations', first from February to April 2016 in the wake of the Bataclan attack in Paris, and for a second time between March and May 2017.[29]

The globalization of insecurity has posed new challenges for the major multinational institutions that underpin today's international order. Specifically, it has challenged policymakers and their diplomats to consider whether such institutions are capable of reacting swiftly enough to rapidly changing requirements for both formal and informal security cooperation. Although such bodies, notably the United Nations, NATO and the International Atomic Energy Agency (IAEA) have found themselves at the forefront of efforts to coordinate international responses to international challenges, their varied performance has prompted vocal criticism from their respective memberships, and illustrated the challenges inherent in cooperation on such a scale.

The UN has been a forum for international discord in recent decades, notably over failure to agree to intervene to end the Rwandan genocide in 1994 or to provide a mandate in support of the invasion of Iraq in 2003. The role of the UN as a forum for security cooperation has been undermined by its determination to be an inclusive body; it has grown from 51 founding members in 1945 to 193 in 2011. As such, member states include several rogue states which pose direct threats to international security, serving as the scene for often bizarre diatribes from autocratic leaders like Muammar al-Gaddafi and Idi Amin, and insisting on holding a minute's silence to mark the death of North Korean dictator Kim Jong-Il in 2011.[30]

In comparison, smaller, more exclusive organizations have arguably proved more successful in coordinating and implementing programmes of security cooperation. Despite enduring a series of at times anguished periods of institutional introspection, NATO managed to redefine its role in post-Cold War international order, moving beyond a listless period of 'constructive ambiguity' to lead the response to 9/11.[31] The so-called War on Terror which followed 9/11 set a new benchmark for institutional security cooperation. The attacks prompted NATO to invoke Article 5 for the first time in the Alliance's history, and to oversee a major multinational troop deployment to Afghanistan in the form of the appropriately named International Security Assistance Force (ISAF).

The new imperative for cooperation

The shifting dynamics that have characterized the globalization of insecurity have created new imperatives for cooperation between states. The complexity of today's strategic threat environment has compelled national governments to pool resources to respond to the greater number of common threats to their collective security. While formal cooperation to counter established state-based threats is still an essential feature, this new imperative has seen a greater emphasis placed on informal forms of cooperation that are characterized by reactive modes of collaboration designed to counter specific non-state threats.

This trend forms part of a 'shifting paradigm' of international security corporation, characterized by a concerted shift from alliance to alignment.[32] This new paradigm challenges normative assumptions over the state's monopoly of the provision of security, as well as the primacy of 'hard power' projection through the deployment of defence assets in support of national security objectives. This offers the potential for a greater role for the private sector, which is able to carry out a large number of security and non-military functions on behalf of the state. In many cases, such as the provision of personnel in support of police operations at major events, this offers the state a more cost-effective option to provide low-level security. In other cases, notably the arena of cyber security, it is the private sector – rather than the state – where the expertise lies, and where innovation occurs. As such, there is now a growing need for states to reassess the potential role for the private sector, and its role in upholding both national and international security.

The rise of the security industry – and particularly of Private Military Security Companies (PMSCs) – has generated significant interest from policymakers, academics and the public alike. It poses fundamental questions, not least over the issue of accountability. While the growth of the security sector is perhaps an inevitable corollary of today's complex security landscape, it also elicits concerns over the ability of the state itself to protect the public. Once described as a 'quiet revolution', the rapid growth of the security sector demonstrates a clear demand for the resources, technology and innovation of the private sector.[33]

Private security personnel now outnumber police in most regions of the world, regardless of their levels of income. Even a decade ago, such personnel outnumbered police by a ratio of 2:1 in the UK and 3:1 in the United States. In Bulgaria, the ratio is closer to 5:1. India's private security personnel now outnumber the army, air force, navy, police and Central Bureau of Investigation combined.[34] Yet as with conventional, 'hard' military power projection, this has not altered a fundamental truth, namely that security – like defence – is available only to those who can afford it.

Such demands have seen even the United States – the world's most powerful and best resourced military – rely heavily upon private contractors. In turn, today's security landscape has become big business. The international security market has grown considerably since the millennium and continues to do so, with growth between 2014 and 2019 anticipated to be between around 11 to 16 per cent.[35] The industry has created significant new commercial entities: Aegis, a private security company founded in 2002, was awarded the Reconstruction Security Support Services Iraq (RSSS-I) contract by the US Department of Defense in 2004 worth $1.3 billion, making it one of the largest security contracts ever awarded.

Therefore, while it remains responsible for *funding* national security, the state no longer has a monopoly on its *provision*. This raises important questions over the nature of civil-military relations, accountability and legitimacy. It requires a fundamental reassessment of the nature of inter-state security cooperation between nations. Such cooperation between states must now be seen as distinct from military cooperation. As the nature of insecurity has evolved to become predominantly asymmetric and kinetic in nature, there is a greater division between what can be characterized as 'soft' security and 'hard' security, as well as what can be considered public and private.

This marks a predictable but important evolution beyond the kind of private sector security architecture provided by PMSCs. Yet it also suggests that states become increasingly reliant upon private security actors in times of public spending constraints: PMSCs themselves first emerged in the United States in response to the reductions in national defence budgets which followed the end of the Cold War in the early 1990s, when it was recognized that shrinking militaries could not meet each and every commitment, and that many of these were not sensitive in nature. Instead, they could be willingly outsourced to private companies.[36]

The advent of PMSCs has fundamentally altered the nature of force projection, not least in the fact that it is no longer monopolized by state actors. While it could be argued that this has long been the case with mercenaries, the use of PMSCs by Western nations such as the United States marks a significant departure from previous practice. Like PMSCs, mercenaries have been much in demand in conflict-affected states, especially in low- and middle-income nations, with implications for regional security, commerce and development far beyond their theatre of conflict; key Tuareg commanders leading the Mali rebellion were known to have received extensive combat experience in Libya, serving as mercenaries for the Gaddafi regime prior to its collapse.[37]

This evolution promises to have a profound impact on states' efforts to foster greater stability within several developing nations which now comprise a new frontline of international security. As elsewhere, such nations have generated commercial interest from the worldwide security industry, as greater stability makes them more attractive investment opportunities, while insecurity creates demand. As the *commercialization of security* has moved beyond PMSCs and mercenaries, it has found fertile ground in insecure territories. Indeed, the growth of the role of the security industry in low- and middle-income states is proportionate to their level of governance and the capabilities and resources of the militaries, police, security and intelligence services.[38] In countries suffering from acute insecurity and devoid of the capabilities they require to confront it, there are abundant commercial opportunities for the private sector. But for such opportunities to be realized – and for the security, commercial and development dividends to materialize – government involvement is not only desirable but essential.

As the nature of insecurity has changed and made security big business, it has offered the prospect of *exporting security*. Historically, such exports were dominated by 'hard' defence exports, known more commonly as 'arms exports', and subject to controversy and state control. Arms exports have long represented something of a fault line within IR, eliciting vigorous debate between Realist, Liberal and Constructivist schools over both their respective merits and demerits. But this is changing. Indeed, the term 'arms exports' is today something of a misnomer, and inadequate to cover the full spectrum of defence and security exports, which now include 'soft' elements as diverse as cybersecurity and training for prison staff.

Trade links – and the role of key strategic exports in particular – have long been a source of leverage, scrutiny, concern and mistrust. Active military support of key allies was a tactical pillar of US foreign policy during the Cold War, with successive administrations arming proxies in a wide array of theatres, from Mobutu Sese Seko in the Congo to the mujahedeen against the USSR in Afghanistan. Consequently, the role of strategic exports in underpinning key relationships between states has received significant attention within IR. The Iran Contra scandal ably demonstrated the impact and political risk inherent in such exports, while arms embargos have been utilized repeatedly as a source of leverage, notably from 1976 against the Argentina junta in response to internal repression, from 1977 against South Africa as a result of Apartheid and from 1989 against China following the Tiananmen Square massacre. Similarly, the illicit trade in key nuclear technologies has enabled nations like North Korea, Pakistan and Iran to seek – and in many cases secure – the bomb.

A greater requirement for governments to involve themselves in trade promotion, coupled with a more complex international security landscape, promises to transform existing notions of security cooperation and the role of both the public and private sectors within it. In an age when states are being required to do more with less to counter threats to national security, an increasing role for the security sector challenges established notions of the state's monopoly over defending its borders, population and national interests.

Conclusion

The comparatively short period since the end of the Cold War has witnessed a fundamental transformation of international relations, and the international security landscape along with it. Although the security challenges that were the hallmark of superpower rivalry between the United States and Soviet Union were numerous and undoubtedly global in scope, they were not *globalized*. The phenomenon of globalization has laid bare the vulnerabilities inherent in the interconnected nature of today's international order. Recent crises, from transnational terrorism, to the global financial crisis, to coronavirus, have all demonstrated the irrelevance of notions of statehood to challenges which pay little or no respect to international borders.

This new strategic threat environment creates an imperative for cooperation among nations states. Nations have been forced to engineer a faster and more nuanced response to the insecurity that confronts them, ensuring that a greater degree of security cooperation between nations is now not just desirable but essential. Threats are simply too numerous, concealed and disparate to be monitored and countered effectively by a single state, regardless of the scale of their resources. The vulnerability of the United States to the 9/11 attacks not only demonstrated the limitations of conventional military power, but also highlighted the challenge involved in monitoring a multitude of security threats in today's state of *persistent conflict*, characterized by low intensity but protracted insecurity.[39]

This new threat environment has upended many of the fundamental normative assumptions which defined concepts of national security, and the international institutions which underpin them. Specifically, it has diminished a series of key distinctions: between *formal* and *informal* cooperation, between *defence* and *security*, between *hard* and *soft* power, between *internal* and *external* threats, as well as between *core* and *peripheral* actors.[40]

Although national security remains the principal responsibility of governments, nations are today more reliant than ever upon partners, from states to the private sector. This process will require them to be more realistic in how they match their resources to today's threat environment, and – crucially – more willing to identify where the private sector can play a role. This new cooperation imperative promises to accelerate the trend towards the use of private contractors in the provision of national security priorities. Beyond filling periodic capability gaps, PMSCs and other private sector entities offer states a new means of wielding influence in the international order, cementing key bilateral relationships, addressing global insecurity and generating revenues.

Today's diplomats are therefore faced with an unenviable challenge: how best to help their nations coordinate the agile, reactive forms of cooperation required to counter the myriad threats to national security. Achieving such a degree of effective coordination will require a greater reliance upon informal means of cooperation, and upon a larger cast of characters than ever before, including those from the private sector. This will require a greater emphasis on a pragmatic approach to diplomatic engagement. In short, such collaboration is likely to be based more upon a synergy of interests than of values. But one thing is certain: effective diplomacy has never been a more indispensable component of national and international security.

Notes

1 US Office of the Director of National Intelligence, *National Intelligence Strategy 2019*, 4–5.
2 Christopher Coker, *Globalisation and Insecurity in the Twenty-First Century: NATO and the Management of Risk* (Oxford: Oxford University Press, 2004), 7.
3 UK House of Lords Select Committee on Soft Power and the UK's Influence, *Persuasion and Power in the Modern World* (London: HMSO, 2014), 25.
4 Thomas Wilkins, '"Alignment," Not "Alliance" – the Shifting Paradigm of International Security Cooperation: Toward a Conceptual Taxonomy of Alignment', *Review of International Studies*, Vol. 38, No. 1 (2012), 53–76.
5 UK Ministry of Defence, *Seven Decades of Security: NATO at 70*, Press Release, 4 April 2019.
6 US Congress (Senate), Committee on Foreign Relations, Hearings on the North Atlantic Treaty, 81st Congress, 1st session (1949).
7 The 'security dilemma' posits that steps taken by nations to enhance their own security, such as entering into alliances or increasing armaments production, can be mistaken as aggressive by potential adversaries. These adversaries then respond in kind, leading to an unintended escalation of tensions. See Richard Jervis, 'Cooperation under the Security Dilemma', *World Politics*, Vol. 30, No. 2 (January 1978), 167–214.

8   Christopher Hughes, 'Reflections on Globalisation, Security and 9/11', *Cambridge Review of International Affairs*, Vol. 15, No. 3 (2002), 421–33.
9   Esteban Ortiz-Ospina and Diana Beltekian, 'Trade and Globalization', *Our World in Data* series, University of Oxford (2014), https://ourworldindata.org/trade-and-globalization
10 Saferworld, *Issue Brief: The Illicit Drugs Trade* (2014), 30.
11 Jennifer Moroney, David Thaler and Joe Hogler, *Review of Security Cooperation Mechanisms Combatant Commands Utilise to Build Partner Capacity* (Washington, DC: RAND, 2013), 18–19.
12 Joseph Nye, 'Get Smart: Combining Hard and Soft Power', *Foreign Affairs*, Vol. 88, No. 4 (July/August 2009), 160–3.
13 'Chinese Theft of Sensitive US Military Technology Is Still a Huge Problem Says Defense Analyst', *CNBC*, 8 November 2017.
14 Donna Lee and Brian Hocking, 'Economic Diplomacy', in R. A. Denemark (ed.), *The International Studies Encyclopaedia* (Oxford: Wiley Blackwell, 2010), 10.
15 Raymond Saner and Lichia Yiu, 'International Economic Diplomacy: Mutations in Postmodern Times', *Discussion Papers in Diplomacy*, Vol. 84, No. 1–31, Clingendael Institute (2003), 2.
16 HM Government, *National Security Capability Review 2018*, 46.
17 UK Intelligence and Security Committee, *Annual Report 2010–2011*, Cm 8114 (London: HMSO, 2011), 10.
18 HM Government, *National Security Capability Review 2018*, 2.
19 See Jonathan Pugh, Clive Gabay and Alison J. Williams, 'Beyond the Securitisation of Development: The Limits of Intervention, Developmentisation of Security and Repositioning of Purpose in the UK Coalition Government's Policy Agenda', *Geoforum*, Vol. 44 (2013), 193–201 and Rita Abrahamsen, 'Blair's Africa: The Politics of Securitization and Fear', *Alternatives: Global, Local, Political*, Vol. 30, No. 1 (January/March 2005), 55–80.
20 UK House of Commons Foreign Affairs Committee, *The UK's Response to Extremism and Instability in North and West Africa*, Seventh Report of Session, 3 Vols., HC86 I–III, Vol. 1, 21 March 2014, 3.
21 Sophie Harman and William Brown, 'In from the Margins? The Changing Place of Africa in International Relations', *International Affairs*, Vol. 89, No. 1 (2013), 69–87.
22 Herbert Wulf, *Security Sector Reform in Developing and Transitional Countries*, Berghof Center for Constructive Conflict Management Occasional Paper (2004), 3.
23 HM Government, *National Security Strategy and Strategic Defence and Security Review 2015*, 39.
24 'Al Qaeda Cartridge Bomb Was Aimed at US', *The Times*, 11 November 2010.
25 'David Cameron Attempts to Defend "Squalid" Deal with Saudi Arabia in Excruciating Interview with Jon Snow', *Independent*, 7 October 2015.

26 'Mike Pompeo Didn't Raise Jamal Khashoggi Murder in Meeting with Saudi King', *The Guardian*, 29 June 2019.
27 Murat Haner, Melissa Sloan, Francis Cullen, Teresa Kulig and Cheryl Jonson, 'Public Concern about Terrorism: Fear, Worry, and Support for Anti-Muslim Policies', *Socius*, Vol. 5 (2019), 1–16.
28 'Coroner Voices Concern over MI5 Tracking of London Bridge terrorist Khuram Butt', *The Times*, 2 November 2019.
29 David Anderson, *Attacks in London and Manchester – March–June 2017: Independent Assessment of MI5 and Police Internal Reviews* (2017), 17–19.
30 'UN Assembly Holds "Minute" of Silence for Kim Jong-Il', *Reuters*, 22 December 2011.
31 Anthony Forster and William Wallace, 'What Is NATO For?', *Survival*, Vol. 43, No. 4 (2001), 107–22.
32 Thomas Wilkins, '"Alignment," Not "Alliance" – the Shifting Paradigm of International Security Cooperation: Toward a Conceptual Taxonomy of Alignment', *Review of International Studies*, Vol. 38, No. 1 (2012), 53–76.
33 Clifford Shearing and Philip Stenning, 'Modern Private Security: Its Growth and Implications', in Michael Tonry and Norval Morris (eds), *Crime and Justice – An Annual Review of Research* (Chicago: University of Chicago Press, 1981), 193–245.
34 Rita Abrahamsen and Michael Williams, 'Security beyond the State: Global Security Assemblages in International Politics', *International Political Sociology*, Vol. 3, No. 1–17 (2009), 2.
35 UK Trade and Investment/Defence and Security Organisation, *UK Defence and Security Export Statistics for 2014* (London: HMSO, 2015), 18.
36 Fred Schreier and Marina Caparini, 'Privatising Security: Law, Practice and Governance of Private Military and Security Companies', Geneva Centre for the Democratic Control of Armed Forces (DCAF) Occasional Paper – No. 6 (2005).
37 UK All-Party Parliamentary Group on Africa, *Security in Africa: An Update* (2012), 16.
38 Abrahamsen and Williams, 'Security beyond the State', 2.
39 Iavor Rangelov and Mary Kaldor, 'Persistent Conflict', *Conflict, Security & Development*, Vol. 12, No. 3 (2012), 193–9.
40 Richard Jervis, 'From Balance to Concert: A Study of International Security Cooperation', *World Politics*, Vol. 38, No. 1 (1985), 58–79, 59.

2

Engaging with proxy groups and indirect state influence in Ukraine and Syria

Dr Samir Puri

Diplomacy has not enjoyed a stellar record in bringing to an end the complex wars that have blighted the last decade. This is not for want of trying, but because of the difficulties faced by diplomatic initiatives that must hack through a tangled undergrowth of proxy wars that have morphed with intractable civil wars. A major complicating factor is the role of proxy armed groups that are deeply embroiled in the fighting, but are one step removed from their patrons, making efforts at conflict resolution especially fraught.

There is nothing new about countries suffering the affliction of a war that is instigated or exploited by outside powers. What is novel during the last decade, if only because of its absence since the end of the Cold War, is the return of genuine geopolitical competition to the world stage. This has unfolded amidst the twilight of an era that began in the 1990s, when the United States and its European allies had greater carte blanche to decide when to intervene militarily abroad, and to choose which sides to back.

The protracted wars in Ukraine and Syria stand as distinct examples of how things have changed. In Ukraine, Russia used its conventional armed forces alongside proxy forces to secure its goals of annexing Crimea in 2014, and stoking a slow-burning war in the Donbas region. The diplomacy surrounding this war has helped to prevent it from escalating but, at the time of writing, has been unable to end the hostilities.

In Syria, the regime of Bashar Assad responded to the Arab Spring protests that began in 2011 with a brutal crackdown. Over time, this escalated into a regional war that has embroiled all manner of state and non-state actor combatants, including the Iranian-backed group Hezbollah, the Russian air force, and Russian private military contractors, all of which have fought to successfully prop up Assad's regime.

Today's proxy wars are shaped by the prevailing geopolitical trend of a relative loss of US global influence to other centres of regional power. While it is true that there is nothing new in getting others to fight on one's behalf, the pertinent questions relate to how this age-old phenomenon presents itself today. This chapter examines the wars in Ukraine and Syria with the following questions in mind. Which proxy forces have featured? What are the implications for modern diplomacy when confronting states that partially or wholly rely on proxies to pursue their war aims? What are the associated implications for multilateral efforts at conflict resolution? And what is novel about the current manifestations of these challenges?

Proxy wars at the twilight of US unipolarity

Speaking in September 2019, the US Defence Secretary Mark Esper bemoaned the fact that neither Russia nor Iran was behaving like 'normal' countries in the international security realm.[1] Setting norms is the preserve of the most dominant countries, but during a time of fluctuating global power balances these norms are inevitably challenged. In years to come, the wars of the 2010's may be looked upon as having set out the terms of recurrent disputes: over which countries have the 'right' to choose local allies when seeking to pursue their national security objectives; and over the legitimacy of different forms of intervention.

Not too long ago, the US government was well acquainted with the temptations and the utilities of engaging in proxy wars. During the Cold War, the probability of a direct conflict between the superpowers declined due to the threat of mutually assured nuclear annihilation. But wars continued to be waged across the developing world, often with a superpower backing one or another faction in Vietnam, Afghanistan, Latin America or elsewhere. As the United States and USSR bid for the allegiances of the newly decolonizing states, arming local allies became the name of the geopolitical game. Each superpower feared that a critical mass of support for their rival in far flung regions might tip the scales of the overall contest.[2] The Cold War was rife with examples of one or the other superpower having its nose bloodied by covert interventions.

The ill-fated Bay of Pigs operation in 1961 remains a notorious instance of US failure, involving CIA support for an uprising of Cuban exiles in a doomed bid to overthrow Fidel Castro's revolutionary regime. Later in the Cold War, in the 1980s, the CIA perfected the formula in Afghanistan when it joined hands with Pakistan to sponsor the Mujahideen guerrillas in their fight against the Soviet Union.

Since then, the tools and technologies of warfare and subversion have advanced in leaps and bounds, not least due to the ubiquity of the internet, which has created new options for online propaganda to shape the narratives around a contentious situation, while at the same time making it much harder to stay covert due to the ease with which digital information diffuses to global audiences. While advanced technologies and the new world they have ushered in draw much attention, there are also important lineages in the art of covert warfare that deserve as much attention. Just compare the CIA's Radio Swan broadcasts that sought to inspire the Cuban insurrection in 1961, and Russia's use of online propaganda to undermine Ukraine's government in 2014. Even if modalities change with the times, subversion and deception are ever present.

However, the most consequential change of all has been in the geopolitical realm, and how the United States has shed the need to engage in covert warfare campaigns. Thanks to the unipolar power it has enjoyed since the end of the Cold War, the United States (and its NATO allies) became accustomed to engaging in overt wars of choice, fighting with their chosen local allies and feeling little need to keep these facts hidden. The United States has felt empowered to sponsor armed groups and factions in civil wars in the name of goals like 'nation building', 'humanitarian intervention' and 'counter terrorism'. By becoming ever more involved in these kinds of military operations, the need for covert action has diminished in favour of openly declared interventions that often had the additional luxury of international mandates from the UN.

Long before the popularization of the term 'hybrid war', a US Army publication in 2002 explained that '*compound warfare* is the simultaneous use of a regular or main force and an irregular or guerrilla force against an enemy'.[3] This concept applied to US support for the Kosovo Liberation Army's war against the Serbian military and paramilitary in 1999, and to when the United States intervened in the Afghan Northern Alliance's war against the Taliban after 9/11. In these operations, US military and intelligence services assisted local groups that performed the bulk of the ground combat. Later, scarred by the ambiguous gains of the *en masse* deployment of its army in Iraq and Afghanistan, the United States defaulted back to deploying lighter footprints and relying on local allies. This was seen in Libya in 2011, as NATO intervened with airpower to help the rebels topple Gadhafi. In another example, under the exigencies of the 'war on terror', France's military intervened in Mali in 2013 to turn the tide against jihadists who were sweeping the country. And the US military has routinely stepped in to help Iraqi and Afghan security forces, as the former faltered against the Islamic State of Iraq and the Levant (ISIL) in 2014, and as the latter reeled during the Taliban's push into Kunduz Province in 2015.

Western states predicated these interventions on the basis of 'partnership' with local actors rather than using 'proxies'. In Russian or Iranian eyes, however, the distinction is unlikely to have been a persuasive one. Bristling at how dominant the United States had been in setting global norms around war and peace, Russia and Iran have each had to bide their time as the era of undisputed US global dominance has played out. To compensate for their weakness relative to the United States, Russia and Iran have each developed their own approaches to proxy warfare.

As the 2010s have progressed, the United States has become less concerned with sustaining multi-year military interventions around the world, and more concerned with guarding its economic pre-eminence from China's rise. This trend was heavily driven by America's exhaustion with its post-9/11 wars. The administration of Barack Obama reduced the momentum of his predecessor George W. Bush's expansive war in Iraq, albeit doing so to briefly escalate the US war effort in Afghanistan. But Obama's strategy was rewarded with only transient gains by the US military against the Afghan Taliban. Later, under the administration of President Donald Trump, US priorities shifted more drastically. Trump has felt no obligation whatsoever to stand by US partners, for example by cutting military and diplomatic support to Syrian Kurdish armed groups in 2019, even after they had engaged in bloody close quarter battles against ISIL, and held ISIL detainees.

Watching these developments with interest, Russia and Iran each have spotted opportunities to grab the low-hanging fruit of greater regional influence. Russia and Iran are very different examples of countries that see their present regional role as incommensurate with their stature and their desire for greater respect. To redress this balance, and to recover the pride they lost during the era of undisputed US unipolarity, they face choices: they can work within the international system, abiding by the norms of its dominant powers and institutions; or, on certain issues, they can subvert the status quo with aggressive foreign policy gambits. In choosing the latter path, the regimes in Moscow and Tehran are nevertheless aware that by episodically defying the United States, they must still assiduously avoid a direct confrontation with its armed forces.

Consequently, Russia and Iran have used proxies and stoked wars in a manner that unfolds below the threshold of a direct state-on-state confrontation. Recently, 'hybrid war' and 'grey zone war' terminologies have become popular for explaining these tactics.[4] These terms refer to governments subcontracting out the dirty work of warfare to its proxies, while accompanying this with subversive measures that aim to confuse and discredit their opponents. Hybrid war is routinely used to explain what is happening at the tactical and operational levels of war. However, at the level of diplomacy and statecraft, it is more instructive to observe how Russia and Iran have integrated their more aggressive gambits into their overall foreign policies.

This has involved the statecraft of hedging: of combining cooperative diplomacy on certain major world issues with violent agitation over others. For example, the year after annexing Crimea, Russia made a vital contribution to the initial success of the 2015 Iran nuclear deal (the Joint Comprehensive Plan of Action – JCPA) alongside the United States and EU states. In another example, Iran used its signature on the nuclear deal as a way to bargain with world powers and to portray itself as a compliant actor, while concurrently endorsing armed groups in Iraq, Lebanon, Syria and Yemen. It is important to contextualize Russian and Iranian proxy wars in this way, since the statecraft of hedging demands something of a diplomatic juggling act: even as proxy wars are waged, active attempts are still made to participate in international affairs, and to avoid total pariah status.[5]

In the eyes of Western governments, this approach carries connotations of deviousness and illegality. Nevertheless, diplomatic challenges abound for the United States and its allies as they seek to expose and counter this activity. Western states can produce intelligence dossiers to validate an allegation of proxy war, and they can muster support for a diplomatic demarche and for sanctions, but to little ultimate avail. Neither private complaints nor public censure has been able to decisively shift the calculus of states like Russia or Iran regarding their respective proxy interventions. In fact, the greater the pressure that has been placed on Russia and Iran, the more stubborn they have become, and the tougher conflict resolution has been in Ukraine and Syria. Such have been the challenges of responding to proxy wars during the twilight of the US unipolar era.

Ukraine's war: The hybridity of diplomacy and deception

This section examines the first five years of the war in Ukraine, which began in 2014. It illustrates the centrality of proxy actors in the onset of the war, in the subsequent conduct of warfare, and how the use of proxies has been used to stymie diplomatic efforts towards conflict management. It is this juxtaposition, between proxy war and the veneer of diplomatic engagement, that has allowed

Russia to stake its claims of authority in Ukraine, and to do so amidst the changing geopolitical tides of eroding US global authority.

The background to the war is best explained in terms of slow burning trends, and an acute moment of crisis. After the dissolution of the USSR in 1991, an independent Ukraine was created next to the Russian Federation. This marked a new chapter in a centuries-long saga of Ukrainians having either lived within or adjacent to different incarnations of Russia's empire, from the tsars until the USSR.[6] In the post-imperial age, Russia's rulers had to accustom themselves to tussling with the West for influence in Ukraine. This tussle culminated in what proved to be a casus belli for war: a political dispute and street protests in the capital city Kiev over whether Ukraine should draw closer to the EU at the expense of its orientation towards Russia.

This drama played out over the winter of 2013–14, leaving Ukraine's civic and political fault lines dangerously open to outside exploitation. For instance, there is great diversity in attitudes across Ukraine: its westernmost and central regions tended to feel greater affinity towards joining the EU; conversely, its easternmost regions retained a greater deference towards neighbouring Russia. And across Ukraine, a general scepticism towards the oligarchic brand of politics being practised in Kiev pervaded. In 2014, these factors contributed to the street protests that forced Ukraine's pro-Russian President Viktor Yanukovych from office, after which he fled to Russia.

Russian President Vladimir Putin's regime interpreted this as a pretext to punish Ukraine. Russia's regime did so by waging a proxy war that sought to turn Ukraine against itself. This involved more than a simple Russian invasion of Ukraine. Even as Russian soldiers and mercenaries crossed the border, there were local people who decided to take up arms against Ukraine's government. Real socio-economic and identity issues were at stake in east Ukraine that had contributed to a local sense of alienation, and exploiting this was essential to Russia's proxy war approach.[7] Ukraine's vulnerabilities acted as a form of kindling onto which Putin's regime could toss a lighted match. Once the fire had ignited, the Kremlin painted the onset of war as a 'separatist' uprising against Kiev's authority.

When war erupted in 2014, the amount of territory that would fall to the Russian-instigated separatist movement could not have been preordained. Nor could the fact that a largely static front line would be drawn across east Ukraine by the year's end. Several Ukrainian cities experienced separatist unrest like Kharkiv, Mariupol and Odessa, the latter being the site of a confrontation at the city's Trade Union House on 3 May 2014 that killed thirty-one people.[8] But it was only the self-proclaimed Donetsk and Luhansk 'People's Republics' where the separatists managed to successfully entrench themselves. Known as the DPR and the LPR, these separatist groups became Russia's proxies. Russian military officer Igor Strelkov's role in organizing the Donbas separatists was notable: 'If our unit hadn't crossed the border, everything would have fizzled out like in Kharkiv, like in Odessa' he later told Russian media.[9]

This was very much an intelligence officer's war, given the nature of Russian proxy backing for the DPR and the LPR. This reflected the principles of Putin's past KGB service writ large – deniability that was achieved via several degrees of separation when executing security operations.[10] Putin publicly sustained the argument that the war was beyond his control and was being waged by local separatists and patriotic Russian soldiers volunteering to fight while on leave. The believability of these arguments proved secondary to the consistency with which they were maintained, and to how quickly Russia could change facts on the ground.

Waging proxy war was an indication not only of Russia's strategic cunning, but also of its weakness as a former superpower that was deniably and hastily securing its national security before it encountered meaningful opposition. Russia seized its main prize with the annexation of Crimea in March 2014. This was ostensibly done to secure Russia's existing Black Sea naval base, which since the USSR's breakup had been leased from Kiev. The seizure of Crimea was a *fait accompli*, achieved without any protracted fighting, and while the international eye was drawn towards the Donbas war where lives were really being lost.

Ukrainian armed forces, caught on the back foot by the outbreak of fighting, moved to a war footing by starting their 'Anti-Terrorist Operation' (ATO) in April 2014. The decision to mount a counteroffensive was one that Kiev's government could scarcely shirk from, having lost a sizeable portion of territory. But the war effort was haphazard, reflecting their lack of battle-readiness. A myriad of 'volunteer battalions' helped in the initial fightback. Some battalions were the armed wings of political movements that had been active in Kiev's street protests, like the Right Sector. Others, like Dnipro-1, were funded by oligarchs, in this case Ihor Kolomoyskyi. These self-starting and self-equipping bands of soldiers bolstered the ranks of pro-Kiev forces. They triumphed in some areas and by July 2014 had retaken cities in the Donetsk region like Kramatorsk and Sloviansk. But the perils of facing Russian-backed forces were illustrated in the battle of Ilovaisk in August 2014, where scores of Ukrainian troops were slaughtered as they attempted to break out of an encirclement.[11]

In the manner of a gambler, Putin's regime had seen a window of opportunity to intervene in Ukraine and seized what it could at the very start of the war – perfectly in tune with the Clausewitz dictum that 'war most closely resembles a game of cards'.[12] After its early gains, Russia continued to wage a limited proxy war, the contours of which were partly drawn by the self-imposed limits of its superficially deniable methods, and by the persistent need to avoid a hypothetical major intervention by Western powers on behalf of Ukraine.

War and peace processes

Even a limited war runs the risk of escalation. On 17 July 2014 it seemed as if the situation was spiralling out of control when a passenger plane, Malaysian Flight MH-17, was shot down as it flew over east Ukraine. In the immediate aftermath of this tragedy, claim and counter-claim were thrown between the governments in Moscow, Kiev and the West. The Russian state denied culpability and obfuscated the matter, despite it being evident that Russian-backed separatists had been shooting down Ukrainian military aircraft and helicopters in prior weeks. A subsequent investigation led by the Dutch government concluded that MH-17 had been downed by a Russian-supplied and operated BUK surface to air missile system. Even as international opinion hardened, Russia continued to deny that its armed forces had any involvement.[13]

The MH17 tragedy had the impact of curtailing the use of aircraft over the war zone. Anyhow, the overt use of Russian airpower in Ukraine would have stretched Putin's deniability to breaking point. Absent of the capability to weaken targets from the air, or to land troops in airborne assaults, the war became bogged down into fixed lines and a contest of infantry, artillery and armour. For all the talk of hybrid war, the ground reality resembled a twentieth-century industrialized conflict. In the bitterest of ironies, on the centenary of the First World War's outbreak, trench lines and shellfire had returned to Europe's eastern edge.

The battlefield stalemate had a direct bearing on diplomatic responses to the war. The highest-level diplomatic push came in the guise of the 'Normandy Format' group, which first met on 6 June 2014. The symbolism of the seventieth anniversary of Operation Overlord and the D-Day landings set the stage for the German Chancellor, the Presidents of France, Russia and Ukraine and their respective foreign ministers to meet and explore the possibility of settling the conflict. The diplomatic push faced an uphill struggle, given the Russian's barefaced lie that it was not responsible for its proxy forces. This created a fundamental contradiction: Russia sat at the top table of diplomatic efforts to manage the conflict, but did so only in the confidence that it would not be named as a party to the ongoing hostilities in any joint declarations.

This theme reared its head in how the Organisation for Security and Cooperation in Europe (OSCE) became involved in the working group and field levels of the diplomatic response. With its roots in the Cold War-era Conference on Security in Europe that took place in the 1970s, when it served as a vehicle for detente, the OSCE was subsequently formalized into a multilateral body. The OSCE had the great virtue of including the Western countries and Russia, making it the most viable multilateral platform through which to foster international action in Ukraine. The OSCE deployed an unarmed Special Monitoring Mission (SMM) across Ukraine after decision was reached on 21 March 2014 by the fifty-seven member states in Vienna, with personnel seconded from most of its member states, including from Russia. The SMM's mandate reflected its status as a non-coercive civilian mission, aimed at 'reducing tensions and fostering peace'.[14]

This set the stage for the first significant diplomatic agreement on the war, known as the Minsk Protocol, due to the OSCE's facilitation of negotiations in Belarus. It was signed on 5 September 2014 by the OSCE, ex-Ukrainian President Leonid Kuchma, Russia's Ambassador to Kiev, the LPR and the DPR. Its provisions included: 'an immediate bilateral ceasefire'; 'monitoring and verification of the ceasefire by the OSCE'; a commitment 'to withdraw illegal armed groups and military equipment … fighters and mercenaries from Ukraine'; and 'decentralisation of power [by Kiev to the] "Particular Districts of Donetsk and Luhansk Oblasts"'. In an addendum a week later, further provisions followed: to 'pull heavy weaponry 15 kilometres back on each side of the line of contact'; and 'to ban flights by combat aircraft over the security zone'.[15]

'Minsk' became a byword for failed diplomacy. The Minsk Protocol embodied the contradiction that while Russia was involved in the diplomatic push, it was still supporting the Donbas separatists in a manner that precluded it from being officially named as a combatant. Thus, the Minsk Protocol treated Ukraine and the separatists as the warring parties, thereby obscuring the war's true dynamics. In reality there was no real way round this conundrum: to have named Russia as an aggressor would have precluded Russian participation in the Normandy meetings and in the OSCE's various efforts – but by being unable to name Russia, the Minsk Protocol was saddled with a debilitating paradox, and would be virtually impossible to fully implement.

This became clear during the winter of 2014–15, as the fighting intensified and concentrated on a set of contested locations. Donetsk Airport was the most totemic: the DPR had hoped to punch out from the airport and push Ukrainian forces further away from Donetsk, their de-facto capital city. So entrenched had both sides become inside the airport that the OSCE even monitored troop rotations, as fresh forces from both sides replaced their exhausted colleagues and casualties.[16] Embattled Ukrainian soldiers were lionized by their countryfolk as 'cyborgs' for holding out in the airport. Eventually they lost their grip, retreated and had to redraw their front line along nearby settlements like Pisky and Avdiivka, amidst continuing artillery fire.

The Minsk Protocol appeared as wrecked as the ruins of Donetsk Airport, which its why in February 2015 an Additional Package of Measures was negotiated (known as 'Minsk II'). This deal stipulated once again for a ceasefire, and for a withdrawal of weapons of a certain calibre by both sides from the front line. At the same time as the negotiations were taking place over the Minsk II agreement, a battle was raging over the strategic rail hub town of Debaltseve. Located in a thin peninsula of Ukrainian government-controlled territory that jutted into rebel held areas, Debaltseve had one side exposed to the DPR, and the other to the LPR (meaning that Russian-backed forces could close on it from all sides). Elsewhere along the frontline Ukrainian forces were not holding back either. At the southern tip of the Donetsk region, the pro-government Azov volunteer battalion spearheaded an offensive out of the coastal city of Mariupol, pushing the 'DPR' east.[17] This created a buffer around Mariupol, which Kiev feared would be the separatist's next target.

Fighting and negotiations were unfolding concurrently. Ukrainian delegates in Minsk had to back the Additional Package of Measures out of desperation, given their armed forces had just lost hold of Donetsk Airport and Debaltseve in quick succession. With Mariupol also threatened, they needed a reprieve. Russian delegates backed the deal more cynically, using the negotiations as a diplomatic smokescreen for their continuing instigation of the violence. Regardless, the 'Minsk II' deal was signed on 11 February 2015.

After this time the front line became increasingly static. The Ukrainian state's loss of Debaltseve was the last *major* change of ownership of territory (at the time of writing).[18] However, the front line was anything but peaceful and fighting has persisted in the form of shelling and probing attacks. Concern around a possible major separatist offensive periodically resurfaced, such as in the weeks preceding the May 2015 seventieth anniversary of Germany's defeat in the Second World War, as the DPR and the LPR stated their intent to parade their military equipment.¹⁹ In the event, summer 2015 passed without any major offensives. Since then, while the intensity of fighting has waxed and waned, it has not escalated sharply. The low intensity of the war has remained an open sore for Ukraine, and also for relations between Western countries and Russia.

How Russia shielded its proxies

After the Minsk deals were signed in 2014 and 2015, the OSCE struggled to monitor a ceasefire that barely existed. SMM personnel were not given sufficient access and baseline inventory data to fully monitor the withdrawal of weapons. There was culpability for this on both sides, and OSCE officials stated that the guns falling silent would be a prerequisite for a more permanent deal.²⁰ In reality, the OSCE SMM was not the only conflict manager in town – a parallel monitoring structure was also in play from 2014 to 2017.

The origin of the 'Joint Centre for Control and Coordination' (JCCC) in June 2014 was shrouded in mystery. It comprised Ukrainian *and* Russian armed forces personnel working cooperatively along the front line, and it 'was established to facilitate bilateral dialogue between Ukraine's Ministry of Defense and military representatives of the Russian Federation', according to the OSCE.²¹ The OSCE also stated that it would 'monitor and report on the work of the JCCC, and on compliance with the Minsk Memorandum'.²²

The Russians had a precedent for such a structure. Years beforehand, a 'Joint Control Commission' (JCC) was established in Transnistria, a strip of land located between Moldova and Ukraine but only recognized as a state by Russia – here, the JCC included Russian, Moldovan and Transnistrian representatives located in the buffer zone.²³ The Russians sought to replicate such a structure in Ukraine, not least because it granted them permission to overtly deploy an official military staff contingent right in the war zone, meaning that a uniformed Russian Colonel-General was in daily face-to-face contact with the DPR and LPR.

Once in place, it transpired that JCCC personnel would operate from fixed locations along the front line, but were unable (or unwilling) to patrol together in order to jointly deescalate the conflict.²⁴ The JCCC lacked a diplomatic mandate and was described by the OSCE as 'neither joint nor coordinated'.²⁵ But the OSCE SMM was also proving ineffective: for two years it failed to mediate between members of the JCCC, and instead grew dependent on the JCCC for its own access to the war zone. Eventually, in May 2016, the OSCE issued this public statement: the 'JCCC is one of few instruments on the ground in Ukraine where direct dialogue takes place. [It] needs to be empowered and work jointly.'[26]

Clearly this was not what Russia wanted, given its need to safeguard its proxies. On 19 December 2017 the Russian Federation made a unilateral decision to withdraw its military delegation to the JCCC. Kiev was indignant: 'Such a step reaffirms that Moscow continues trying to force Ukraine to begin a so-called "direct dialogue" with the militants of the illegal armed formations that conduct their activities in the temporarily occupied areas of Donetsk and Luhansk under total control and with full support by Russia.'[27]

Ukraine's government could identify Russia's proxies in this way, but it was loath to afford them any legitimacy. Kiev duly created a post entitled 'Minister for Temporarily Occupied Territories and Internally Displaced Persons' (who from April 2016 was Vadym Chernysh). The use of 'temporary' emphasized Kiev's intent to recover all of Donetsk and Luhansk. As Russia withdrew its JCCC personnel, Chernysh offered this view: 'It clearly shows that Russia wants to do everything possible even on this level to not even appear to be a party to the conflict and make us go down the path of dialogue with incomprehensible people who were installed by Russia itself in these breakaway areas of Donetsk and Luhansk.'[28] His frustration reflected the fact that Russia was doing what it could to shield its proxies as the war simmered.

The struggle to end Ukraine's war

What can be made of half a decade of faltering efforts to manage the war in Ukraine? Russia's proxy war was only sustainable because Moscow has accompanied it with a half-hearted investment in conflict management. Having said, while it is possible to see 'Minsk' as a byword in insincere peacemaking, this overlooks the distinct possibility that Ukraine's war could have been far worse without the diplomatic response. The Minsk Process and the OSCE have helped to contain the war by erecting a shaky diplomatic scaffold that has held the warring parties more or less at the battle lines that were reached in 2015.

In moments of despair, Ukrainian President Poroshenko (2014–19) called for a peacekeeping mission by the UN or EU.[29] To no avail of course, since Russia would hardly countenance a UN mission, while the EU's perceived role in provoking Russia's intervention ruled it out as a platform. In response, Russia had suggested that the OSCE monitors be armed, but these proposals did not go far. Russia has demonstrated that it is conformable with sponsoring the OSCE in Ukraine, and this deserves further reflection.

The OSCE has proved its worth in its rapid response to the crisis, and for providing a forum for Russia, Ukraine and Western governments to talk. Calls to strengthen the OSCE are sensible,[30] but the cumbersome nature of its fifty-five-member consensus decision-making, and Russia's active participation, has inadvertently turned it into a diplomatic vehicle through which to slow down conflict management to a snail's pace under the veneer of meaningful diplomacy. Overall, its involvement in the OSCE has allowed Russia to burnish its conflict management credentials while concurrently waging its limited proxy war.

It is also apparent that Kiev's government has had little incentive to fully implement the provisions of Minsk II,[31] leading Russian officials to heap blame onto Kiev for the unresolved war.[32] Poroshenko was unable to persuade the Verkhovna Rada (parliament) to support the Minsk deal, because its provisions would have allowed local elections in the Donetsk and Luhansk regions. This would have been tantamount to a surrender bill in the eyes of Ukraine's political right, who have fervently opposed any recognition of the Donbas rebel republics, fearing this would allow them to become de-facto Russian dependencies. These political fissures have reduced Kiev's room for a compromise with Russia over what happens to areas held by the DPR and LPR. Thus, Minsk II has effectively been unimplementable.

The West has concluded that since the war cannot be ended, Ukraine must be strengthened by training its armed forces, reforming its institutions and helping its economy.[33] But reforming an oligarchical politico-economic system cannot unfold quickly enough to match the needs of conflict management. In 2019 Poroshenko lost to Volodymyr Zelenski in Ukraine's presidential election. Upon taking office, Zelenski tried to ease Kiev's relations with Moscow through exchanges of prisoners of war. This generated brief respite and goodwill, but Zelenski soon found that like his predecessor, his government had little diplomatic space to bargain with Russia over ending the Donbas war, without surrendering east Ukraine to Russian influence.

The longer the war persists, the trickier it will be to reunify the parts of Ukraine bisected by the front line. There is a narrative favoured by some patriotic Ukrainians and their Western supporters that Ukraine's populace has united in national solidarity against Russian malevolence.[34] This is true to a point, but it ignores the matter of Kiev's future relationship with the people of the Donbas. War always exacerbates xenophobias and, even if they are not card-carrying separatists, a general sense of alienation from Kiev intensifies the further east one travels. A national dialogue between Kiev and the Donbas regions will have to reverse years of prejudices between the east and west of the country.[35] Intercommunal mistrust has only been exacerbated by the internal displacement of an estimated at 1.36 million people (as of 2018).[36] There is grass roots work that needs to be done to bridge the fissures in Ukraine's populace that gave succour to Russia's intervention.

All of this is testament to how perilously difficult it has been be to deal with Russia's cleverly orchestrated proxy war. Russia's war aims were achieved by seizing the Crimea, and by stoking an ongoing armed conflict that would prevent Ukraine from being able to join the EU or NATO. Russia's diplomatic top cover, in which it played for time through the OSCE and at Minsk, has also been vital to these outcomes.

It is true that Russia has been punished by Western sanctions against its leadership, and by expulsion from the G8. Russia has also faced deterrence measures by NATO to curtail the possibility that it intervenes in the Baltic States in a similar way to what it has done in Ukraine, or that it threatens Poland or Romania.

However, Russia's influence on east Ukraine has not been reversed, and the Kiev government is no closer to regaining its pre-2014 territory. It is not inconceivable that fighting in Donbas persists for years and, even if the violence eventually tapers off, that Kiev's government never fully regains control of the Donetsk and Luhansk regions. Such are the outcomes of the proxy war that has been inflicted on Ukraine, in which Russia has employed diplomacy in full service of the deception surrounding its military operations.

Syria's war: The Gordian knot of civil and proxy war

Despairingly, it seems an oxymoron to talk of conflict management in the Syrian context. Diplomatic efforts have repeatedly faltered in the face of so much fighting, loss of life, displaced people, terrorism and foreign intervention. Initially, President Bashar al-Assad's regime attempted to crush a rebellion against his rule in 2011. This instigated a war that escalated by sucking in neighbouring states, great powers and foreign jihadists alike. Studies on civil wars convey how tough it can be to end such a multidimensional war, where there are multiple outside backers for the principal protagonists,[37] and Syria's war tragically bears this out.

With so many participants, Syria's war has come to resemble a hellish Rubik's cube, a metaphor that conveys how conflict management efforts may only ever been able to match one set of colours at a time.[38] A fluid military picture has serially imposed itself on the diplomatic processes that have been underway. The following analysis focuses on the first five years of the war (2011–16), and explains why diplomatic efforts in this time repeatedly ran aground over issues of foreign military intervention.

Syria became a theatre of proxy war involving a great many regional and international powers. The different ways in which proxies have been used is of importance, with some being engaged overtly by their sponsors, while others have been assisted indirectly and deniably. For example, the Lebanese-based armed group Hezbollah intervened in the war at Iranian behest, giving Tehran's government a considerable amount of indirect influence in Syria. Conversely, the United States overtly backed – and later abandoned – Kurdish armed groups that it partnered with to fight the jihadists of ISIL. The contrast between methods of direct and indirect proxy support, and the consequent impact on conflict resolution, is the focus here.

Picking proxies amidst an escalating civil war

The Assad regime was implacable in the face of the 2011 uprising. A generation beforehand, in 1982, Hafiz al-Assad had brutally defended his regime by reducing the city of Hama to rubble when its inhabitants revolted.[39] His son Bashar followed this precedent to defend the sectarian support base of the Assad dynasty, in which the minority Allawite Shia dominated the majority Sunni populace.[40]

The first attempt to broker peace was led by the Arab League, a regional organization of twenty-two states, which took on the task due to its status within the Middle East, and in the context of Arab Spring uprisings that had gripped the region. In accordance with its draft peace plan, a monitoring mission was deployed. In January 2012, the mission withdrew as fighting intensified.[41] Some 5,000 lives had already been lost by this point according to UN estimates, as some members of Syria's army defected to join the opposition Free Syrian Army, and as the uprising metamorphosed into a full-blown civil war.

Conflict management efforts moved from a regional to an international platform. The UN appointed Kofi Annan as 'Joint Special Envoy for the UN and Arab League'. He launched a peace plan in March 2012, but left the role after just five months. Annan explained: 'When the Syrian people desperately need action there continues to be finger-pointing and name-calling in the Security Council … It is impossible for me or anyone to compel the Syrian government, and also the opposition, to take the steps to bring about the political process.'[42]

At this time there was extra uncertainty as to whether the United States would intervene against Assad's regime. President Obama, however, resisted the clamour for action from US liberal interventionists, but also from regional powers wanting to overthrow Assad, like Turkey and Saudi Arabia (keen to see an Iranian ally removed). Instead, the United States opted for arms-length condemnation of Syria's regime, convening a 'Friends of Syria' group in February 2012 to diplomatically isolate Assad's regime.

Two major powers defied the United States. Iran considered Assad's regime to be among its few allies in the region. Russia had a history of arming the regime of Hafiz Assad, back when Syria had been a client state of the USSR. For Iran, backing Syria was crucial to its regional position. Russia had other motives: to rebuild its long absent influence in the Middle East, and to checkmate the United States in the process.

Russia was still seething after feeling misled by UN Resolution 1973 over Libya's civil war in 2011, which had paved the way for NATO's aerial intervention and Gadhafi's fall. Over Syria, Russia wanted to block another US-led regime change. To bridge the dispute, Finland's Martti Ahtisaari brokered a succession plan in Syria, alleging he had Russian support for his proposal – something refuted by a Western diplomat to the media: 'I doubt the P3 [US, UK and France] refused or dismissed any such offer at the time. The questions were more to do with sequencing and with Russia's ability to get Assad to step down.'[43]

The matter of Assad's political fate would bedevil what was known as the 'Geneva Process'. In June 2012, Russian Foreign Minister Sergei Lavrov and US Secretary of State Hillary Clinton agreed a draft communiqué on a political transition in Syria. The United States interpreted this to mean Assad would step down; Russia's interpretation was that Assad could remain in power if Syrians wished him to.

As the diplomacy became deadlocked, the main Syrian opposition bloc at this time, the Transitional National Coalition, realized it was not going to receive categorical US military backing. US policy vacillated from talking about regime change, to arming only those rebels it deemed moderate.[44] This created a vacuum that was exploited by the Gulf States as they became major backers of the rebels. Motivated by the cause of backing Sunni co-religionists, the Gulf States now pushed for a Muslim Brotherhood-affiliated rebellion.

Conversely, Assad's backers were more equivocal in the support they offered his regime. Hezbollah, the Iran-backed armed group had deployed from Lebanon to fight on behalf of the regime. An estimated 7,000 Hezbollah fighters were active in Syria and, while likely to have been involved in some way ever since 2011, only confirmed their involvement in 2013. Six years later they were still fighting alongside the Syrian army against the remaining rebel forces.[45]

Russia offered a vital diplomatic reprieve for Assad's regime. On 21 August 2013, Syria's regime used chemical weapons in Ghouta, a rebel-held suburb of Damascus.[46] Obama declared a red line in order to reinforce the taboo against using non-conventional weapons. Rather than punish Assad with force, the United States responded to a Russian proposal to act jointly to remove all stocks of chemical weapons from Syria, through the UN's Organisation for the Prohibition of Chemical Weapons. By accepting Russia's offer, Obama never followed through to defend his red line. Then, in September 2013, UK Prime Minister David Cameron was defeated in a parliamentary vote after he suggested military strikes against the Assad regime for its chemical weapons uses. As the prospect of Western military strikes diminished, so did Western diplomatic leverage, which could only have been maximized if the prospect of military intervention had remained on the table.

There was another diplomatic push. With the successful precedent of the chemical weapons removal plan, Russia and the United States met once again in Geneva in early 2014 in a process that was known as 'Geneva II'. At the UN level, Annan's successor, Lakhdar Brahimi, served in the lead diplomatic role until May. In July 2014, Steffan de Mistura was appointed the new UN envoy to the Syrian conflict.

Diplomacy was still a sideshow because the nature of the proxy war had mutated. In September 2015 Russia deployed its air force to support Syria's regime. This game-changing intervention stabilized Assad's precarious military position, after his army had suffered reverses in Idlib and Palmyra. Now, with Russia and Hezbollah both fighting on its behalf, the Assad regime benefited from a mix of overt and covert backing. As the battlefield fortunes of Assad's army improved, the appetite of the Syrian regime for talks dampened.

A fresh diplomatic drive duly floundered. In October 2015, an ad hoc group of states met in Vienna as the 'International Syria Support Group', or ISSG (including the United States, UK, Russia, Iran, Saudi Arabia, Turkey and others – but *not* Syria's regime). In December 2015, the UN Security Council passed Resolution 2254, which required the UN to broker talks between Syria's opposition and its regime, with a view to establishing 'credible governance' by summer 2016, and a new constitution in 2017. A 'nationwide cessation of hostilities' was announced by the ISSG as commencing on 27 February 2016.[47] The cessation was an interim measure, aimed at allowing humanitarian access to several war-ravaged cities. The hope – soon forlorn – was for a pause in bloodshed to give way to a more formal ceasefire.

However, the nature of the proxy wars being waged in Syria wrecked the UN's attempts at conflict management. Failing to address the reality of proxy interests proved fatal for diplomatic efforts to find a lasting settlement. UN brokered intra-Syrian talks involving the Assad regime and the rebel groups took place in Geneva. Mediated by De Mistura, his team ran working groups to break the issues down and operate on the basis of proximity talks, rather than getting all parties in one room. But the uninvited ghost at the Geneva talks was the outside sponsors of the civil war's various factions. Lacking unity, the rebels presented a weak negotiating front. The High Negotiating Committee (HNC), a cluster of opposition groups that had coalesced with Saudi backing, vied for influence with the Syrian Kurdish groups, and with Salafist groups like Ahrar al-Sham. Assad regime representatives were in no mood for compromise, not least since Russia and Iran were its backers. UN talks began in February 2016, but the Syrian regime simultaneously began a military offensive to retake Aleppo, forcing rebels such as the Free Syrian Army (which was being represented by the HNC) to ask for weapons from the Saudis and Turkey.

Fighting and negotiating had come to define Syria's war. Just as it had practised this formula in Ukraine, Russia was encouraging the Assad regime to use diplomacy as a smokescreen to cover its intensifying military actions. The signs were ominous when just days before the February 2016 cessation of hostilities began, Assad was so emboldened as to declare his intention to forcefully retake all of Syria.[48]

A joint Syrian/Russian bombardment of Aleppo (Syria's largest city) intensified in 2016. Watching this unfold, fifty-one US State Department officials expressed frustration in a joint letter: 'None of us sees merit in a large-scale US invasion of Syria ... But we do see merit in a more militarily assertive US role ... based on the judicious use of stand-off and air weapons, which would undergird and drive a more focused and hardnosed US-led diplomatic process', and to 'enforce the Cessation of Hostilities'.[49]

Bereft of Western military intervention to reshape the battlefield at this crucial moment, multilateral diplomacy stood little chance of untying this Gordian knot of overlapping enmities. The politics of proxy war had long since overtaken the politics of peace, leaving the UN talks subordinate to the whims of the most powerful intervening governments, and a prisoner to the latest battlefield developments.

The proxy war over who counts as a 'terrorist' in Syria

In 2014, the battlefield picture was further complicated by the sudden advance by ISIL's forces across Syria and Iraq. ISIL has taken advantage of the chaos in Syria to establish its self-declared Caliphate, and to perpetuate sectarian and anti-Western terrorism. The success of ISIL greatly alarmed the US and European governments, especially after ISIL distributed gruesome videos in which its members beheaded Western journalists and aid workers that had been captured in Syria. Reflecting its own priorities, the West duly fixated on the jihadist threat.

For example, the February 2016 cessation of hostilities agreement text sought to ring-fence and refocus the war effort against jihadist groups: 'Military actions, including airstrikes, of the Armed Forces of the Syrian Arab Republic, the Russian Armed Forces, and the US-led Counter ISIL Coalition will continue against ISIL, Jabhat al-Nusra, and other terrorist organizations designated by the UN Security Council.'[50] This resulted in the curious situation of a cessation of hostilities including within it a provision to intensify the war against ISIL, while also trying to deescalate the regime-versus-rebel fighting. In effect, it bifurcated the war into one facet that to escalate and another facet to resolve.

Russia took advantage of this, consistently arguing that Assad's regime provided a bulwark against the jihadists, and that *all* the rebel groups it has been striking can be seen as 'terrorists'. The United States, on the other hand, now threw its lot in behind the Kurdish groups as its favoured proxy for engaging ISIL in a ground war that would be assisted by the US air force and special forces. The Kurds fought hard, culminating in a series of protracted battles that eventually helped to erode the territorial hold of ISIL in Syria.

The problem was that each intervening country had its own understanding of which actors counted as 'terrorists' in Syria. Turkish government concern was triggered by the prominent role of Kurdish armed groups in fighting ISIL, and how this might inspire Turkey's Kurds. This was due to Turkey's own long-standing war against Kurdish separatists, which had been underway since the 1980s. Consequently, Ankara deemed that United States backing for the Kurdish groups was an intolerable development.

Turkey eventually got its way when in October 2019, after the purported defeat of ISIL (as measured by the loss of its territorial Caliphate), President Trump abruptly ended US support for the Syrian Kurds. Trump had acquiesced to Turkish demands that it needed to attack the Syrian Kurds in order to clear out a buffer zone along the Turkish-Syrian border. Seeing the United States effectively surrender the last of its leverage in Syria, Russia stepped in to broker an ad hoc diplomatic agreement involving Turkey and the Syrian Kurds.

Taking stock of the confusing strands of the Syrian conflict, a number of observations are notable. First, multilateral efforts at conflict resolution were repeatedly frustrated because of the sheer number of overlapping proxy interests at play. The UN, attuned to mediating a civil war, was incapable of dealing with a civil war that had morphed with proxy war. Second, Russia accrued considerable diplomatic leverage by sticking to its clear objective of backing Assad's regime, and by manoeuvring into a position of bilateral influence with other major intervening powers like Iran and Turkey. Third, the United States ultimately lost its diplomatic leverage over the conflict as a whole by prioritizing its counterterrorism aim of fighting ISIL via the Kurds, a position that it could not sustain in the face of growing Turkish pressure. Fourth, Iran emerged in a strong position because of its proxy backing of Hezbollah, and by ending up on the winning side in the war. Conversely, Saudi Arabia and other Gulf States saw their Sunni rebel proxies on the losing side. In sum, with so many conflicting interests at play, the only route to diplomatic leverage over Syria was to back a successful warring faction. As the politics of proxy war continually triumphed over the politics of peace, Syria's misery was compounded by the conflicting priorities of outsiders.

Updating the age-old notion of getting others to fight on your behalf

This chapter began by contextualizing the age-old notion of proxy warfare according to prevailing geopolitical trends, and by pointing out that proxy wars today have unfolded at a time of relative loss of US global influence to other centres of regional power. This was followed by detailed consideration of the wars in Ukraine and Syria, with each case study presenting a different manifestation of common questions. Who has the normative right to back certain factions in a war? And how can conflict resolution approaches adapt to the modern realities of proxy wars? To conclude, while it is true that there is nothing new in getting others to fight on one's behalf, the pertinent questions relate to how this age-old phenomenon presents itself today.

These questions implore us to examine who offers proxy sponsorship, and why they are doing so. The political boundaries of proxy war are just as important as the operational realities, and this is why an excessive focus on the operational modalities of proxy war distorts our understanding of the phenomenon.

A rejoinder is therefore needed to avoid being carried away with the apparent novelty of so-called hybrid and grey zone warfare. The buzzwords continue apace: 'surrogate warfare' is another, involving 'delegation and substitution of warfare, partially or wholly, to a deputy. In an effort to minimise the exposure of one's own troops to the operation risks of war and thereby minimise the political risks for policymakers, states increasingly share these risks with proxies, auxiliaries, and technological platforms'.[51] This definition is more expansive – and not especially useful – because it shoehorns in almost every instance under the sun of getting an ally to fight on one's behalf, before heaping in state-sponsored cyber-attacks for good measure.

Rather than catch-all buzzwords, it is important to consider the different reasons as to why war by proxy is chosen. And to refocus attention on the role of diplomacy as an enabler for those waging proxy war, and as a tool in the response of those who are seeking to counter it. After all, war is ultimately a political act, and proxy war is no exception.

In this regard, Ukraine's war shows how a cleverly orchestrated proxy war campaign relies as much on 'hybrid war' tactics as it does on Russia's use of supporting diplomacy. The real hybridity at play here is between the tactics of subversion and covert war on the one hand, and the subsuming of these tactics into the wider dynamics of Russian diplomacy and statecraft, such as through the OSCE. Syria's war offers up very different lessons: it serves up comparative examples of Russian, Iranian, Turkish, Saudi and US efforts at picking local allies and proxies to further their respective objectives. Each of these countries met with varying degrees of success, but all were buttressed by the relative successes and failures of their diplomatic efforts to carve out space for their proxy war gambits.

The fact that the United States has emerged sidelined in each scenario is a striking set of outcomes. Unless the United States finds a way of countering proxy war in scenarios like Ukraine, and finds ways to impose its will in competitive proxy war scenarios like Syria, the next decade may see further erosions in its global influence. Ultimately, the era of undisputed US unipolarity may give way to a more anarchical environment in which governments routinely try to intervene abroad, and then wash their hands of the blame, because they have mastered the art of clearing out diplomatic space for their proxy wars.

War is akin to a garden weed – no matter how neat and solid the paving stones placed to constrain its growth appear to be, its shoots will reach through, find air and grow. The diplomatic arrangements of the post-Cold War world, once so self-assuredly guaranteed by US power, are presently finding this to be the case regarding proxy wars.

Notes

1. Esper speaking 'A Conversation with the Defence Secretary', Royal United Services Institute (RUSI), London, 6 September 2019.
2. J. L. Gaddis (2006), *The Cold War: A New History* (New York: Penguin), 123.
3. Thomas M. Huber (ed.), *Compound Warfare: That Fatal Knot* (Honolulu: University Press of the Pacific, 2004), 1.
4. Ministry of Defence, MCDC Countering Hybrid Warfare Project, 3.
5. I fully develop this concept in Samir Puri (2017), 'The Strategic Hedging of Iran, Russia, and China: Juxtaposing Participation in the Global System with Regional Revisionism', *Journal of Global Security Studies* 2, no. 4, 307–23.
6. Puri, *The Great Imperial Hangover* (London: Atlantic, 2020), chapter entitled 'Russia's Embrace of Empire'.
7. Shaun Walker, *The Long Hangover: Putin's New Russia and the Ghosts of the Past* (Oxford: Blackwells, 2018), 220.
8. BBC News, 'Ukraine Crisis: Dozens Killed in Odessa Fire amid Clashes', 3 May 2014; *The Economist*, 'Ukraine's Turmoil: Chaos Out of Order', 3 May 2014, pp. 31–2; 'The war in Ukraine (2): Closing in', 2 August 2014, 26.
9. *The Moscow Times*, 'Russia's Igor Strelkov: I Started War in East Ukraine', 21 November 2014.
10. Fiona Hill and Clifford G. Gaddy, *Mr Putin: Operative in the Kremlin* (Washington, DC: Brookings, 2013), chapter entitled 'The Case Officer'; Julie Fedor, *Russia and the Cult of State Security: The Chekist Tradition, from Lenin to Putin* (London: Routledge, 2013).
11. *The Economist*, 'War in Ukraine: The Turn of the Tide', 12 July 2014, 31–2.
12. Clausewitz, *On War*, 86.
13. *The Guardian*, 'MH17 Report Suggests Efforts Were Made to Cover Up Causes of Disaster', 13 October 2015.
14. OSCE, 'Deployment of an OSCE Special Monitoring Mission to Ukraine', 21 March 2014.
15. OSCE, 'Protocol on the Results of Consultations of the Trilateral Contact Group, Signed in Minsk', 5 September 2014; BBC News, 'Ukraine Deal with pro-Russian Rebels at Minsk Talks', 20 September 2014.
16. OSCE SMM, 'Latest from the SMM Based on Information Received as of 12 December, 18:00', 13 December 2014.

17   *BBC News*, 'Ukraine Conflict: Battle Rages Ahead of Minsk Talks', 10 February 2015.
18   At the time of this writing, September 2019.
19   OSCE SMM, 'Latest from the OSCE SMM Based on Information Received as of 21 April, 18:00', 22 April 2015; 'Latest from the OSCE SMM Based on Information Received as of 9 May, 18:00', 9 May 2015.
20   UN, 'Statement by Ambassador Heidi Tagliavini and Ambassador Ertugrul Apakan', 7395th meeting of the Security Council on the situation in Ukraine, 27 February 2015.
21   Ukraine Crisis Media Centre, 'OSCE Mission to Ukraine to Augment Monitoring Capacity', 13 October 2014.
22   OSCE SMM, 'Latest from the SMM Based on Information Received as of 18:00, 16 October', 17 October 2014.
23   Government of Republic of Moldova, 'The Delegation of the Republic of Moldova to the Joint Control Commission'.
24   OSCE SMM, 'Latest from the SMM Based on Information Received as of 18:00, 20 October', 21 October 2014.
25   OSCE Principal Deputy Chief Monitor Alexander Hug's comments quoted in Ukraine Crisis Media Centre, 'Last week the SMM OSCE have recorded over 700 ceasefire violations with the use of arms prohibited by Minsk agreements', 8 April 2016.
26   Twitter, SMM Principal Deputy Chief Monitor Hug, 'OSCE SMM Ukraine'|@OSCE_SMM May 27'.
27   Government of Ukraine, 'Statement by the Ministry of Foreign Affairs of Ukraine in connection with the unilateral decision of the Russian Federation to withdraw military personnel of the Russian Armed Forces from the JCCC'. 18 December 2017.
28   Chernysh quoted in *Interfax*, 'By withdrawing from JCCC, Russia trying to force Ukraine into dialogue with militants'. 19 December 2017.
29   *BBC News*, 'Ukraine Conflict: Poroshenko Calls for UN Peacekeepers', 19 February 2015.
30   OSCE, 'Back to Diplomacy: Final Report and Recommendations of the Panel of Eminent Persons on European Security as a Common Project', 3 December 2015.
31   International Institute for Strategic Studies, *Armed Conflict Survey 2017*, p. 324.
32   Government of Russia, 'Vladimir Putin Addressed the Eighth Meeting of Russian Federation Ambassadors and Permanent Envoys at the Russian Foreign Ministry', 30 June 2016.
33   Lough and Solonenko, 'Can Ukraine Achieve a Reform Breakthrough?', Chatham House Report.
34   Cleary, 'Halfway There on National Unity in Ukraine', *Atlantic Council*, 29 September 2015.

35 OSCE Project Coordinator in Ukraine, 'Report of the Eastern Ukraine Forum "Reconstruction through Dialogue," 13–14 May 2015, Kramatorsk'.
36 Figures from the Government of Ukraine, UN Human Rights Monitoring Mission and the IISS, as presented in *Armed Conflict Survey 2019*, 147.
37 Patrick M. Regan, 'Third-party Interventions and the Duration of Intrastate Conflicts', *Journal of Conflict Resolution*, Vol. 46, No. 1 (2002), 55–73; David E. Cunningham, 'Veto Players and Civil War Duration', *American Journal of Political Science*, Vol. 50, No. 4 (October 2006), 875–892.
38 Puri, 'What Does Progress in Resolving Syria's War Look Like?', *The Telegraph*, 17 February 2016.
39 Raphael Lefevre, *Ashes of Hama: The Muslim Brotherhood in Syria* (London: C Hurst & Co, 2013).
40 Emile Hokayem, *Syria's Uprising and the Fracturing of the Levant* (London: Routledge, 2013), 39–69.
41 Ibid., 158–62; *BBC News*, 'Arab League Suspends Syria Mission – Nabil el-Arabi', 28 January 2012.
42 *BBC News*, 'Kofi Annan Quits as UN-Arab League Envoy', 2 August 2012.
43 *The Guardian*, 'West Ignored Russian Offer in 2012 to Have Syria's Assad Step Aside', 15 September 2015.
44 Vacillation in US policy to arm Syria's rebels is described in a junior CIA officer's part-redacted memoir: Laux, *Left of Boom, 2017*, 263–76.
45 IISS. *Armed Conflict Survey 2019*, 195.
46 *BBC News*, 'Syria Chemical Attack: What We Know', 24 September 2013.
47 US Department of State, 'Joint Statement of the US and the Russian Federation, as Co-Chairs of the ISSG, on Cessation of Hostilities in Syria', 22 February 2016.
48 *BBC News*, 'Syria conflict: Bashar Assad Vows to Retake Whole Country', 12 February 2016.
49 *New York Times*, '51 US State Department Officials Express Their Disagreement with US Policy towards Syria', 22 June 2016.
50 Op. cit., US Department of State, 'Joint Statement of the US and the Russian Federation'.
51 Andreas Krieg and Jean-Marc Rickli, *Surrogate Warfare: The Transformation of War in the Twenty-First Century* (Washington, DC: Georgetown University Press, 2019), 3.

3

Approaches to strategic resets in diplomacy: The case of the Fifth Marquess of Lansdowne

Dr Andrew Ehrhardt

During a career that spanned three decades at the end of the nineteenth century, the Fifth Marquess of Lansdowne held some of the most coveted and influential positions within the British Empire, including Viceroy of India, Secretary of State for War and Secretary of State for Foreign Affairs. For many in the twentieth century, however, Lansdowne – also known as Henry Petty-Fitzmaurice – was best remembered for his infamous 'peace letter' of November 1917. Published in the pages of the *Daily Telegraph*, his letter called for a peaceful settlement with Germany in order to 'avert worldwide catastrophe', which he believed inevitable if the war continued apace. 'We are not going to lose this war, but its prolongation will spell ruin to the civilised world', he warned. In order to ensure that Germany was clear as to British intentions, he recommended that it be known that 'we do not desire the annihilation of Germany as a Great Power … [and] we have no desire to deny Germany her place among the great commercial communities of the world'.[1] Should this be accepted by both powers, he felt, the war could be brought to a peaceful end and the post-war recovery might begin.

The letter sparked outrage in the British press and public and marked an unfortunate end to the political career of one of Britain's most transformative foreign secretaries.[2] Indeed, Lansdowne's tenure between November 1900 and December 1905 has long been overlooked, but his policies initiated one of the most significant periods in British diplomatic history. He had inherited a grand strategy of non-alignment which, while largely successful in previous decades, was quickly becoming an outdated policy as a result of a changing international environment. The future of the international order, which was now beset with rising powers such as the United States, Germany and Russia, was uncertain; yet one thing was clear: Britain's past predominance was fading.

Against this backdrop, Lansdowne broke with the traditional foreign policy of his predecessor, the iconic Lord Salisbury, and settled longstanding disputes to repair historically strained relations and forged alliances to shore up British vulnerabilities.[3] His three major achievements – the Anglo-Japanese Alliance of 1902, the Anglo-French Entente of 1904 and the rapprochement with the United States – contributed to a transformation in British grand strategy which guided the government's foreign policy at the turn of the century.[4]

The benefits of this period in diplomatic history are often overlooked by students and practitioners of statecraft, yet it is here that one can extract a number of valuable insights for present challenges in international politics. Despite more differences than similarities between the UK at the turn of the twentieth century and the United States today, leaders in Washington might better understand the way in which a global hegemon manages the inevitability of its own relative decline. Similarly, contemporary British policymakers might also find that their own grand strategy, undoubtedly in need of a reset after leaving the European Union, can benefit from adopting certain approaches of their predecessors. The chapter explores these lessons, and will close with suggestions for the way in which American and British statesmen might look to the tenure of Lansdowne, which represents a case study in pragmatic and innovative policymaking during a period of strategic reset.

A risk of 'Stranded Isolation'

By 1900, the elaborate celebrations that had marked Queen Victoria's Diamond Jubilee in June 1897 were soon overshadowed by increasing doubt as to Britain's position in a changing geopolitical landscape. A series of embarrassing setbacks against the Boers in South Africa began to cast a grim shade over the imperial apex of the late Victorian period. The irregular fighting forces of the South African Republic (the Transvaal) and the Orange Free State exposed the shortcomings of a frail, ill-prepared British military numbering more than 250,000 men.[5] Despite a string of victories in the first year of the war, the conflict soon became protracted, due in large part to tactics of guerrilla warfare adopted by the Boer republics. The inability to quickly and resolutely win the war led to public fatigue for the effort and a crisis of confidence within the British military and diplomatic ranks. To make matters worse, Whitehall was mired in a financial crisis, with its credit declining and public taxes increasing in order to pay for the mismanaged campaign.[6]

These difficulties were exacerbated by a number of concurrent international problems. The Boxer Rebellion was underway in China, a conflict which, since November 1899, threatened the advantageous 'Open Door' policy in that region.[7] Russian forces – along with those from Britain and Germany – had played a key role in quelling the Boxer insurrection; but by the end of the year, those same troops remained in Manchuria, raising suspicions that the Tsar harboured his own expansionist aims in China. An earlier agreement between the Chinese and Russian governments in 1898 – one which leased Port Arthur to Russia for the next twenty-five years – had already led some British diplomats to warn that Moscow held expansionist aims in the Far East and Central Asia.[8]

Across the Atlantic, the United States had recently established itself as a global power after an overwhelming victory in the Spanish-American War. Not only had this conflict confirmed America's place as the predominant player in the Western Hemisphere, but American leaders were also adopting a somewhat bullish approach to relations with the UK, particularly in the northern Caribbean basin.[9] Anglo-American relations had undoubtedly improved from the nadir of the Venezuelan Crisis in 1895, a boundary dispute which led Lord Salisbury to contemplate the possibility of another war between the countries.[10] Several outstanding disputes, however – namely those involving the boundaries of the Alaskan territory and access to fisheries in New England – remained unresolved between leaders in Washington and London.

Closer to home, Spain was threatening Gibraltar as a result of Britain's 'benevolent neutrality' towards the Americans during the Spanish-American War.[11] Similarly, relations with France, which had ebbed and flowed throughout the nineteenth century, were fraying. In 1898, the Channel neighbours had squared off over control of the Nile River Valley, in what nearly erupted into a larger military confrontation. The Fashoda Incident, as that dispute was known, was eventually resolved; but France now had its forces interspersed in the disputed areas of Algeria and Morocco and leaders in Paris were threatening to challenge British predominance in the north of the continent. Meanwhile, rumours were spreading to London that France and her Dual Alliance partner Russia, perceiving a brittle overstretch by the British in South Africa, could challenge the British Empire in various regions, from the Far East to India.[12]

More alarming to some officials in Whitehall were the developments in Germany. Since 1890, when Otto von Bismarck was forced from his post as Chancellor, there had been uncertainty and suspicion as to German intentions in Europe, Africa and the Far East. Under Wilhelm II's policy of *Weltpolitik*, Germany sought to expand its influence throughout the world. The government, following the recommendations of Grand Admiral Alfred von Tirpitz, increased its fleet to an extent that the British Admiralty was forced to withdraw warships in the Far East and Western Hemisphere in order to defend European waterways.[13] By 1901, Kaiser William II declared that Germany had obtained its own 'place in the sun', and that going forwards, it needed to accept that its future greatness 'lies upon the water'.[14] It was a statement that officials in London viewed as a direct challenge to Britain's supremacy on the seas.

Thus, as Britain looked across to the European continent, the situation was distressing. The competing German-led Triple Alliance and Franco-Russian Alliance meant that the UK was starved of friendly relations on the continent and effectively locked out of Europe.[15] The journalist W.T. Stead reflected the alarmism sweeping through various quarters of Whitehall, 'the Empire stripped of its armour, has its hands tied behind its back and its bare throat exposed to the keen knife of its bitterest enemies'.[16]

This moment of internal doubt and existential anxiety had been building. Throughout the 1890s, naval technology and armaments had increased steadily among the great powers.[17] The Triple Intervention by Russia, Germany and France to end the First Sino-Japanese War in 1895 had been an exposition of naval strength which revealed not only these countries' capabilities on the high seas, but also their collective interest in China.[18] To counter the rise of hostile navies and maintain its traditional dominance of the seas, Britain had enacted an Act of Parliament in 1889 which declared that the Royal Navy must have a naval size equal to the next two powers combined – in this case France and Russia. The 'two power standard', as it was known, became a pillar of British grand strategy in the 1890s.[19] As the decade wore on, however, this policy seemed not only costly but also unrealistic. As France, Russia, Germany, Japan and the United States continued to build their fleets, it became clear that Britain's supremacy on the high seas was deteriorating.[20] Only a decade after the introduction of the two-power standard, the director of Naval Intelligence, Reginald Custance, lamented that the dominance which the British had exercised in the Atlantic, the West Indies and the Pacific had declined.[21] To make matters worse, the Royal Navy could not afford to maintain its size without severe domestic consequences. Lord Selborne, recently appointed head of the Admiralty in 1900, was sobered by the Chancellor of the Exchequer's warning that the department would be forced to 'cut its coat according to its cloth'.[22] Questions such as where to position a scaled back fleet now left some quarters of the Empire more exposed.

The changing international order forced a re-evaluation of British foreign policy more broadly. The policy of non-alignment with powers on the European continent – referred to as 'Splendid Isolation' by members of the press and government ministers such as the Colonial Secretary Joseph Chamberlain – had been one of the guiding principles of British grand strategy since the second premiership of Benjamin Disraeli in the 1870s.[23] Although more of a policy of non-alignment than strict isolation, it was based primarily on maintaining the Empire, avoiding continental entanglements and acting, periodically, as the arbitrating weight in the European balance of power. In other words, Britain would throw its support either to the Dual Alliance (composed of France and Russia) or Triple Alliance (composed of Germany, Austria-Hungary and Italy) in order to deter the aggressive bloc in a given diplomatic standoff. It was a strategy which relied at once on a predominant navy and an avoidance of binding military alliances.

The staunch champion of the policy throughout the 1890s was the third Marquess of Salisbury, who had served for three non-consecutive terms in his dual role of Prime Minister and Foreign Secretary.[24] In defending his aversion to committing Britain to alliances, he wrote,

> Except during [Napoleon's] reign we have never even been in danger; and, therefore, it is impossible for us to judge whether the isolation under which we are supposed to suffer, does or does not contain in it any elements of peril. It would hardly be wise to incur novel and most onerous obligations, in order to guard against a danger in whose existence we have no historical reason for believing.[25]

Not only did he think alliance building a dangerous game, but he felt that the maintenance of peace on the European continent could best be attained by Britain acting as the arbitrating weight between the Dual and Triple alliances. By this time, however, Salisbury had grown disillusioned by the fact that Britain's power was waning as its threats multiplied. In this unnerving existence, his policy of 'Splendid Isolation' risked devolving into a reality of *stranded isolation* in which the British Empire might be cast adrift in a sea of hostile powers.

Alliances to help share the burden

The election of November 1900 offered a referendum on both the South African War and, more broadly, the future direction of British foreign policy. As the Liberal MP and former leader of the opposition, William Vernon-Harcourt, argued, 'The result of the Government's policy … is that we are now the best-hated country in the world and burdened with the accumulated debt and an increased taxation.'²⁶ Fortunately for the Conservatives, their Liberal opposition was bitterly divided over the Boer war, a conflict which, due to recent gains by British military, was now viewed as more worthwhile by large sections of the public. As a result, the Conservative party returned to government with an electoral mandate for a period in which British foreign policy would change in fundamental ways. Despite Salisbury's pleasure with the election result, pressure from his own Cabinet ministers – along with his deteriorating health – would not allow the iconic statesman to maintain his dual role of Prime Minister and Foreign Secretary. The latter position Salisbury had always coveted, but his views on the direction of foreign policy, in particular, left him increasingly isolated from some members of his Cabinet, most notably Chamberlain and Lansdowne.²⁷

With the relinquishment of his beloved role, Salisbury promoted in his stead one of the more unpopular members of his government at the time – the Secretary of War, the Marquess of Lansdowne. Lansdowne took over the Foreign Office in November 1900 absorbing widespread criticism due to his failures during the ongoing war. First hearing of the appointment on 31 October, many in the British press expressed their dismay with the decision. The *National Review* felt that the entire Cabinet reorganization was 'a first-rate joke on the nation', while the *Standard* felt that it was an 'inconceivable blunder', and noted that the new Foreign Secretary had 'neither the character, qualifications, nor experience for such a position'. The *Daily Mail* was perhaps the most foreboding, writing that, 'If Lord Lansdowne is appointed Foreign Secretary and some other man of agreeable manners is made First Lord of the Admiralty, the country may lament a great opportunity lost forever.'²⁸

The outrage from some members of the press was countered within the walls of Downing Street where Lansdowne was respected by many of his colleagues. A veteran of governments dating back to Gladstone, Lansdowne had, by that time, held some of the most esteemed positions within the British Empire – experiences which provided him with a unique perspective into British diplomacy.²⁹ As Governor-General of Canada, Lansdowne learned first-hand how the divisive questions of access to fishing grounds and the location of the Alaskan boundary led to recurring tensions between Washington and London. Years later, as the Viceroy of India, he suffered no illusion of the threat that Russia posed to Persia, Afghanistan and most importantly, India. More recently, as Secretary of State for War during the early fiascos of the Second Boer War, Lansdowne learned all too well how an overstretched military could produce strategic shortcomings.³⁰ His career, by 1900, had exposed him both to the external threats facing the

British Empire and to the increasingly limited abilities the country retained in defending against potential aggressors. The combination of these experiences helped to shape his diplomatic perspective and directly influenced his own approach to British foreign policy.

By the time of his ascension to Foreign Secretary, he accepted that the maintenance of the Empire could not rest on the incumbent grand strategy. In response to Lord Salisbury's defence of his isolationist policy in 1901, he wrote:

> I fully admit the force of the Prime Minister's observation, that this country has until now fared well in spite of its international isolation. I think, however, that we may push too far the argument that, because we have in the past survived in spite of our isolation, we need have no misgivings as to the effect of that isolation in the future.[31]

For Lansdowne, British survival and influence in the twentieth century would instead rest on the construction of new strategic relationships.[32] With whom these new relationships would be formed was far from certain, however.

In his first year at the Foreign Office, Japan and France – despite being two of the countries with whom Britain would eventually reset relations – were not the first choice of the new Foreign Secretary. As one historian of British diplomacy in the period has noted, Lansdowne had one 'preconceived idea' and that was to strengthen relations with Germany.[33] This view was shared by other members of the Cabinet but opposed by the Prime Minister, who, despite being on the periphery of foreign policymaking in these years, poured cold water on the proposal in May 1901. In line with his views of why non-alignment should be the preferred policy, Salisbury warned that such an agreement might bind an unwilling public to war.

> I do not see how, in common honesty, we could invite other nations to rely upon our aids in a struggle, which must be formidable and probably supreme, when we have no means whatever of knowing what may be the humour of our people in circumstances which cannot be foreseen.[34]

Ultimately, it was the opposition to an Anglo-German agreement which carried the day. Yet despite the breakdown in negotiations, the problem of how to shore up Britain's vulnerabilities in China and the Far East remained. Even Salisbury, who many thought to be 'aloof' in these later years, wrote to a friend in September 1901 that, 'Other statesmen are acutely watching the chessboard of Europe'.[35] He felt that while states such as Germany and France might be able to offer Russian territorial concessions to stem their expansionist desires, Britain could ill-afford to appease the Tsar, lest his aspirations turn to the vitally important British interests in Persia, Afghanistan and India. Regardless of the deteriorating negotiations with Germany, Lansdowne remained adamant that the way forward was for Britain to bring in other powers to help bear its burden.

Russian actions in the Far East, in particular Manchuria, had become more pronounced since the Boxer Rebellion. The intransigence displayed by Moscow in exiting Manchuria under the Boxer Protocol alarmed Japan, who not only had a 'strong sentimental dislike' of Russian presence in the Chinese province, but also feared Russian designs for Korea.[36] It was in the Japanese anxiety towards Russia that Lansdowne found a strategic opening. By July, he was in conversations with the Japanese minister in London, Baron Hayashi, over shared concerns of Russian action in the Far East. As Lansdowne wrote after an early exploratory conversation with Hayashi, 'There was so much resemblance between the policy of our two Governments', including the absence of territorial ambitions and a preference for the status quo. As such, Lansdowne admitted that Hayashi 'would find me ready to discuss the matter with him with a view to the possible establishment of an understanding between our two countries'.[37]

In Japan, Lansdowne found a willing partner. Manchuria and Korea may have been the more immediate concerns, but officials in Tokyo harboured old grudges against Russia, Germany and France. In 1895, these states had combined to end the Sino-Japanese War, a move which helped the three European powers establish a foothold in China. The intervention – an embarrassing defeat for Japan – left the country bitter, distrustful and determined to avoid such a European coalition in the future. In London, officials were also wary of such a European coalition directed against British interests in the Far East. A series of memoranda by Lord Selborne, First Lord of the Admiralty, in the fall of 1901 laid bare British strategic vulnerabilities, especially at the hands of combined Franco-Russian power.

> As long as France and Russia continue their present scale of new construction, we cannot lessen ours, nor is it possible for us to ignore the growth of naval power all the world over. The real fact is that we have run our margin of naval strength to a finer point than prudence warrants, because our stakes are out of all proportion greater than those of any other Power. To defeat us in a maritime war would mean a disaster of almost unparalleled magnitude in history.[38]

Selborne's recommended policy was to continue with the Anglo-Japanese negotiations in the hopes of arriving at a settlement. Such an alliance would 'effectively diminish the probability of a naval war with France or Russia singly or in combination'.[39]

In spite of the objections from some in the British Cabinet – most notably from Salisbury and Chamberlain – the Anglo-Japanese Alliance was signed on 30 January 1902, marking the first time that Britain had signed a peacetime alliance in over a century.[40] Importantly, the text of the agreement was carefully worded, pledging future British actions only under certain circumstances. It was a case of diplomatic craftsmanship that would serve the government well in the coming years. Under the terms of the agreement, Britain and Japan promised neutrality if either power was involved in a war over China or Korea with *one* adversary. Should either power find themselves in a war with *two* states, the alliance partner would be required to offer military assistance in the conflict. For example, if France joined Russia against Japan, then Britain would be forced to come in on the side of Japan. But if Japan and Russia fought a war between themselves – as was soon to happen – Britain might avoid being dragged into such a conflict provided France and Germany remained neutral.

The agreement served British interests in four ways. First and most important, it became a deterrent to Russian aggression against British interests in China and the Far East. Since July 1901, Lansdowne had made it clear that his desire was to see the regional status quo maintained.[41] Second, the alliance with Japan eased concerns that Japan might one day reach an agreement with Russia.[42] Despite their mutual hostility, a Russo-Japanese settlement on outstanding issues was not out of the question, and such an agreement would leave British interests completely exposed in the Far East. Third, the alliance provided Britain with added military muscle for future diplomatic negotiations with Russia. There was still a desire within Whitehall to reach an understanding with Russia which might alleviate fears of her expansion into Persia, Afghanistan and India. Thus, it was hoped that the Anglo-Japanese agreement would immediately deter Russia from aggressive actions and hopefully bring the Tsar around to a wider settlement in the future.[43] Fourth, the alliance reduced the British naval requirement in the Far East, which allowed the Royal Navy to shift its focus to more pressing geopolitical concerns, namely the protection of the British Isles in the face of increased naval armament by Germany and France.[44] As Lord Selborne later admitted in 1903, 'We cannot be stronger than every Power on every coast simultaneously'.[45]

In both countries, the agreement was received with widespread support, and three years later it was renewed and extended.[46] In defending this policy before the House of Lords shortly after the signing of the alliance, Lansdowne again put forwards the case for a move away from Britain's traditional policy of non-alignment. Given the changing power dynamics in the European and wider international order, Lansdowne pressed the need for a strategy suited for the times, a strategy which would become the hallmark of his time as Foreign Secretary.

> In these days war breaks out with a suddenness which was unknown in former days, when nations were not, as they are now, armed to the teeth and ready to enter on hostilities at any moment ... I would entreat your Lordships to look at this matter strictly on its merits and not to allow your judgment to be swayed by any musty formulas or old-fashioned superstitions as to the desirability of pursuing a policy of isolation for this country. If considered on its merits, I venture to suggest that what you have to take into account in regard to an alliance of this kind is, first, whether the ally is a desirable ally, an in the next place whether the objects of the alliance are commendable, and last, but not least, whether the price you pay for the alliance is greater than you ought to pay.[47]

Although the formation of an alliance with Japan represented the most notable departure from the policy of Salisbury, Lansdowne, for the remainder of his time as Foreign Secretary, also sought to realign British foreign policy through other methods. One of his more significant initiatives was improving relations with the United States, a country which, in the previous two decades, had joined the ranks of the great powers. The 1880s and 1890s, however, had been a period of tense relations between Washington and London, with disputes over fishing rights in Newfoundland and the Venezuela boundary almost bringing the countries into open conflict.[48] While these differences had been resolved by the time of Lansdowne's move to the Foreign Office, there remained a number of outstanding issues, most notably over the construction of an Isthmian Canal, the Venezuela Crisis of 1902 and the location of the Alaskan boundary.

In one of his early decisions, Lansdowne resuscitated stalled negotiations over the construction of a canal to link the Pacific Ocean with the Caribbean basin. Such a waterway had become a priority for American military officials, who, during the Spanish-American War, were hamstrung by the need to sail around Cape Horn in order for commercial and military vessels to move from the Atlantic to the Pacific. The signing of the Canal Treaty in November 1901 paved the way for the development of a canal and led Lansdowne to remark that 'a new chapter had been opened' between Britain and 'our brothers across the ocean'.[49] Lansdowne and others in the Cabinet supported the agreement with a full understanding that it would be viewed as an unequal concession on the part of the British. Taking into account the American persistence regarding this issue and Britain's weakened position in the Western Hemisphere, Lansdowne sought a foundational agreement that might lead to additional settlements of outstanding disputes between the countries, most notably over the Alaskan territory boundaries which had been a source of tension earlier in his career. As he told the House of Lords in February 1904, the boundary issue was a 'long-standing and dangerous international difference' which could at 'any moment have brought us into serious and acute controversy with the United States'.[50]

For Lansdowne, timing was an essential aspect of his diplomacy. In his view, the British Empire was in an inevitable relative decline, and the window through which London could exert its power and influence without submitting to conflict was closing. The time was ripe for a reset of Anglo-American relations. As Lansdowne wrote to the British Ambassador in Washington Julian Pauncefote in December 1901,

> We should not delay much longer taking up the Alaska boundary and other questions ... The conditions are favourable and indeed they may never be more so. How delightful it would be if you should be able, before you leave Washington, to give us that clean slate which we all so much desire.[51]

Before the Alaska boundary issue could be taken up, however, there was another diplomatic crisis between the United States and Great Britain over Venezuela. In December 1902, British, German and Italian ships imposed a naval blockade of Venezuelan ports in response to the government's refusal to pay debts owed to the European powers. The conflict escalated when British and German vessels began firing on Venezuelan ships and military positions on the coast. While initially President Theodore Roosevelt did not view the combined European action as a challenge to the Monroe Doctrine, he eventually grew wary of European military action against Venezuela; and when the Venezuelan President Cipriano Castro asked him for assistance, he took up the opportunity to exert American influence in the region. This move, however, was welcomed by the British, who were now resigned to the fact that America was predominant power in the Western Hemisphere.[52] This reality was never lost on Lansdowne, who early in the conflict, spoke of not provoking the United States during the conflict with Venezuela. 'Nothing should be done to give offence to the susceptibilities of the United States, or to indicate to them that we have any desire to impugn the Monroe Doctrine.'[53] The conflict was eventually resolved, due in large part to the British decision to work with the United States. The avoidance of war in favour of arbitration, one historian has noted, represented 'a profoundly unusual restraint between a hegemon and a rising power.'[54]

On the issue of the Alaska boundary, Lansdowne took a similar conciliatory approach, knowing that a prolonged dispute – much less a future conflict – would serve only to stall improved Anglo-American relations, now viewed as essential to Britain's wider foreign policy. Even after President Roosevelt's nomination of political cronies to the Alaskan Tribunal, Lansdowne remained determined to reach a settlement built on this clean slate.[55] Speaking in Parliament in early February 1904, Lansdowne stated that Britain would continue to defend its Empire, but this would not be the result of blind, doctrinal intransigence. Strategically insignificant issues should and would be sacrificed for the maintenance and improvement of more essential strategic relationships.

> The question at issue is a question not merely of the frontier of Canada, but of the frontier of the British Empire ... [and] I do not think that anyone seriously expected that we should obtain a favourable verdict on all points; and I am inclined to find some consolation in the fact that our military and naval advisers tell us confidently that the two islands in the Portland Channel which, under the award were given to the United States, are of no strategical value whatever.[56]

Already three years into his tenure at the Foreign Office, Lansdowne had worked to improve relations with Japan and the United States, each comprising a pillar of the larger post-Salisbury British grand strategy based on harnessing new relationships to secure key British interests. The reality remained, however, that Britain had few friends in Europe. What is more, there was a lingering fear of Russian provocations within key quarters of Whitehall. In July 1903, the War Office had circulated a memorandum which raised numerous concerns over Russian activity in Manchuria. The Russians, the memorandum warned, 'are perfectly in earnest in their intention to gradually obtain the mastery over the country until it shall have ... become a Russian province'.[57] That Russia was viewed as the most pressing threat facing Great Britain in these months was no secret. The warnings from the Japanese foreign minister and the War Office had confirmed fears long held by Lansdowne, namely that Russian hunger for territory and influence would eventually bring London and St Petersburg into direct conflict with one another. The Anglo-Japanese Alliance, while helping to alleviate British vulnerabilities in the Far East in 1902, had never been enough to calm Lansdowne's fears over Russian intentions in India and Persia.[58] In his mind, the ideal scenario would be an agreement between the two powers.

> If Russia would put us in full possession of her ideas, and if she would bear in mind that for any concessions which she obtained from us we should expect corresponding concessions from her, I believe that we might put an end to the unfortunate rivalry which had so long prevailed between us in China and in other parts of Asia.[59]

It was in line with his approach to foreign policy, namely that by governments sitting down respectfully and earnestly to discuss their interests and aspirations, resolutions could be found. But just how such an agreement might be broached remained the central question. It had been hoped that the Anglo-Japanese Alliance would bring the Russian bear to the table, but recent events had proved otherwise. Now it was hoped that by fostering better relations with Russia's Dual Alliance partner, Britain might be able to bridge the hostile divide.[60] As Lansdowne wrote in September, reaching an agreement with France 'would not improbably be the precursor of a better understanding with Russia'.[61]

In the coming months, Lansdowne would lead negotiations with the French Ambassador Cambon and his counterpart in Paris, Delcasse. The French request for predominance in Morocco was countered by British demands over Egypt, while additional points were raised on access to fisheries in Newfoundland, territory in Gambia and spheres of influence in Siam.[62] There was significant progress made in the fall and winter of 1903; and after a delay, the two countries signed of a number of agreements on 8 April 1904. Later christened the 'Entente Cordiale', the treaties marked a revolution in Anglo-French relations, and like the Anglo-American rapprochement, offered a 'clean slate' upon which the future relationship could prosper.[63]

Lansdowne saw the agreement as the first step in what could become a 'comprehensive scheme' to improve Anglo-French relations over the long term.

> [The agreements] remove the sources of long-standing differences, the existence of which has been a chronic addition to our diplomatic embarrassments and a standing menace to an international friendship which we have been at much pains to cultivate, and which, we rejoice to think, has completely overshadowed the antipathies and suspicions of the past.[64]

The benefits of the Anglo-French Entente can be split into direct and indirect achievements, with the latter being arguably the most important for Lansdowne. The direct benefits included the alleviation of potential sources of conflict between the powers – particularly on the African continent and in the fisheries surrounding Newfoundland – all while avoiding the binding of Britain to a formal European alliance. These resolutions Lansdowne deemed important in and of themselves, and worthy of a settlement regardless of the ramifications it had on the international order. Britain gained control over Egypt while France obtained the same in Morocco. Elsewhere, the French renounced claims to fisheries in Newfoundland, boundary disputes in Nigeria and Gambia were settled in France's favour, while both powers settled longstanding disputes over Siam in Southeast Asia. In a speech a year later, Lansdowne admitted the pragmatism inherent in this policy.

> If we claim any credit to ourselves for having arrived at a good understanding with the French Republic, it is not because we contend for a moment that our diplomacy has been particularly profound, but because we do think that we have been able to arrive with our brilliant neighbours at a good, simple, straightforward, business-like understanding.[65]

At the same time, there were also a number of indirect benefits of the agreement that had important consequences for powers such as Russia and Germany, and herein lies the strategic dimension of the British effort. Lansdowne believed from the start that closer relations with France might facilitate better relations with St Petersburg. While Lansdowne cannot be credited with the Anglo-Russian Entente of 1907, his work on the Anglo-French rapprochement – accompanied by a series of aggressive diplomatic moves by Germany, as well as a successor adamant on further solidifying relations with France – first set this in motion.[66]

Applying the history

Squeezed between two anchors of British diplomatic history – Salisbury and Sir Edward Grey – Lansdowne's tenure in the Foreign Office has been undervalued not only by diplomatic historians but also by those concerned with contemporary international affairs. Few commentators and fewer practitioners invoke the work of the Marquess of Lansdowne, who, when he became Foreign Secretary in 1900, inherited a British foreign policy that was stagnant and ill-suited to a changing international environment. The international hegemon for long stretches of the nineteenth century was now subject to new political and economic challenges from rising powers. The way in which Lansdowne responded to these changing realities offers important insights for diplomats of every ilk, but none more so than American and British statesmen who face their own unique challenges in the present day.

In the course of every nation's existence, there are moments requiring a distinct change in strategy. Recognizing these moments and initiating such recalibrations, however, are often where leaders fall short. The need for a strategic reset can be due to external phenomena, such as the recent rise of China and the effect this has had on American calculations; or it can stem from domestic events, such as the British public's decision to leave the European Union in 2016.

While questions facing British and American policymakers are very different in nature, both powers are undoubtedly at an important crossroads; and the fate of their future influence hinges on whether their leaders can first accept the need for a strategic reset and then implement an appropriate policy.

It is here that certain aspects of Lansdowne's approach might best be applied. First is his realistic and unsentimental assessment of the international environment. As he reflected on the realities facing British foreign policy towards the end of his career, he wrote:

> We have only to look at what is passing in other parts of the world. Other nations are grouping themselves together. Other nations are also arming themselves to the teeth, and in these days the shock of war comes with much greater suddenness and rapidity than it came in the days of our forefathers. I venture to say to you that in these times no nation which intends to take its part in the affairs of the civilized world can venture to stand entirely alone.[67]

After assessing the shape and direction of international politics at the turn of the century, Lansdowne then worked towards implementing a strategy which he believed accounted for Britain's relative weakness and advanced Britain's chief objective: the safety and prosperity of the Empire. And herein lies the second key aspect of Lansdowne's approach – the ability to deliver a decisive strategic reset which harnesses the power of diplomatic relationships. The fundamental principle of Lansdowne's new grand strategy was a movement away from strict non-alignment and towards the creation or restoration of relationships with other great powers. Importantly, alliances, so long as these agreements were carefully worded, were no longer viewed as diplomatic traps but strategic pillars.

The view of such relationships is very different in the Washington of 2020. American leaders today have spoken of a 'return of great power politics' and renewed great power competition in ways that resemble some of the assumptions taking place within Whitehall at the turn of the twentieth century. The modern American approach, however, is a far cry from the strategic recalibration undertaken by members of the Foreign Office and Ministry of War. Although leading American statesmen, and most notably President Donald Trump, have sought to distance themselves from the policies of their predecessors, they have often done it in a petulant and whimsical manner, with little regard for wider strategic implications. The result has been an approach that alienates traditional allies and accumulates dangerous adversaries. Western European allies, for example, are left uncertain of the American commitment to NATO, while accusations of military provocation in the South China Sea, tit-for-tat retaliatory measures on trade, and even exchanges of blame for the Covid-19 pandemic are reflections of the tension which, despite being avoidable, now define Sino-American affairs.[68]

Furthermore, the idea of conducting diplomacy in a 'business-like' manner – something that Lansdowne often advocated – is one which has returned to contemporary discussions of statecraft. President Trump, a successful businessman himself, appeared to some to be the champion of such a pragmatic and straight-talking approach. Yet to someone like Lansdowne, the actions of the American President – such as calling the North Korean leader 'Rocket Man' – would appear to be more of a detriment than stimulus to successful negotiations.[69] Disputes between states, Lansdowne argued earlier in a 1902 speech, could be rectified if powers 'would use a little more frankness to one another – if, instead of scowling at one another from different sides of the fence, they would tell one another fairly and squarely what it was they wanted, and endeavour to settle the business upon business-like principles'.[70] Such a conservative approach to the methods of statecraft, a hallmark of Lansdowne's tenure as Foreign Secretary, seems now to be a lost art among those who might otherwise benefit the most.

Across the Atlantic, the UK, while not engaging in as abrasive a diplomacy as the United States, is in danger of succumbing to what has, in recent years, been a listless foreign policy. Between the public's vote to leave the European Union in July 2016 and the country's formal departure in March 2020, there was little focus on the future strategic direction of the country, due in large part to the uncertainty surrounding the time-frame and severity of the separation. The British government's current position, however, marks one of the most challenging strategic resets since the end of the Second World War. But the odes to 'taking back control' and 'going it alone', which made up much of the chorus championing an exit from the European Union, must be checked by those responsible for the larger direction of British statecraft. These policymakers would do well to channel some of Lansdowne's ability to recognize the changing landscape in international affairs – as well as Britain's position within that system – and to offer a cohesive strategy for the years ahead. Related to this is another crucial insight, namely Lansdowne's warning from 1905 that 'no nation ... can venture to stand entirely alone'. It is a reflection that rings especially true today, as Britain, now firmly in the ranks of the medium powers, seeks to shore up its influence either through realignment or renewals of its economic and security partnerships.

In applying history to present problems, one must always be wary of analogies and sceptical of concrete 'lessons'. The differences between historical and contemporary political questions are often greater than the similarities, yet in examining specific individuals and events in history, one's perspective of diplomacy – in particular the challenges, opportunities and potential pitfalls – broadens to give an intellectual foundation which is at once grounded and innovative. It is this kind of historical approach to statecraft which can offer students and practitioners valuable insight when addressing the most pressing questions of foreign policy.

Notes

1   Lord Lansdowne, 'Coordination of the Allies' War Aims', *Daily Telegraph*, 29 November 1917, reprinted in Goldsworthy Lowes Dickinson (ed.), *Documents and Statements Relating to Peace Proposals and War Aims* (London: George Allen and Unwin, 1919), 84–9.
2   One of Lansdowne's biographers, Simon Kerry, has written that while Lansdowne's reasoning behind the 'peace letter' has been misunderstood, it nonetheless served to tarnish his political reputation. See Simon Kerry, *Lansdowne: The Last Great Whig* (United Kingdom: Unicorn Publishing Group, 2017), 315.
3   The argument made in this chapter contrasts with those put forwards by other historians, such as John Charmley, Zara Steiner and Keith Neilson, who have argued that Lansdowne did not have an overarching or distinct strategy. Charmley writes that 'There is no sign that Lansdowne regarded his actions as marking a caesura in British diplomatic history'. John Charmley, 'Splendid Isolation to Finest Hour: Britain as a Global Power, 1900–1905', *Contemporary British History*, Vol. 18, No. 3 (2004), 130–46, here 135. Steiner and Neilson have written that, 'In finding these ad hoc solutions, Lansdowne had not, except in the case of Japan, departed markedly from his predecessors' efforts to seek accommodations with potential and actual rivals.' Zara Steiner and Keith Neilson, *Britain and the Origins of the First World War*, 2nd ed. (Basingstoke: Palgrave Macmillan, 2003), 34. See also G. W. Monger, 'The End of Isolation: Britain, Germany and Japan, 1900–1902: The Alexander Prize Essay', *Transactions of the Royal Historical Society*, Vol. 13 (1963), 120–1; Ian Nish, 'British Foreign Secretaries and Japan, 1892–1905', in B. J. C. McKercher and D.J. Moss (eds), *Shadow and Substance in British Foreign Policy, 1895–1939: Memorial Essays Honouring C.J. Lowe* (Edmonton: The University of Alberta Press, 1984), 74–5. Nish builds on an argument put forward by Cedric Lowe in *The Reluctant Imperialists: British Foreign Policy, 1876–1902* (London: Routledge & Kegan Paul, 1967).
4   Charmley writes of 'the quiet diplomatic revolution of the Lansdowne era', and notes that 'By 1905 Britain's diplomatic position was better than it had been for

a decade'. John Charmley, 'Splendid Isolation to Finest Hour: Britain as a Global Power, 1900–1905', pp. 141, 135. See also Charmley, *Splendid Isolation?: Britain, the Balance of Power and the Origins of the First World War* (London: Faber and Faber, 2009). Similarly, Zara Steiner has written that 'Lansdowne proved to be an adroit foreign secretary at a particularly difficult period in British history ... A large measure of the credit for Britain's stronger continental position after 1904 was due to the Foreign Secretary's response to these occurrences'. Zara Steiner, *The Foreign Office and Foreign Policy, 1898–1914* (Cambridge: Cambridge University Press, 1969), 46–7.

5   Richard Hart Sinnreich, 'About Turn: British Strategic Transformation from Salisbury to Grey', in Williamson Murray, Richard Hart Sinnreich and James Lacey (eds), *The Shaping of Grand Strategy: Policy, Diplomacy, and War* (Cambridge: Cambridge University Press, 2011), 129–31.

6   In early 1902, the war was costing Britain an estimated £5.5 million per month. It is estimated that the three-year war cost Britain £223 million. See Andrew Roberts, *Salisbury: Victorian Titan* (London: Weidenfeld & Nicolson, 1999), 809–10. See Alfred Havighurst, *Britain in Transition*, 4th ed. (Chicago: University of Chicago Press, 1985), 10.

7   As Lord Salisbury wrote at the time, 'It may be said that the policy of this country is effectively to open China to the commerce of the world, and that our estimate of the section of other powers in the Far East depends on the degree to which it promotes or hinders the attainment of this object.' The Marquess of Salisbury to Sir Nicholas O'Conor, 28 March 1898, in G. P. Gooch and Harold Temperley, *British Documents on the Origins of the War, 1898–1914, Vol. I: The End of British Isolation* (London: His Majesty's Stationary Office, 1927), No. 41, 27–8. For an overview of the debates that this conflict caused in the British Cabinet, see T. G. Otte, '"Heaven Knows Where We Shall Finally Drift": Lord Salisbury, the Cabinet, Isolation, and the Boxer Rebellion', in Gregory C. Kennedy and Keith Neilson (eds), *Incidents and International Relations: People, Power, and Personalities* (Westport: Praeger, 2002), 25–45.

8   For one example, see Sir Nicholas O'Conor to the Marquess of Salisbury, 18 March 1898, in Gooch and Temperley, *British Documents on the Origins of the War, 1898–1914, Vol. I*, No. 23, pp. 16–17. There were also reports in late 1899 that Russian troops were moving to the border with Afghanistan. In conversation with Sir F. Lascelles, the German Foreign Minister Bernhard von Bülow said that Russia could 'scarcely be doubted' of her intention to obtain a port on the Persian Gulf. See Sir F. Lascelles to the Marquess of Salisbury, 20 December 1899, in Gooch and Temperley, *British Documents on the Origins of the War, 1898–1914, Vol. I*, No. 302, 243–4.

9   See, for example, Grover Cleveland, 'Message to Congress Regarding Venezuelan-British Dispute, 17 December 1895'. A copy of this speech is in J. F. Watts and Fred

L. Israel (eds), *Presidential Documents: The Speeches, Proclamations, and Policies That Have Shaped the Nation from Washington to Clinton* (New York: Routledge, 2000), 181–4.

10 Lord Salisbury wrote to a friend that, 'A war with America – not this year but in the not distant future – has become something more than a possibility'. Lord Salisbury to Sir Michael Hicks Beach, 2 January 1896. Quoted in Roberts, *Salisbury: Victorian Titan*, 617.

11 See Kori Schake, *Safe Passage: The Transition from British to American Hegemony* (Cambridge, MA: Harvard University Press, 2017), 198–212.

12 Lord Selborne to Lord Curzon, 23 December 1899, in D. George Boyce (ed.), *The Crisis of British Power: The Imperial and Naval Papers of the Second Earl of Selborne, 1895–1910* (London: The Historians' Press, 1990), 98–9.

13 In June 1897, Tirpitz wrote to the Kaiser that, 'For Germany the most dangerous enemy at the present time is England. It is also the enemy against which we most urgently require a certain measure of naval force as a political power factor'. Quoted in Paul Kennedy, *The Rise of the Anglo-German Antagonism, 1860–1914* (London: George Allen and Unwin, 1980), 224.

14 Kaiser Wilhelm II, 'Speech to the North German Regatta Association, 1901', see C. Gauss, *The German Kaiser as Shown in His Public Utterances* (New York: Charles Scribner's Sons, 1915), 181–3.

15 The Triple Alliance between Germany, Austria-Hungary and Italy was signed May 1882. The Franco-Soviet Alliance was formalized in January 1894.

16 Quoted in Kennedy, *The Rise of the Anglo-German Antagonism*, 242.

17 Paul Kennedy, among other historians, has highlighted the relative decline for the UK in this period, paying particular attention to economic and industrial factors. Noting that Britain had fallen behind both the United States and Germany in terms of industrial manufacturing, Kennedy writes that British decline was 'not because it wasn't growing, but because others were growing faster'. Paul Kennedy, *The Rise and Fall of the Great Powers: Economic Change and Military Conflict from 1500 to 2000* (London: Unwin Hyman, 1988), 228.

18 Ibid., 227.

19 Richard Hart Sinnreich, 'About Turn: British Strategic Transformation from Salisbury to Grey', in Williamson Murray, Richard Hart Sinnreich and James Lacey (eds), *The Shaping of Grand Strategy: Policy, Diplomacy, and* War (Cambridge: Cambridge University Press, 2011), 118–19.

20 As Paul Kennedy has written, 'The spread of industrialization and the changes in the military and naval weights which followed from it weakened the relative position of the British Empire more than that of any other country, because it was the established Great Power, with less to gain than to lost from fundamental alterations in the status quo'. Kennedy, *The Rise and Fall of the Great Powers*, 226.

21 Aaron L. Friedberg, *The Weary Titan: Britain and the Experience of Relative Decline, 1895–1905* (New Jersey: Princeton University Press, 1988), 167.
22 Ibid., 161.
23 Erik Goldstein and Brian McKercher, 'Introduction', in Erik Goldstein and Brian McKercher (eds), *Power and Stability in British Foreign Policy, 1865–1965* (London: Frank Cass, 2003), 2.
24 Lord Salisbury served as Prime Minister from June 1885–January 6; July 1886–August 92; June 1895–July 1902. He served as Foreign Secretary from April 1878–April 80; June 1885–February 6; January 1887–August 92; June 1895–November 1900.
25 Memorandum by the Marquess of Salisbury, 29 May 1901, in G. P. Gooch and Harold Temperley, *British Documents on the Origins of the War, 1898–1914, Vol II: The Anglo-Japanese Alliance and the Franco-British Entente* (London: His Majesty's Stationary Office, 1927), No. 68–9, 86.
26 Quoted in 'Boer War Cost 100,000,000: Liberals, in Election Manifestos, Criticise the Government's Policy – Say War was Unnecessary', *New York Times*, 22 September 1900.
27 T. G. Otte, 'A Question of Leadership: Lord Salisbury, the Unionist Cabinet and Foreign Policy Making, 1895–1900', *Contemporary British History*, Vol. 14, No. 1 (2000), 1–26.
28 Quoted in Roberts, *Salisbury: Victorian Titan*, 789; The *Standard* and the *Daily Mail* were quoted in 'Lansdowne Not Liked: British Press Oppose New Foreign Minister', *Chicago Tribune*, 1 November 1900, 5.
29 The Fifth Marquess of Lansdowne served as Foreign Secretary from 1900–5; Secretary of State for War from 1895–1900; Viceroy of India from 1888–94; and Governor General of Canada from 1883–8.
30 Steiner, *The Foreign Office and Foreign Policy, 1898–1914*, 53–4. Ian Nish has written that 'Because of his War Office experience … he was inclined to bring in the strategic element'. Ian Nish, 'British Foreign Secretaries and Japan, 1892–1905', in B. J. C. McKercher and D. J. Moss (eds), *Shadow and Substance in British Foreign Policy, 1895–1939: Memorial Essays Honouring C.J. Lowe* (Edmonton: The University of Alberta Press, 1984), 61.
31 Memorandum by the Marquess of Lansdowne, 11 November 1901, in Gooch and Temperley (ed.), *British Documents on the Origins of the War, 1898–1914, Vol II*, No. 92, 76–9.
32 Zara Steiner, 'Great Britain and the Creation of the Anglo-Japanese Alliance', *The Journal of Modern History*, Vol. 31, No. 1 (1959), 27.
33 T. G. Otte, 'The Elusive Balance: British Foreign Policy and the French Entente before the First World War', in Alan Sharp and Glyn Stone (eds), *Anglo-French Relations in the Twentieth Century: Rivalry and Cooperation* (London: Routledge, 2000), 12–13.

34 Memorandum by the Marquess of Salisbury, 29 May 1901, in Gooch and Temperley (ed.), *British Documents on the Origins of the War, 1898–1914, Vol II*, No. 86, 68–9.
35 Roberts, *Salisbury: Victorian Titan*, 812.
36 See the Marquess of Lansdowne to Mr. Whitehead, 31 July 1901, in Gooch and Temperley, *British Documents on the Origins of the War, 1898–1914, Vol II*, No. 102, 90–1.
37 Ibid.
38 Memorandum by Lord Selborne, 'The Navy Estimates and the Chancellor of the Exchequer's Memorandum on the Growth of Expenditure', 16 November 1901, in Boyce (ed.), *The Crisis of British Power*, 129–36.
39 Memorandum by Lord Selborne, 'Balance of Naval Power in the Far East', 4 September 1901, in Boyce (ed.), *The Crisis of British Power*, 123–6. See also Steiner, *The Foreign Office and Foreign Policy, 1898–1914*, 53–4 and 'Great Britain and the Creation of the Anglo-Japanese Alliance', 29–31.
40 Roberts, *Salisbury: Victorian Titan*, 812.
41 The Marquess of Lansdowne to Sir C. MacDonald, 30 January 1902, in Gooch and Temperley, *British Documents on the Origins of the War, 1898–1914, Vol II*, No. 124, 113–14.
42 Steiner, *The Foreign Office and Foreign Policy, 1898–1914*, 47.
43 As Zara Steiner and Keith Neilson note, 'The treaty had been concluded with Russia in mind. In the three years that followed it was Russia that remained at the centre of strategic planning'. Steiner and Neilson, *Britain and the Origins of the First World War*, 30.
44 Steiner, *The Foreign Office and Foreign Policy, 1898–1914*, 47; Paul Kennedy, *The Realities behind Diplomacy: The Background Influences on British External Policy, 1865–1980* (London: Fontana Press, 1989), 116–17.
45 Selborne to Lansdowne, 20 October 1903. Quoted in Anthony Best, 'Race, Monarchy, and the Anglo-Japanese Alliance, 1902–1922', *Social Science Japan Journal*, Vol. 9, No. 2 (2006), 171–86, here 172.
46 Nish has pointed out that even Lansdowne was surprised at the support it received early on. Ian Nish, 'The First Anglo-Japanese Alliance Treaty', paper presented at The Suntory Centre symposium on the Anglo-Japanese Alliance, 22 February 2002. Discussion paper No. IS/02/432, April 2002. The renewed treaty in 1905 stipulated that both powers would pledge support if the other was attacked by just one power, as opposed to two. It also gave special mention to Britain's interests in India and Japan's interests in Korea.
47 Lansdowne speaking on the Anglo-Japanese Alliance in the House of Lords, 13 February 1902. See *Hansard*, House of Lords Debate, Vol. 102, cols. 1172–81, 13 February 1902.
48 Roberts, *Salisbury: Victorian Titan*, 617, 632.

49 'Lord Lansdowne at Darlington', *The Times*, 28 November 1901. See also Iestyn Adams, *Brothers across the Ocean: British Foreign Policy and the Origins of the Anglo-American 'Special Relationship', 1900–1905* (London: Tauris Academic Studies, 2005), 34. This treaty, known as the Hay-Pauncefote Treaty, was signed on 18 November 1901. Zara Steiner has noted that by signing the treaty, 'The British recognized the supremacy of the Americans in Western waters and subsequent crises in Anglo-American relations never fundamentally upset the basic understanding'. Steiner, *The Foreign Office and Foreign Policy, 1898–1914*, 47.
50 *Hansard*, House of Lords Debate, Vol. 129, cols. 6–51, 2 February 1904.
51 Lansdowne to Pauncefote, 31 December 1901, Lansdowne MSS FO 800/144. Quoted in Adams, *Brothers across the Ocean*, 224.
52 Schake, *Safe Passage*, 147–9.
53 He added, 'I certainly am able to say that during the whole course of these negotiations not one single word was said or written by the United States Government which was not thoughtful and friendly and considerate towards this country. That is true of our relations with the United States Government.' *Hansard*, House of Lords Debate, Vol. 118, cols. 1043–88, 2 March 1903.
54 Schake, *Safe Passage*, 150.
55 Adams, *Brothers across the Ocean*, 107.
56 *Hansard*, House of Lords Debate, Vol. 129, cols. 6–51, 2 February 1904. See also Adams, *Brothers across the Ocean*, 121.
57 'Note on Russian Position in Manchuria' by Lieutenant-Colonel Wingate, 29 July 1903, in Gooch and Temperley (ed.), *British Documents on the Origins of the War, 1898–1914, Vol II*, No. 211, 241.
58 Added to this was the fact that India had stated their opposition to Japanese assistance in the event of a Russian attack. Paul Jacques Victor Rolo, *Entente Cordiale: The Origins and Negotiation of the Anglo-French Agreements of 8 April 1904* (London: Macmillan, 1969), 201–2.
59 The Marquess of Lansdowne to Sir C. Scott, 29 July 1903, in Gooch and Temperley, *British Documents on the Origins of the War, 1898–1914, Vol II*, No. 242, 212.
60 For a discussion on the linkages between the Anglo-Japanese Alliance and the Anglo-French Entente, see E. W. Edwards, 'The Japanese Alliance and the Anglo-French Agreement of 1904', *History*, Vol. 42, No. 144 (1957), 19–27.
61 Quoted in Avner Cohen, 'Joseph Chamberlain, Lord Lansdowne and British Foreign Policy 1901–1903: From Collaboration to Confrontation', *Australian Journal of Politics & History*, Vol. 43, No. 2 (1997), 122–34, here 128.
62 The French produced a draft agreement on 21 July 1903, on which the two governments based their negotiations.
63 The agreement was welcomed on both sides of the Channel, with *The Times* reporting that the entente had brought 'tidings of great joy' to England. *Le Journal des Débats* celebrated the moment as one of 'historical importance', and one in

which France had been able to obtain its interests without a resort to force. 'The Anglo-French Agreement', *The Times*, 11 April 1904. *The Times* quoted passages from French papers, including *Le Journal des Débats*. See also Rolo, *Entente Cordiale*, 271–2.

64 The Marquess of Lansdowne to Sir Edmund Monson, 8 April 1904, in Gooch and Temperley, *British Documents on the Origins of the War, 1898–1914, Vol II*, No. 416, 364–73.

65 'Lord Lansdowne on Foreign Affairs', *The Times*, 7 November 1905.

66 The Anglo-Russian Convention was signed in St Petersburg on 31 August 1907. See Rose Louise Greaves, 'Some Aspects of the Anglo-Russian Convention and Its Working in Persia, 1907–14', *Bulletin of the School of Oriental and African Studies, University of London*, Vol. 31, No. 1 (1968), 69–91; Zara Steiner, 'British Power and Stability: The Historical Record', in Erik Goldstein and B. J. C. McKercher (eds), *Power and Stability: British Foreign Policy, 1865–1965* (London: Frank Cass, 2003), 25 and Steiner, *The Foreign Office and Foreign Policy, 1898–1914*, 47; Keith M. Wilson, *The Policy of the Entente: Essays on the Determinants of British Foreign Policy, 1904–1914* (Cambridge: Cambridge University Press, 1985), 74.

67 'Lord Lansdowne on Foreign Affairs', *The Times*, 7 November 1905.

68 Hilde Eliassen Restad, 'Whither the "City upon a Hill"? Donald Trump, America First, and American Exceptionalism', *Texas National Security Review*, Vol. 3, No. 1 (2019), 62–92.

69 President Trump first used the term 'Rocket Man' in a speech to the United Nations General Assembly. 'Rocket Man is on a suicide mission for himself and for his regime. The United States is ready, willing and able, but hopefully this will not be necessary.' Donald Trump, 'Remarks by President Trump to the 72nd Session of the United Nations General Assembly', 19 September 2017.

70 'Lord Lansdowne on Foreign Affairs', *The Times*, 13 December 1902.

4

The Middle East and North Africa in the twenty-first century: An analysis of social media impact and corresponding diplomatic trends

Negah Angha and Inga Kristina Trauthig

Over eight years have passed since the civil society uprisings that came to be known as the 'Arab Spring' swept across the Middle East, leaving parts of the region in civil war (most notoriously Syria), others in turmoil (such as Libya), and one embedded in democratic processes (Tunisia).[1] There has been much debate about the specific causes and timing of the instability and violence and the unresolved enigma of whether the demonstrations inflicted harm in the region or might still lead to a more positive future.[2] Although the reasons are multi-faceted, the ability of new communications technologies and social media to electrify and mobilize people, especially the Arab youth, has become an unchallenged component when discussing the Arab Spring and more recent political developments.[3] Social media in 2011 functioned as a catalyst for repressed societies but more practically was an unprecedented tool for organizing masses of people for demonstrations.

Typically, diplomacy has been heavily formalized and institutionalized, which results in a rigid mechanism with little room to react instantly, handle technological campaigns in a timely manner or connect with civil society. It is not that Western governments or diplomats were unaware of the Iranian-led online campaigns which focused on the corrupt political system – ultimately making the 2009 protests in Iran the largest since 1979.[4] Rather, they were both institutionally and technically unprepared to engage and support civil society

Negah Angha is currently on a sabbatical from the US Department of State. The views presented here are her own and do not necessarily reflect those of the Department of State.

in the region – limited by the rules of diplomatic engagement and unfamiliar with the tools that were in the hands of nearly every young person across the globe. This chapter offers an assessment of diplomacy in the MENA region regarding new technologies, as well as looking to the future and providing recommendations.

The interconnectedness that had developed between the populations in the Middle East by 2011 was exposed with the eruption of the Arab Spring. As Howard et al. describe it,

> No one could have predicted that Mohammed Bouazizi would play a role in unleashing a wave of protest for democracy in the Arab world. Yet, after the young vegetable merchant stepped in front of a municipal building in Tunisia and set himself on fire in protest of the government on December 17, 2010, democratic fervour spread across North Africa and the Middle East.[5]

In hindsight, it is not certain that the instability that erupted was, in fact, 'democratic fervour'. Yet the sparks of anger among the region's rapidly growing cohort of young people facing unresponsive governments and diminishing economic opportunities were spread and fanned by social media, providing social solidarity and tools for mobilization. Facebook, Twitter and YouTube retold the individual stories of political and economic repression across the MENA region in ways that inspired young people to organize protests.[6] For example, on Twitter, several million tweets with the hashtags #Libya or #Egypt were retweeted during 2011, either by local activists or participants and sympathizers from further afield.[7] It is important to note, however, that well before the protests in North Africa in late 2010 and early 2011, similar small-scale protests fuelled by social media against political leadership had taken place in Belarus, Iran, Philippines and Thailand. In June 2009, Twitter became the medium of choice for national and international activists to challenge the election result in Iran; the hashtag #iranelection was employed to the point that the Iranian protests were dubbed a 'Twitter revolution', albeit an unsuccessful one.[8]

For diplomacy, social media technologies are a considerable factor, both theoretically and practically. Although social media has been widely adopted by governments for policy articulation and explanation, as well as outreach to national citizens abroad, what should be the accepted diplomatic terms for use of social media in policy advocacy directed towards overseas publics (sometimes called 'public diplomacy 2.0')?[9] As people around the world have adopted social media tools for their political mobilization and action, governments have been drawn to these same tools to advocate for their interests and communicate with new audiences. Therefore, the practice of public diplomacy needs to develop new accepted practices.

There are limits to the acceptable use of social media by governments to engage overseas publics. Current public discussions about the unattributed or duplicitous efforts by foreign governments, such as Russia in the 2016 US election, to use social media to sow dissatisfaction, or to disrupt or alter the outcomes of political choices or processes, demonstrate the need for an evaluation of accepted practices.[10]

This chapter examines how the rapid changes in communications technologies have changed diplomatic practices in the MENA region. Firstly, it discusses the adoption of new communications technologies for political mobilization in the MENA region and situates the social media hype in 2011 in a broader historical context. Secondly, it describes technological developments in the context of US diplomacy, examining how previous US administrations responded to the realization that social media was a powerful tool for informing and mobilizing mass audiences. Thirdly, it examines the region-wide instability which began in 2011 and the US response. To conclude, it addresses how these new communications technologies have altered the basic patterns of diplomatic practices since the Arab Spring. In so doing, it assesses the possible revolutionary potential they hold for diplomacy in the Middle East and North Africa, a region of extraordinary diplomatic challenge where young people have demonstrated extraordinary prowess in using social media for political communication. In addition, it provides recommendations with regard to the MENA region, pinpointing the priorities and challenges for the region. This chapter uses a qualitative approach, considering primary sources such as the US Department of State's twenty-first-century statecraft agenda, academic literature, social media data, statistical evidence recorded by international organizations, and the insights of current and former members of the diplomatic corps. Bringing together the issue of social media and its importance in the Arab Spring with the quandary of how Western public diplomacy should engage with this trend in the MENA region, this chapter fills a unique gap in the literature.

Diplomacy in the digital age

The literature on diplomacy suggests that its practice is more art than science, as policy decisions and actions are often dependent on individual leaders and their perceptions or context. There is a lack of formal theories to guide the practice of public diplomacy and an absence of effective mechanisms to evaluate policy once implemented.[11] Discussion about public diplomacy and the use of social media, therefore, becomes a struggle to offer more than anecdotal evidence and a demonstrated affinity for new trends. With the evolution of technology, digital diplomacy became a complementary tool for traditional diplomacy, sometimes dubbed public diplomacy 2.0.[12] It is reflected in how foreign ministries have come to rely on the tools of social media to communicate policy positions directly to individuals, without the traditional government and conventional filters and how everyday individuals can communicate directly with, and perhaps influence, foreign governments. Sandre sees the evolution of a new phase – public diplomacy 3.0 – where pluralities of players meet and discuss issues[13] and where technology has dispersed power to people or groups based on the strength of their networks.[14]

Many analysts have written about how social media complements traditional diplomacy, making it more inclusive by extending its reach. Others have argued that it is an untenable disruption. This conversation is not new. Journalism scholars Bill Kovach and Tom Rosenstiel suggest that there have been significant disruptions in communications technology throughout history from the invention of the printing press, the telephone and the telegraph, radio and television, to the internet.[15]

In general, foreign ministries have been careful to observe formal diplomatic practices that avoided the appearance of 'meddling in the internal affairs' of other countries. The frustration that non-practitioners and political activists – and many diplomats – often felt in the mind-bending language of diplomacy often led to the impression that messages were being soft-pedalled or lacked meaningful impact. Social media provided an extraordinary new tool which invited governments to communicate directly with citizens abroad, over the heads of their leaders, which at times infuriated.

Social media allows diplomats to be in the mix, with everyone exchanging information. It gives diplomats the means to influence the countries they work in on a massive scale, not just by communicating to the elites.[16] Getting it wrong can have consequences, but getting it right can rewrite the diplomatic rulebook. Démarches, though digital, still must take place. But facilitating conversations and listening to the people and civil society are key. Foreign ministries are already attempting to change their means of delivery, nowhere more than in the MENA region. However, while foreign ministries can try to engage in discussions in host countries, in doing so they raise concerns about meddling even in open societies with friendly governments. Governments that retain power, even repressive governments, are closer to their people and exert more pressure on them than foreign ministries of other countries. We also have to take into account the limits of what social media engagement can achieve in foreign countries too.

Except for Bahrain, no significant uprising has occurred within the Gulf Cooperation Council (GCC) states, yet all have high internet penetration rates: for example, Saudis are the most active per capita uses of Twitter, YouTube, Snapchat and Instagram globally. Saudi Crown Prince Mohammed bin Salman, dubbed 'the prince of the internet generation', runs the government on the social media messaging site WhatsApp, according to academic Afshin Molavi.[17] However, very little has been done by GCC foreign ministries to reach out to their citizens and beyond. Every Gulf country monitors political activists closely and loose interpretation of laws makes it difficult to speak out against the ruling monarchies. The emerging findings of an ongoing study by academic Banu Akdenizli on how foreign ministers in the Gulf use Twitter suggest that Gulf states are not using it to engage and develop relationships with their citizens, but rather follow typical autocratic society rules that reflect only the agenda of the state and not of interacting with or seeking information from its citizens or followers. The GCC countries' diplomatic cohorts will most certainly lose opportunities in securing long-term domestic and foreign public opinion if it avoids interactive communication.

Some countries, such as the United States and UK, have invested in being recognized as having tech-savvy foreign ministries, but their effectiveness has never been satisfactorily measured.[18] The same might be said for the more clandestine efforts by Russia, China, Iran, Saudi Arabia, Syria and other governments seeking to affect actions by foreign publics. Others such as the Gulf monarchies have done very little.

The Silicon Valley effect

US and Western diplomats were aware that the rapid changes in communications technologies and social media were altering patterns of news gathering, public discussion and political mobilization in Iran in 2009 and beyond, but they were not positioned to take advantage of these new tools and dynamics. Although diplomats had long struggled to keep up with the tempo of a news cycle driven by non-stop cable and satellite TV, during the pre-social media era they still enjoyed a 'cushion of time' between decisions and manoeuvres, policy and responses.[19] Today, most Western diplomats still believe that effective foreign ministry policymaking requires reliable intelligence and dialogue with partners, the consideration of options and an approval process that assures the support of political leadership. That all takes time, regularly frustrating political leadership and publics who criticize foreign policymaking as archaic. Effective diplomacy cannot be conducted on a whim – it takes hours of back-and-forth conversation and an ability to listen and respond thoughtfully.

Although there has not yet been sufficient time for thorough academic analysis, the regular and vigorous use of Twitter by US President Donald Trump has clearly had an impact on foreign policymaking.[20] President Trump has regularly engaged in personally and directly articulating foreign policy messages. Irrespective of whether the President's Twitter diplomacy has successfully advanced his administration's foreign policy goals, it is clear that the policymaking process itself will never be the same as Twitter has now become the norm to obtain and share information by leaders.

Aside from policy articulation, social media channels have added a new element to public diplomacy practice – they enable two-way interaction between foreign ministries and their social media followers. The strategy offers the prospect of meaningful engagement between foreign ministries and attentive international publics, both listening and learning from foreign perspectives while using the engagement to advocate for policy support.[21]

Real-time, publicly visible international negotiations

In recent years, social media has increasingly been used as a means of direct communication between states.[22] Diplomats are also looking at new ways of relaying information about their decisions and actions during negotiations, particularly during periods of crisis.

Twitter became a public outlet that allowed parties to negotiate in parallel with formal channels during the fraught P5+1 nuclear negotiations with Iran between 2013 and 2015.[23] It also became an outlet that allowed the world to become party to the high-level negotiations that were taking place. Duncombe portrays one component of the completion of the 2015 nuclear deal with Iran, which was the Twitter engagement by US and Iranian diplomats on the respective negotiating teams.[24] Social media enabled each party to communicate publicly, signal intentions and develop trust when traditional face-to-face diplomacy between Iran and the United States was limited. Each exchange occurred before a global viewership, which provided a window into the negotiations and an understanding of the potential impacts on Iranian citizens and private companies looking to invest in a more accessible Iranian market. It also provided ammunition to opponents of the deal, who were able to convince presidential candidate Donald Trump that the deal represented a failure of diplomacy.

Many other key US diplomats have used social media to provide up-to-date information to citizens and pundits on issues they are working on and to dispel misinformation. Social media provides an important tool – and a challenge – in crises where there are few sources of reliable information. Faced with the vigorous use of social media by advocates of the terrorist Islamic State of Iraq and al-Sham (ISIS) group, governments were obliged to step up their own efforts to counter-message. The Global Coalition to Defeat ISIS created a special communications working group through which governments coordinated their public and social media messaging directed at ISIS supporters and seeking to blunt the attraction of ISIS for domestic and international audiences.[25] Former Special Envoy Countering ISIS Brett McGurk was particularly active in using social media to convey US policy towards multiple leaders in the region, calling attention to military or humanitarian crises and correcting rampant misinformation in what had become a media-poor environment with few reliable professional news outlets. Targeted Tweets and updates allowed citizens to stay engaged and sought to dispel misinformation.

The essence of diplomacy is the discreet delivery of confidential communications through accepted practices. It is therefore unsurprising that some governments, particularly those which prefer to control the flow of news and information to their publics, do not welcome direct communications to their citizens by foreign governments. Nevertheless, for Western governments, this practice is likely to continue although such methods open each message and policy position to dissection and interpretation by potentially unhappy governments and other social media users and those seeking to galvanize opposition to those policies.

Implications for the MENA region

Rapid changes in communication technologies have radically altered the MENA region's media landscape. Although governments were able to assert control over the terrestrially based national radio and television networks after independence, the era of satellite broadcasting followed by the rise of social media brought dramatic new sights and ideas to Arab publics and challenged political narratives spawned by the region's autocratic governments. The publicly stated purposes of social media companies to connect the world for good and the widely held belief that riding the wave of new technologies was important for the future of national economies diverted attention from the disruptive potential of widespread social media use. Arab governments came to understand this too late.[26]

The post-independence media landscape and its state entanglements

The resistance movements across the Arab world that pushed for decolonization in the early years of the twentieth century and the former imperial powers weakened by two world wars led to an era of independence and national pride across the MENA region. This was accompanied by state-building efforts by the newly independent countries, including the creation of national media institutions. Until then, these countries had been dominated by media input from the ruling power.[27] The King of Morocco, Mohammed V, commissioned Africa's first news agency and set the example for neighbouring countries.[28] These state linkages with news agencies were neither disputed nor controversial as they both mimicked the tools formerly wielded by colonial powers and were connected to the aim of creating strong, independent states in post-colonial MENA.[29] With this came practical issues such as direct funding by governments to promote a nationalist agenda, and wield power through the control of the main communication channel. Understandably, the new Arab governments sought to speak directly to their people and not through what they saw as colonial voices such as the BBC. For many years, these institutions were able to operate almost unchallenged while being tied directly to the government.[30] In 1975, the Federation of Arab News Agencies (FANA) was established with eighteen member states: Algeria, Egypt, Iraq, Jordan, Kuwait, Lebanon, Libya, Mauritania Morocco, Oman, Palestine, Qatar, Saudi Arabia, Syria, Sudan, Tunisia, the United Arab Emirates and Yemen.[31] Journalist and former Washington bureau chief for Al-Arabiya, Hisham Melhem, summarized the situation in a 1993 interview:

> Since World War II, in most Arab countries, the main media outlets and practically all the news agencies have been operated by the state. Before the Iraqi invasion, the Kuwait News Agency was not controlled directly in the way the Iraqi or Saudi or Syrian agencies are. But there was a chain of command, and it ended at the palace.[32]

However, by then the transnational potential of fraternization and mobilization via media channels was well understood – the pro-Nasser Egyptian Sawt al-Arab (Voice of the Arabs) radio was, until 1967, highly influential and widely listened to, spanning countries from Morocco to the Gulf states.[33] This dynamic pre-empts the social media era that transcended national borders in 2011.

The spread of satellite TV: The emergence of Al-Jazeera and its effects

The confluence of nationally guided news sources closely tied to their respective governments began to crumble in the mid-1990s when first the US broadcaster CNN and then the Qatari Al-Jazeera and other channels became available via satellite. They opened up new space for political communication, hampering governments' abilities to monitor the spread of information and dominant points of view.[34] A number of new satellite television channels emerged in the early 1990s. The Saudi-owned Middle East Broadcasting Center (MBC) was a leader in news after its launch in London in 1991, but it exhibited close ties with the Saudi regime. Eclipsed by Al-Jazeera's sensational coverage, it shifted to focus mostly on entertainment programming. Another important player was the Lebanese Broadcasting Corporation (LBC). Initially launched in 1985 as a terrestrial channel by the Lebanese militia during the civil war, it developed into a widely watched entertainment channel reaching an international audience.[35]

While LBC was hugely popular, it was the Qatari-owned and based Al-Jazeera that became the MENA region's 'must-watch' TV channel, making waves across the region for its news and debate programmes.[36] By the time of the 1998 Iraq bombings, Al-Jazeera was broadcasting interviews with senior Iraqi officials, including President Saddam Hussein. Operationally, the launch of Al-Jazeera was tied to political processes initiated by the young Shaykh Hamad bin Khalifa. Among other things, he wanted to launch an all-news channel that would compete with BBC Arabic.[37] These media developments worked towards unifying Arab public opinion through shared Arab concerns such as the second Gulf War, Lebanese instability, the Palestinian struggle or the lack of reform in the region. As a tool of Qatari policy, Al-Jazeera sought to become a cradle for a shared understanding of Middle Eastern values and galvanized anger over offences to Arab issues and ideals.[38] Early on, Al-Jazeera served as a catalyst for political protest movements, permitting social groups to air their messages free of national censorship. Advocates of political Islam were given a powerful new voice, and reformers were given broad opportunities to criticize corruption and incompetence in governance. However, advocates for parliamentary democracy and criticism of Qatar's leaders were off-limits. Precursors of the 2011 protests that spread across the region with similar narratives were covered on live television during the 2000–2 Israeli-Palestinian war and the 2003 American-led invasion of Iraq. Although these initial protests were impressive and sensational at the time, providing a vision of what was in store for the region, the imminent local political effects were minimal and no governments were severely disrupted.[39]

The wide-reach of satellite TV was captured by Eutelsat,[40] and by 2002, the proportion of households receiving satellite channels, including in Algeria, Lebanon and Saudi Arabia, was 70 to 90 per cent. Although the MENA region was facing a changing media landscape, pan-Arabic satellite TV demonstrated the potential for technological change to radically alter how Arab public opinion was formed and how political action could be mobilized. Although MENA governments faced new challenges in managing news and information in the early years, they did not anticipate and could hardly expect to control the flood unleashed by social media, which liberated each person to 'share' and 'like' information and opinions.

The role of social media in the Iranian uprisings and Arab Spring

In addition to the changed TV news landscape, the widespread and vigorous use by young Arab protesters of social media channels such as Facebook, Twitter and YouTube was significant to the dynamics sweeping the region in 2011. Although social media were not the decisive tools for these revolutionary movements, they were a key factor facilitating criticism of national governments, the articulation of demands and the sharing of information among protesters.[41] These equal access platforms nurtured novel developments such as the emergence and independence of female voices in leading and shaping the protests' public positions.[42] Technology was not central to the emergence and spread of the uprisings, neither was the leadership of any individual or political party, but it was striking how the technology and the messages communicated via social media resonated in various local environments.[43]

Satellite TV channels such as Al-Jazeera were drawn into becoming participant observers in regional conflicts. For example, in Libya Al-Jazeera was dragged into what many analysts described as a 'media war', in which the channel's coverage adopted a profoundly anti-Qaddafi slant and by March 2011 reported several hours a day on the unfolding conflict.[44] While this coverage was important, especially for international attention and to promote the legitimacy of the rebels, social media was more important on the ground in political organization and demonstrating solidarity.

The internet's regional penetration was the necessary precondition for unleashing social media's potential, and it accelerated in the years preceding the Arab Spring. In 2003, the number of internet users in all Arab countries was a mere 1.6 per cent of the population,[45] yet these numbers do not portray the actual relevance of the internet in the Arab world due to the under-reporting of internet use at cyber cafes.[46] In the early 2000s, bloggers across the region quickly latched onto internet access as a vehicle for personal expression and communication with like-minded people in both the region and the West. The surge in interest culminated in Iran's 'Green revolution' (the 'Twitter revolution') in 2009, which dramatically brought the power of social media to world attention.[47] Although most of the Libyan population was considered to be offline in 2011 (with internet penetration between 5.5 per cent and 14 per cent), between 400,000 and 900,000 people still succeeded in accessing the internet. Since a number of these connections were based on multiple-user cyber cafes, the number is likely to be even higher. In addition, this scope was widened by the high level of mobile phone connectivity: Libya reached 100 per cent mobile phone penetration as early as 2008.[48] This dynamic hastened the arrival of youth communication in particular. Across the Arab world, Facebook had more than 21 million users by 2011, more than the estimated total number of newspaper readers, with both Egypt and Tunisia displaying particularly high levels of membership.[49] In Libya, the Facebook Group 'Day of Anger' had 15,000 followers by 14 February 2011[50] and the hashtags #17Feb and #Benghazi were trending globally on Twitter.[51] Today, the relevance of the internet in people's daily lives is easily seen. According to Internet World Stats, by 2019 Libya had almost 60 per cent internet penetration.[52]

Internet access and the rapid adoption of smartphones cannot be seen as the causes of revolutions or even anti-regime protests in the Arab world. Significantly, the Gulf states have been ranked highest for WiFi technologies, but have barely seen protests since 2011. The numerical level of internet, smartphone and social media penetration is not the crucial explanatory variable. These are grounded in local conditions, culture and how local populations react to events on social media.[53]

However, these technological developments have advanced rapidly, and governments could not keep up – this rings true in other parts of the world.[54] Civil society actors were able to use the internet more effectively to overcome their limited resources. Therefore, in organizational terms, social media addressed two crucial hurdles for people in repressive states: it decreased the costs of communication, regardless of gender or background, and enabled people to raise their voices against regimes privately or even anonymously.[55] Social media, therefore, has been an accelerator, working alongside more traditional means of organization in the Arab world, such as Friday sermons at mosques.[56]

Historically new technologies have contributed to ground-breaking political and social transformations[57] and in 2011 in the Arab world, access to the internet and to social media-enabled protesters to circumvent obstacles to anti-regime mobilization.[58] As of 2019, some argue that social media has turned from a blessing into a curse;[59] however, its relevance and influence undeniably remain. Most importantly, the transformation of communications technology contributes to the evolution of 'old' public diplomacy to 'new' public diplomacy. The internet and social media have increased the tempo of international relations and the scale of engagement among states, societies, firms and individuals. National entities such as state governments are therefore pressured into adapting to the importance of the internet and other new media tools in promoting their public diplomacy efforts.

The role of social media in the West's response

Digital outreach by Western government towards hard to reach global citizens

Recognizing the ability of online tools to reach audiences directly, US diplomats broke new ground in diplomatic technological advancements when, in December 2011, Virtual Embassy Tehran was launched.[60] Although there have not been formal diplomatic relations between the United States and Iran for more than forty years, informal ties suggested that – beyond the frosty government-to-government relations – many people in Iran were interested in the United States, seeking information about the United States, regarding travel, study, politics or culture. Virtual Embassy Tehran is a website designed to provide a direct access Persian language channel for US outreach and engagement with interested Iranians without intermediaries. According to a State Department official involved in the project, it was originally conceived as a platform for two-way communication, enabling users in Iran to leave comments or ask questions. But it was determined that this would leave the site vulnerable to hacking by

Iranian cyber agents altering text or context, which could be damaging to the US government.⁶¹ To facilitate two-way communication, US diplomats direct Virtual Embassy Tehran users to a suite of social media platforms, which are also in Persian, such as Facebook, Instagram and Twitter. This allows US diplomats to manage both the opportunity of speaking to Iranian youth and the risk of compromise of its platforms.⁶²

Even while the State Department and the US embassies around the world were taking their first tentative steps at using social media to engage audiences, Virtual Embassy Tehran provided a unique case study for how a foreign ministry might seek to engage in public diplomacy towards countries where there is no physical embassy presence. It also tested the previously understood boundaries of diplomatic engagement by demonstrating how diplomats anywhere could reach beyond traditional bilateral discussions and open media to directly and privately engage with the citizens of other countries.

The Virtual Embassy Tehran website attracted more than 300,000 visitors in its first three months.⁶³ It was not surprising that the Iranian government, already locked in a confrontational posture with the United States, would react negatively to such efforts to affect popular opinion in their country, launched technical efforts to block the site. But undertaking communications with Iranian citizens over the objections of their government raised more challenges than simply taking regularly updated security measures to protect the site. It also raised important considerations for the US and other foreign ministries hoping to undertake similar projects. These included whether the cyber agents of Iran or other host countries would seek to monitor or gather intelligence on citizens who engaged the site, leading to possible harassment, arrest and imprisonment, or whether they would engage in meddling on the platforms.

Iranian internet users learned quickly to use new technological tools to avoid detection online, using proxy servers and virtual private networks (VPNs) to gain access to Virtual Embassy Tehran and related social media accounts.⁶⁴ The proliferation of circumvention tools such as *Psiphon* allows Iranian users to visit the site from inside Iran while evading the Iranian government's attempts to block or restrict access.⁶⁵ According to Sullivan, traffic at the web site is not routinely very high, but visits spike during times of heightened domestic unrest and demonstrations in Iran, or whenever Iranians are looking for uncensored content.

The question derived from the US' experimental digital outreach to Iran is whether it can evolve with new communications technologies to other forms of diplomatic engagement. In the case of the United States, social media programmes have been embraced at MENA regional embassies or for direct communications in countries where diplomatic or security considerations proscribe the sending of diplomats such as Libya and Syria. An interesting ongoing experiment has been the US-UAE Sawab Centre, a joint online counter-messaging programme that engages young people across the MENA region to challenge the vision being sold to them by violent extremists.[66]

While social media companies often describe themselves as leaders in bringing people together, they have yet to develop to the point where foreign ministries can turn over functions to online diplomats at embassies in stable countries. Despite its challenges, with the lack of resources to establish resident embassies in every country, a new generation of virtual embassies could become an attractive alternative, similar to what was meant to facilitate dialogue between US diplomats and Iranian citizens.[67] With the ongoing conflicts in the MENA region, this could be a way to overcome the limitations of traditional diplomacy. Studies suggest, however, that virtual embassies have failed to elicit dialogue or create relationships between diplomats and foreign populations.[68] Yet as Bjola et al. suggest, this may change in the future as the virtual reality route may create a more realistic and intimate experience in which diplomats meet 'face-to-virtual-face' with foreign citizens in countries with high social media engagement, talking to them in real-time and even engaging in joint projects. The United States is currently experimenting with virtual exchange programs, linking groups in the United States and the MENA region for education and engagement through a public-private partnership managed by the Aspen Institute.[69]

The ongoing struggle: To tweet or not to tweet?

As countries have expanded their use of digital platforms, they are struggling to adjust their online presence and learn how to use social media more effectively in a public manner to advance their foreign policy priorities.[70] Foreign ministries are still struggling to identify key nongovernment actors and to meaningfully engage them. Direct contacts will always upset host governments; the question is whether it is worth it from a national interest point of view and how far foreign ministries can have direct engagement without the current model of government-to-government dialogue. The current trend clearly points to major changes in the traditional rulebook of diplomatic practices, but it is unclear whether governments will ever reach consensus on acceptable strategies to conduct 'public diplomacy 2.0'.

In 2012, the US embassy in Cairo, experimenting with its then-nascent Twitter account, ran afoul of the Egyptian presidency over tweets linking to the *Daily Show*'s John Stewart's account. Stewart had raised concerns over the arrest of political commentator and comedian Bassem Youssef, who had been charged with insulting Islam and President Mohammed Morsy. The official Egyptian presidency tweet,[71] directed at the US Embassy and the *Daily Show*, read: 'It's inappropriate for a diplomatic mission to engage in such negative political propaganda'. The Muslim Brotherhood's Freedom of Justice Party put out a similarly terse tweet, stating: 'Another undiplomatic & unwise move by @USEmbassyCairo, taking sides in an ongoing investigation & disregarding Egyptian law & culture'.[72]

Max Fisher, a former writer and editor at *The Atlantic*, aptly wrote in 2012: 'Twitter is a social medium, and it both encourages informality and rewards users who embrace that more conversational style. It does not reward users who put out only staid press releases and official statements'. To be credible, diplomats do not necessarily need to descend to the lowest form of discourse, but they do need to communicate colloquially and authentically to be seen as legitimate members of the online community. However, if diplomats are to engage as ordinary people rather than as faceless bureaucrats, how are they to do so without having to face the challenges posed by host governments, or even their own government?

One of the problems revolves around governments' ability to really listen and engage with their foreign interlocutors. The implementation of a social media programme that allows governments to listen and understand their audiences should be a top priority. Former British Ambassador Tom Fletcher articulates it as follows: 'diplomacy is action not reportage, so diplomats will need to show that they can use these new tools to change the world, not just describe how it looks'.[73] How foreign ministries move beyond simple sentiment analysis to a position where social data can provide valuable insights into the crafting of a veritable digital diplomacy presence as a tool to articulate a country's foreign policy agenda, remains an open question. Many diplomatic communities are unable either to organize digital outreach or to effectively operate as digital communicators in host countries without falling foul of host country governments and their elites.

Conclusion

In the nineteenth century, 'upon receiving his first telegram in the 1840s, then British Foreign Minister Lord Palmerston reportedly exclaimed: "By God, this is the end of diplomacy!"'[74] However, the work of the diplomat has survived and expanded, as has the complexity of international engagement, as new communications technologies have evolved.

In mid-2017, Denmark named an ambassador to Silicon Valley, breaking new ground by putting 'techplomacy' on the political map.[75] The ambassador's assignment is to engage with technology companies in the same way as any ambassador would engage bilaterally with any host country. This is not an entirely new role, given that the San Francisco-based UK and Ireland consuls-general began working closely with technology companies five years earlier and in 2015 the US State Department appointed a representative to Silicon Valley to work with tech companies.[76] Nevertheless, this new level of presence in Silicon Valley begins a new chapter in the diplomatic rulebook.

Now technology is a driving force in changing diplomatic engagement, what more can be done to allow diplomats to engage freely with host country citizens without seeming like faceless bureaucrats? Although the two-dimensional nature of diplomacy endures, digital technology sheds new light on the tension between the public and private spheres of diplomacy. The digital revolution offers a positive-sum contribution to world affairs, with a reduction of distance and increased potential for understanding, but this must be weighed against the challenges.

The same tools that allow governments to speak directly to citizens around the world and increase space for underrepresented voices in policy debates also provide podiums for the spread of global populism and amplify discontent around the real or imagined impacts of globalization. Foreign policy can only be further enriched if diplomats can operate without being stuck in the confines of government-to-government dialogues.

The former UK ambassador, Tom Fletcher, notes in his book, *The Naked Diplomat*, that the use of technology and innovation in multilateral organizations such as the United Nations makes their work more 'meaningful and accessible to the public. More than a hashtag and a civil society event'.[77] Allowing citizens to follow foreign policy decisions and negotiations directly from the source provide more meaning and a personal stake for them.

The traditional structures of diplomacy make it too rigid and slow to react in a timely manner to technological campaigns or advancement made by the civil society it seeks to protect or connect with. It is not that Western governments or diplomats were unaware of the Twitter campaigns that prompted and played out during the 2009 protests in Iran or the uprisings in Egypt in 2011. A lack of flexibility meant they were unable to engage with civil society, proscribed, as they were, by the rules of diplomatic engagement. Diplomats need to be protected and indemnified, even if in a small measure, from their host governments to operate. Otherwise, the bilateral tensions make it harder for diplomats to pursue larger goals and objectives.

Times are changing, with leaders of nations – small and large – taking to social media to directly engage with global citizens – and the MENA region is a particularly noteworthy example to follow. Foreign ministries can change and redefine their engagement with social media in a more colloquial manner. As this will be an ever-growing issue, a long-term study is needed to assess the feasibility of such online, direct engagement and what the new diplomatic rules of engagement could look like going forwards.

Notes

1 N. J. Brown, 'Tracking the "Arab Spring": Egypt's Failed Transition', *Journal of Democracy*, Vol. 24 (2013), 45–58.
2 Clifton Martin and Laura Jagla, *Integrating Diplomacy and Social Media* (Washington, DC: The Aspen Institute, 2013); H. H. Khondker, 'Role of the New Media in the Arab Spring', *Globalizations*, Vol. 8 (2011), 675–79.
3 Andrey V. Korotayev, Leonid M. Issaev, Sergey Yu. Malkov and Alisa R. Shishkina, 'The Arab Spring: A Quantitative Analysis', *Arab Studies Quarterly*, Vol. 36 (2014), 149–69.
4 F. Tusa, 'How Social Media Can Shape a Protest Movement: The Cases of Egypt in 2011 and Iran in 2009', *Arab Media and Society*, Vol. 17 (2013), 1–19.
5 P. N. Howard, D. Duffy, D. Freelon, M. M. Hussain, W. Mari and M. Maziad, 'Opening Closed Regimes: What Was the Role of Social Media during the Arab Spring?' Working Paper Series (2011), National Science Foundation, University of Michigan.
6 Ibid.
7 A. Bruns, T. Highfield and J. Burgess, 'The Arab Spring and Social Media Audiences: English and Arabic Twitter Users and Their Networks', *American Behavioural Scientist*, Vol. 57 (2013), 871–98.
8 Ibid.; A. Burns and B. Eltham, 'Twitter Free Iran: An Evaluation of Twitter's Role in Public Diplomacy and Information Operations in Iran's 2009 Election Crisis'. in Franco Papandrea and Mark Armstrong (eds), *Record of the Communications Policy & Research Forum 2009* (Sydney: Network Insight Institute, 2009), 298–310 [PDF, pp. 322–34].
9 C. Hayden, 'Social Media at State: Power, Practice, and Conceptual Limits for US Public Diplomacy', *Global Media Journal*, Vol. 11 (2012), 21.

10 R. Mueller, *Report on the Investigation into Russian Interference in the 2016 Presidential Election* (Washington, DC: US Department of Justice, March 2019); P. W. Singer, E. T. Brooking, *Like War: The Weaponization of Social Media* (Boston, MA: Houghton Mifflin Harcourt Publishing Company, 2018).

11 R. M. Entman, 'Theorizing Mediated Public Diplomacy: The US Case', *The International Journal of Press/Politics*, Vol. 13 (April 2008), 87–102; E. Gilboa, 'Searching for a Theory of Public Diplomacy', *Annals of the American Academy of Political and Social Science*, Vol. 616 (2008), 55–77; P. Pahlavi, 'Evaluating Public Diplomacy Programs', *Hague Journal of Diplomacy*, Vol. 3 (2007), 255–81; Efe Sevin and Diana Ingenhoff, 'Public Diplomacy on Social Media: Analyzing Networks and Content', *International Journal of Communication*, Vol. 12 (2018), 1–23.

12 Hayden, 'Social Media at State', 21.

13 A. Sandre, *Digital Diplomacy: Conversations on Innovation in Foreign Policy* (Lanham, MD: Rowman & Littlefield, 2015).

14 Ibid.

15 Bill Kovach and Tom Rosentiel, 'The Elements of Journalism', *Covenant Journal of Communication (CJOC)*, Vol. 1 (December 2013), 1–6.

16 Philip M. Seib, *Real-Time Diplomacy: Politics in the Social Media Era* (Malden, MA: Polity Press, 2012), 86.

17 A. Molavi, 'Social Media and the Gulf States: A Revolution That Is Not Revolutionary', *The Caravan*, Vol. 1714 (2017), 7.

18 E. Metzgar, 'Is It the Medium or the Message? Social Media, American Public Relations & Iran', *Global Media Journal*, Vol. 12 (2012), 2; E. Gilboa, 'Searching for a Theory of Public Diplomacy', *Annals of the American Academy of Political and Social Science*, Vol. 616 (2008), 55–77; P. Pahlavi, 'Evaluating Public Diplomacy Programs', *Hague Journal of Diplomacy*, Vol. 3 (2007), 255–81; Efe Sevin and Diana Ingenhoff, 'Public Diplomacy on Social Media: Analyzing Networks and Content', *International Journal of Communication*, Vol. 12 (2018), 1–23.

19 Philip M. Seib, *Real-Time Diplomacy: Politics in the Social Media Era* (Malden, MA: Polity Press, 2012), 86.

20 For example, *Did Twitter Help Stop War with Iran?* https://www.wired.com/story/donald-trump-iran-twitter-war/

21 I. Manor and E. Segev, 'America's Selfie: How the US Portrays Itself on Its Social Media Accounts', in C. Bjola and M. Kornprobst (ed.), *Digital Diplomacy: Theory and Practice* (Abingdon: Routledge, 2015), 7.

22 C. Duncombe, 'Twitter and Transformative Diplomacy: Social Media and Iran-US Relations', *International Affairs*, Vol. 93 (2017), 546.

23 Ibid.

24 Ibid.

25 Authors' interview on 19 August 2019 with former US Diplomat and public diplomacy expert Larry Schwartz.

26 P. Ward, 'What Google's "Don't Be Evil" Slogan Can Teach You about Creating Your Company's Motto', *Forbes Magazine*, 5 January 2018.
27 J. R. Cole and D. Kandiyoti, 'Nationalism and the Colonial Legacy in the Middle East and Central Asia: Introduction', *International Journal of Middle East Studies*, Vol. 34 (2002), 189–203.
28 LIJAF, Ligue internationale des journalistes pour l'Afrique, *L'état de la presse en Afrique. Rapport 2005. Les agences africaines de presse à l'ère du multimedia* (Paris: Mediane, 2005).
29 T. Guaaybess, *Télévisions arabes sur orbite*. Un système médiatique en mutation (1960–2004) (Paris: CNRS Editions Paris, 2005).
30 Guaaybess, 'Télévisions arabes sur orbite'.
31 At the time of writing, FANA consists of sixteen state agencies, having lost some previous members such as Mauritania but gained others, such as Bahrain. For more, see their official site, https://www.fananews.com/en/
32 J. Stork and S. Ethelston, 'Politics and Media in the Arab World: An Interview with Hisham Milhem', *Middle East Report*, Vol. 180 (1993), 16–19.
33 E. Ghareeb, 'New Media and the Information Revolution in the Arab World: An Assessment', *The Middle East Journal*, Vol. 54 (2000), 395–418.
34 M. Lynch, *The Arab Uprisings Explained: New Contentious Politics in the Middle East* (New York: Columbia University Press, 2014).
35 Ghareeb, 'New Media', 395–418.
36 Ibid.; N. Sakr, 'Media Development and Democratisation in the Arab Middle East', *Global Dialogue*, Vol. 6 (2004), 98–107.
37 Ibid.
38 Lynch, *The Arab Uprisings*.
39 Ibid.
40 *Eutelsat* is one of the world's leading satellite operators, with a powerful fleet of satellites serving users across Europe, Africa, Asia and the Americas. For more information, see https://www.eutelsat.com/en/home.html
41 Martin and Jagla, *Integrating Diplomacy*.
42 N. Eltantawy, 'From Veiling to Blogging: Women and Media in the Middle East', *Feminist Media Studies*, Vol. 13 (2013), 765–9.
43 N. Eltantawy and Julie B. Wiest, 'Social Media in the Egyptian Revolution: Reconsidering Resource Mobilization Theory', *International Journal of Communication*, Vol. 5 (2011), 1207–24; G. Wolfsfeld, E. Segev and T. Sheafer, 'Social Media and the Arab Spring: Politics Comes First', *The International Journal of Press/Politics*, Vol. 18 (2013), 115–37.
44 R. Weighill and F. Gaub, *The Cauldron: NATO's Campaign in Libya* (Oxford: Oxford University Press, 2018).
45 UNDP Arab Human Development Report 2003, http://hdr.undp.org/sites/default/files/rbas_ahdr2003_en.pdf

46 Sakr, 'Media Development'.
47 Lynch, *The Arab Uprisings*.
48 Freedom House, 'Report Freedom Net: Libya', https://freedomhouse.org/country/libya/freedom-net/2019, last accessed July 2019.
49 Lynch, *The Arab Uprisings*.
50 The Libyan revolution is credited as having started on 17 February 2011, the proclaimed 'day of anger', which witnessed powerful protests in the country.
51 Weighill and Gaub, *The Cauldron*.
52 Internet World Stats, 'Usage and Population Statistics: Libya', https://www.internetworldstats.com/africa.htm, last accessed July 2019.
53 C. A Frangonikolopoulos and I. Chapsos, 'Explaining the Role and the Impact of the Social Media in the Arab Spring', *Global Media Journal: Mediterranean Edition*, Vol. 7 (2012), 10–20.
54 Ghareeb, 'New Media'.
55 For more on unexpected revolutions, see Susanne Lohmann (1994) and Timur Kuran (1991), who suggest that one of the major obstacles to mass protest is the falsification of online preferences.
56 D. Della Porta and L. Mosca, 'Global-Net for Global Movements? A Network of Networks for a Movement of Movements', *Journal of Public Policy*, Vol. 25 (2005), 165–90; L. Langman, 'From Virtual Public Spheres to Global Justice: A Critical Theory of Internetworked Social Movements', *Sociological Theory*, Vol. 23 (2005), 42–74.
57 Ghareeb, 'New Media'.
58 M. M. Aman and T. J. Jayroe, 'ICT, Social Media, and the Arab Transition to Democracy: From Venting to Acting', *Digest of Middle East Studies*, Vol. 22 (2013), 314–47.
59 Some have argued that social media's availability and anonymity have led to abuses by extremists and state-sponsored political manipulation. D. Welsh and S. A. Zway, 'A Facebook War: Libyans Battle on the Streets and on Screen', *New York Times* 4 September 2018.
60 In the authors' interview with one of the creators of the website, US diplomat Gregory Sullivan, he noted that the United States declared its intention to launch the site in July 2011. By September 2011, there were approximately 800 news articles regarding the Virtual Embassy. It went viral and it surpassed its expectations – raising awareness of Iranian censorship activities and directing young Iranians to engage with the United States on platforms it operated on.
61 Authors' interview on 8 August 2019 with US diplomat Gregory Sullivan.
62 Ibid.
63 Metzgar, 'Is It the Medium or the Message?', 6.
64 Ibid.
65 Ibid.

66 Authors' interview on 19 August 2019 with former US Diplomat and public diplomacy expert Larry Schwartz.
67 C. Bjola, J. Cassidy and I. Manor, 'Public Diplomacy in the Digital Age', *The Hague Journal of Diplomacy*, Vol. 14 (2019), 83–101.
68 Ibid., 6.
69 Authors' interview on 19 August 2019 with former US Diplomat and public diplomacy expert Larry Schwartz.
70 Sandre, *Digital Diplomacy*.
71 https://twitchy.com/2013/04/02/us-embassy-cairo-angers-egyptian-presidency-by-tweeting-video-defending-bassem-youssef/
72 http://www.thetower.org/egypts-muslim-brotherhood-takes-to-twitter-to-lash-out-against-obama-state-dept/
73 T. Fletcher, *The Naked Diplomat* (London: HarperCollins, 2017), 9.
74 https://blogs.wsj.com/digits/2015/02/24/diplomats-on-twitter-the-good-the-bad-and-the-ugly/, last accessed 16 July 2019.
75 N. Nikolov, 'Denmark Hired a Tech Ambassador. After What Happened with Facebook, Maybe Every Country Should', *MashableUK*, https://mashable.com/2018/04/10/casper-klynge-tech-ambassador-silicon-valley-denmark/?europe=true, last accessed 16 July 2019.
76 P. Blumenthal, 'Big Tech Companies Are So Powerful That a Nation Sent an Ambassador to Them: Introducing the Danish Envoy to Silicon Valley and Beyond', *Huffington Post*, https://www.huffingtonpost.co.uk/entry/silicon-valley-ambassador-nations_n_5b2aed12e4b00295f158ef8f?ncid=other_twitter_cooo9wqtham&utm_campaign=share_twitter, last accessed 16 July 2019.
77 Fletcher, *The Naked Diplomat*, 9.

5

Defining environmental interest: Identity, discourse and American engagement with global environmental frameworks

Dr Harris Kuemmerle

One would have to spend a very long time trying to come up with even a single contemporary global concern that does not have at least one central environmental, climatic, geographic, resource, pollution or energy aspect.[1] We see the environment in one form or another in all diplomatic endeavours, and climate change is the biggest political and diplomatic issue we as humans are confronted with in terms of both scope and complexity. That being said, some forms of modern diplomacy are more overtly 'environmental' in context than others so the distinction, while somewhat misleading, is appropriate for our purposes. Likewise, humans have also been acutely aware of the intense interrelation of societies and environment for as long as we have had societies with early examples of environmental protections, and policies related to the environment, going back millennia.

One particularly notable example of this recognition is the fourteenth-century Italian jurist, Bartolus, who penned the treatise *Tractatus de Fluminibus seu Tyberiadis* which dealt explicitly with the complex implications that the dynamic movement of the Tiber River presented for the established territories, sovereignties and relations in northern Italy at the time.[2] His work is remarkable for a number of reasons; however, what is perhaps most compelling is that he was one of the first thinkers to recognize and critically explore the idea that political systems, human relations and economic structures are fundamentally determined by environmental features, processes and spaces. His insights into the dialectical nature of human interaction with the Tiber River predates by centuries the later concept of the hydro-social cycle which has risen to prominence in the study of hydropolitics in recent years.[3] Indeed, the questions he asked remain of profound importance and have clear direct relevance to a whole host of contemporary environmental diplomacy issues – from the riparian politics of the Indus, Nile and Mekong to the complex legal questions emerging as a result of the opening up of the arctic to a whole host of new activities which would have never been possible before the Anthropocene.[4] This work, while but one example, is emblematic of a wider recognition throughout history that environment and terrain play a huge role in defining and shaping human interactions and legal systems across scales.

This chapter concerns itself with exploring how discourse, identity and politics shape both how a state conceptualizes what the environment is and how it defines what its environmental interests are. In doing so, it draws upon established concepts and principles within the fields of critical geopolitics, political will and environmental identity to present an emergent understanding of environmental diplomacy and state behaviour grounded in domestic-level political and economic discourse. This discussion is framed around the case of American involvement in global climate change mitigation and prevention frameworks with further insight drawn from the case of Pakistani hydropolitics. On the 1st of June 2017 President Donald Trump announced that the United States would be withdrawing from the 2015 Paris Climate Agreement. The fact that such an action came to fruition at all brings into sharp relief a number of key questions about the politics of environmental diplomacy and of participation in global climate change adaptation and mitigation frameworks, which scholars and practitioners still grapple with. That central question is how, and under what conditions, local and national governments 'have sufficient will and capacity' to push through *durable* environmental policies – a question to which 'we currently have no systematic answer'.[5] The notion of political will is a core component of this question which presents a number of conceptual and methodological crossovers with key aspects of environmental identity and critical geopolitics which I argue (when leveraged together) presents considerable opportunities to effectively interrogate Bernauer's original query.

In these pages I make the following key arguments. Firstly, I argue that specific environmental interests are an emergent phenomenon tied to the environmental identities of specific groups across the political and cultural spectrum. Secondly, I argue that different actors and groups all possess their own environmental identities – which are in constant competition to become 'common-sense' environmental identities within society – that have a direct impact upon their understandings of national environmental interest. Finally, I argue that specific environmental identities have had the effect of redefining how the United States understands what the environment is, and what its environmental interests are. The idea that environmental protection and economic growth are incompatible is the product of a particular environmental identity which (in this specific guise) emerged within the Republican Party and has become a common-sense understanding which has defined American environmental interests in opposition to global engagement on these issues. This affects political will and has made diplomatic efforts less politically possible while fundamentally altering how the United States approaches environmental policy.

Environmental diplomacy

The term 'environmental diplomacy' is a comparatively recent invention, only emerging towards the end of the twentieth century with Carroll's *Environmental Diplomacy* being one of the earliest examples of the term in academic literature.[6] Other subsequent key texts in the development of the idea were by Susskind and Tolba & Rummel-Bulska.[7] These works were influential, with Susskind providing key insights into the range of competing domestic and global influences at play in environmental negotiations. He argued that the influences and interests at play include political actors, competing agencies, commercial and industrial forces, and nongovernmental groups and interests which

> range from out-and-out conservationists who oppose any further development in sensitive areas to 'free marketeers' who believe that only pricing strategies and financial incentives, not regulations, will be effective in achieving greater environmental protection. Other nongovernmental interests, whether represented on the negotiating committee or not, will work to push the committee in still other directions: consumer advocates will fight to ensure that environmental regulations do not increase the burdens on the poor and the disadvantaged; real estate developers worry that local investment options could be limited by new environmental restrictions contained in international treaties; bankers are wary of the impact that new environmental regulations might have on economic growth; and spokespeople for various scientific groups want to ensure that all policy decisions take account of the 'best' technical research available – especially the work that they have done.[8]

His work provided an early insight into the multi-layered interests embedded within these negotiations which have in recent decades become a hallmark of track-II strategies and stakeholder engagement initiatives.

Before continuing, there is a more basic question to address: what exactly defines and encompasses environmental diplomacy as opposed to other forms of diplomacy? Broadly speaking, there are eight general categories of global issues which all require what could be understood as 'environmental' diplomacy to effectively manage and govern. The first of these – in no particular order – is atmospheric and environmental pollution which encompasses agreements which are primarily concerned with the regulation of atmospheric particulates including greenhouse gas emissions and other airborne pollutants, including noise and light pollution. Major examples of these agreements include the Framework Convention on Climate Change and the 1987 Montreal Agreement on Ozone depletion. The second is water and food security which includes frameworks such as the Water Convention for the management of transboundary freshwater sources and the Convention on Biological Diversity. The third category is climate and extreme weather which encompasses a range of environmental issues whose effective management is largely tied to the frameworks regulating atmospheric pollution mentioned previously. The fourth is environmental protection and ecosystem conservation, which is intimately tied to the issue of food and water security and is one of the cornerstones of the modern environmental movement. The fifth category is the health and management of polar and marine zones. This issue encompasses both specific marine and environmental protection frameworks such as the MARPOL 73/78 agreements regulating maritime pollution as well as the wider laws of the sea codified within the framework of the United Nations Convention on the Law of the Sea.

The sixth category is resource sharing and extraction. Governance on the issues of resource sharing and extraction depends largely upon what aspects of the natural world we define as a 'resource'. For example, the Mekong River Commission regulates the shared use of the water resources of the Mekong River between Cambodia, Laos, Thailand and Vietnam. The collective body of regulations on the management of fisheries and fish stocks represents arguably the biggest single example of a shared resource upon which it is difficult for any one nation to claim universal ownership. The seventh category is energy security which covers both the availability of energy resources (such as oil, gas or solar potential) alongside the regulation of the effective disposal of energy by-products (such as nuclear waste) in a safe and environmentally sustainable manner. Examples of these include both the Comprehensive Test Ban Treaty and the Convention on Civil Liability for Nuclear Damage.

Finally, the eighth category is public health and the management of microbial environments. There has been a growing recognition in recent decades that public health is fundamentally an environmental issue. Most aspects of public health – from disease, to health consequences of pollution, to efforts against malnutrition and dehydration – are fundamentally driven by environmental factors and require globally comprehensive environmental protection and governance frameworks. These exist in some cases, such as in the Agreement Concerning Cooperation in the Quarantine of Plants and Their Protection against Pests and Diseases, and the Constitution of the European Commission for the Control of Foot and Mouth Disease – alongside the range of frameworks on limiting pollution. However, in general the links to public health remain one of the most underdeveloped aspects of global environmental protections.

All of the above areas encompass issues and considerations which require extensive multi-scalar negotiations and governance frameworks from a local to global scale in order to effectively manage – which all tap into, and have profound implications for, nearly every aspect of human societies.[9] Naturally, given the extensive overlaps between these and other issues it is a futile – and ultimately unhelpful – exercise to delineate specifically what is and is not 'environmental' diplomacy. However, within the scope of our purposes it is sensible to understand environmental diplomacy as being negotiations where these issues play a leading role.

The notion of the global commons is also central, and while it is not within the scope of this discussion to go over the concept in great detail it should be noted that negotiations and diplomacy are typically only required in situations where there is a common shared resource which more than one actor relies upon – such as fish stocks, the atmosphere or water supplies.[10] Moreover, what is and is not a shared resource changes across scales. For example, at the national scale the Tennessee River is a common resource which the United States shares with no other nation state. However, at the subnational scale of the federating units, the Tennessee River becomes a common resource shared amongst a range of different actors with a resulting dispute between states over its waters reaching such a peak that it resulted in the creation of the Tennessee Valley Authority in 1933. This example highlights both how resources and environments change across scales and how political, economic and governance structures can often serve to define and delineate certain geographic or natural spaces along particular scalar geopolitical parameters which often run contrary to naturally existing environmental processes and systems.[11]

Contemporary environmental diplomacy, as now understood, began during the Cold War. Early examples include the Partial Test Ban Treaty (1963), the Convention on International Trade in Endangered Species of Wild Fauna and

Flora (1973/75), Convention on the Conservation of Migratory Species of Wild Animals (1979), Antarctic Treaty System (1959) and the Convention on Long-Range Transboundary Air Pollution (1979/83) amongst many others. Some scholars have argued that the general antipathy of the Soviet Union towards environmental initiatives in favour of economic and industrial development resulted in the Cold War period seeing fewer environmental agreements than could have been hoped.[12] However, others, such as Stephen Brain, argue that the decline of international environmental agreements since 1991 can be attributed to

> the fall of the Soviet Union, the end of the Cold War, and the collapse of a rival ideological, political, and economic system to capitalist democracy ... [which] ... greatly changed (and perhaps destroyed) the diplomatic setting in which environmental compacts had previously evolved and flourished. The replacement of a multipolar world power structure with a unipolar structure has greatly reduced the pressure felt by the remaining superpower to support environmental legislation.[13]

Regardless, the history of American environmental diplomacy after 1991 is characterized largely by periods of indifference or outright hostility to international environmental agreements, with only occasional engagement.

Environmental diplomacy regards negotiations and agreements pertaining to a range of primarily environmental issues. These processes encompass a wide range of influences across scales and are likely driven by a mixture of geopolitical dynamics, economics, international norms and subnational politics. That being said, scholarship on environmental politics has typically centred around inter-state negotiations with the varying influences which affect a state's negotiating position seen within this lens. While not disregarding geopolitical or more global-scale strategic considerations – such as those highlighted by Brain – I propose that specific environmental interests are not borne out of the act of diplomacy itself but can be better understood as an emergent phenomenon tied to the environmental identities of certain constituent groups. In this regard, the competing interest in international environmental negotiations is simply another front in a wider conflict between different environmental identities playing out across the political and cultural spectrum. Underpinning this assertion are two core concepts. These are the issues of political will in environmental diplomacy and how certain policies become politically possible. And the second is the role of environmental identities. The next section will interrogate these two concepts in greater detail.

Environmental identity and political will

Political will is often described as a key consideration in the successes or failures of international environmental agreements and frameworks. Post, Raile and Raile define it as a situation where a '(1) sufficient set of decision makers (2) with a common understanding of a particular problem on the formal agenda (3) is committed to supporting (4) a commonly perceived, potentially effective policy solution'. Under this definition, political will is both binary and open-ended, a dialectical relationship between two or more loose groupings of individuals and ideas. This model provides valuable insight into the nature by which political will is achieved.[14] However, it also presents some important questions, namely, what exactly is a 'common understanding' or common 'perception'. How are these states achieved, what do they look like and what ideational factors are involved in this process? In this section, I consider the concepts of environmental identity and critical geopolitics as a way of shedding further light on the notion of 'common' environmental understandings.

Critical geopolitics is centred around understanding how foreign policy (and global politics) is made politically possible, for example, in Agnew, Ó Tuathail & Agnew and Ó Tuathail.[15] Scholars of critical geopolitics argue that policymakers, along with all humans, have a certain set of assumptions and that these assumptions are 'socially constructed ... in different historical geographical circumstances and ... [provide] ... the basis for geopolitical rationales to social and political purposes that are anything but simple reflections of a natural geopolitical order'.[16] Three key areas have been identified by scholars in the construction of these assumptions: practical, formal and popular geopolitics. Practical refers to the assumptions inherent in the practice of geopolitics and foreign policy; formal refers to the traditional assumptions of geopolitical actors; while popular critical geopolitics refers to the geopolitical assumptions which are created within the area of everyday practices and popular culture. Dodds, Sharp and Dittmer have all highlighted the key role of discourse in shaping geopolitical assumptions, while Ó Tuathail and Agnew posited a concept of intellectual statecraft that suggests the world is built around various discourses, narratives and identities which, in turn, form an intrinsic part of a process of othering.[17] In such a view, foreign policy is not rational but the product of a complex set of discursive assumptions, identities and loyalties which question contemporary understandings of geopolitics.[18] Moreover, the role of culture and discourse must also be considered with McFarlane & Hay arguing that instruments of popular culture (including the mass media) help shape the terrain within which 'high politics' can be played out. They give space to some groups and interests. They marginalise others ... Dominant geopolitical actors map out lives and practices on a terrain of (inter)national consciousness – a hegemonic 'common sense' – to which they and the mass media, through their representational practices, have contributed.[19]

This idea of the hegemonic common sense is of particular importance as it illustrates how individual groups each can have their own 'common-sense' environmental identities and conceptualizations of environmental interest while also illustrating how certain ideas win out over others.

When understood alongside the idea of the hegemonic common sense, the assumptions of policymakers proposed within critical geopolitics establish a clear connection between what is politically possible and what are the dominant common-sense understandings of environmental identity and environmental interest within the society. This helps us to understand that national environmental interests are not solely the inevitable result of economic, strategic and/or geopolitical factors,[20] but are instead enabled and made politically possible through the elevation of certain environmental identities and interests over others through political, discursive or cultural means within a state's domestic sphere. This provides further insight into how a common understanding can emerge; however, we also need to grapple with the concept of environmental identity in relation to this.

Locating environmental identity is a difficult, and often fraught, task. Closely related to environmental identity are a range of concepts including 'emotional affinity towards nature,'[21] nature relatedness,[22] concern for the self in relation to nature and environmental issues,[23] and nature connectedness.[24] Taken together, these complimentary concepts form a key aspect of how environmental identities are shaped with Schmitt, et al. arguing that what these ideas 'share in common are the subjective sense of oneness with the natural world and self-definition as part of the natural world'.[25] Further studies have highlighted the role of reflection and education in developing environmental identities.[26] Likewise, a key study by Holland argued that personal 'sentiments' – such as a personal affinity for nature or passion for outdoors activities – are meaningless without a more foundational ideational connection and that 'sentiment becomes significant for sustained and generative environmental action only when it is transformed into a sense of self to which one is emotionally attached'.[27] These works suggest that environmental identities are an internally emergent phenomenon in that particular sentiments, to borrow Holland's terminology, may come to us through education, geographic location or upbringing, but it is ultimately through a combination of the above that we develop our own individual environmental identity through a process of self-reflection.

The above suggests environmental identities are an internally emergent process dependent upon individual sentiments and experiences. However, Schmitt et al. conversely argue that we should understand environmental identities as being the result of complex interpersonal interactions between individuals and groups – asserting that

> politicized environmental identification was a stronger direct predictor of environmental activism than was identification with nature. In other words, our findings suggest that environmental activism is driven less by feeling a part of the natural world, and more directly motivated by feeling a part of a collective of people who comes together to create pro-environmental social change. More generally, our work suggests that people's environmentally relevant behaviour is not exclusively or even primarily a function of people's attitudes toward the natural world. Rather, it depends to a large degree on people's conceptions of human social relations and within what human identities they situate themselves.[28]

While sentiments and nature connectedness are important for priming individuals towards certain environmental identities over others, it is ultimately this politicized process of environmental identification which cements identities and transfers sentiments 'into a sense of self to which one is emotionally attached'.[29]

These two concepts of critical geopolitics and environmental identity allow us to understand that different actors and groups all possess their own environmental identities. These emerge in a dialectical process of identity formation between the individual and the group, with the 'conceptions of human social relations' being the dominant force. The environmental identities of different groups are in constant conflict within the maelstrom of domestic-level political and cultural discourse with only some identities able to breakthrough and become a 'common-sense' environmental identity – or conceptualization of the environment – shared amongst the majority of individuals and groups. Critical geopolitics also reminds us that the identities (or assumptions) of policymakers have a direct impact upon their understandings of national environmental interest, and in the next section I will explore this further using the example of American engagement with environmental frameworks.

American environmental politics

All the major groups in American politics have an environmental identity and dominant environmental interests.[30] In the interests of time and available space, I will be considering only the two main American political parties. However, neither of these groups are homogeneous and are each composed of myriad smaller groups, ideological camps, and political and economic actors. The environmental identities of the two main American political parties (the Democratic and Republican parties) have evolved considerably over the last century. Historically, open to environmental protections (and the founder of the US Environmental Protection Agency), the Republican Party has evolved into a party which largely opposes environmental protections and advocates a policy on climate change that oscillates between scepticism and outright denial. The Democratic Party, by contrast, has positioned itself as the party of environmentalism and climate change prevention in opposition to the Republican Party. It is beyond the scope of this discussion to explore in-depth the evolution of environmentalism within US politics, or provide a detailed history of the environmental policies of the American political parties.[31] That being said, an understanding of the concept of environmental identity helps us to recognize that since the mid-1980s and especially since the end of the Cold War, the main parties have become focal points for two wildly divergent environmental identities which have served as the main spaces in which people have understood their social relations and situated their identities to draw upon the terminology of Schmitt et al.[32] This process has led to a considerable gap in the environmental identities between the two parties with an impact on the evolution of the environmental interests of the two parties.

What are America's 'environmental interests'? Are these interests self-evident, or are they the emergent result of political and discursive processes? American environmental interests are not fixed, or logical points, but are rather at times arbitrary manifestations of specific moments of common-sense environmental identities and interests which achieved dominance within the American political and cultural discourse. To understand better the nature of this process, it is helpful to highlight how American environmental interests have been understood since 1989. This discussion will be centred around American engagement with the Kyoto Protocol and Paris Agreement.

The Kyoto Protocol was signed in 1997 as the direct result of intensive negotiations beginning around 1995.[33] The United States had been an active participant in these negotiations under Democratic President Bill Clinton –

and in particular, Vice-President Al Gore – where it was argued by the then administration that participation in the protocol was in the United States' best interests.[34] Indeed, the United States was one of the original signatories of the Protocol in 1997. However, there were two main obstacles to full ratification of the Protocol by the United States. The first was the Byrd–Hagel Resolution, which passed the Republican-controlled Senate in 1997. The Resolution declared that

> (1) the United States should not be a signatory to any protocol to, or other agreement regarding, the United Nations Framework Convention on Climate Change of 1992, at negotiations in Kyoto in December 1997, or thereafter, which would–
> (A) mandate new commitments to limit or reduce greenhouse gas emissions for the Annex I Parties, unless the protocol or other agreement also mandates new specific scheduled commitments to limit or reduce greenhouse gas emissions for Developing Country Parties within the same compliance period, or
> (B) would result in serious harm to the economy of the United States; and

> (2) any such protocol or other agreement which would require the advice and consent of the Senate to ratification should be accompanied by a detailed explanation of any legislation or regulatory actions that may be required to implement the protocol or other agreement and should also be accompanied by an analysis of the detailed financial costs and other impacts on the economy of the United States which would be incurred by the implementation of the protocol or other agreement.[35]

This effectively outlawed US ratification of the Kyoto Protocol. The weight and importance given to scenario 'B' highlight a sea change in environmental identity, and perceptions of American environmental interests, within the Republican Party and members of the American right which had been underway since the Reagan Administration – with environment being secondary, ultimately in service to economic growth.[36]

The Byrd–Hagel Resolution was passed unanimously, enabled by the support of Democratic senators. This led Krogstrup and Svendsen to argue that 'supporting the Protocol would be irrational for [any] Senate members because of the potential risk that it could shutdown factories and lay off workers in their constituencies'.[37] While I do not deny that political calculus was a factor in the passing of this Resolution, I argue that this calculus is more reflective of the general success which the Republican Party has had in framing American environmental interests along zero-sum lines, with an implied assumption being that Americans must choose between the economy or the environment, and that the economy must always take priority.[38] Regardless of the validity of this framing, it further highlights how perceptions about what are and are not in the environmental interests of the United States have been shaped largely to reflect the environmental identities of key elements of the American Right which have recently come to dominate the Republican Party. Finally, the change in leadership in the White House in 2000, with the election of the Republican President George W. Bush, effectively ended any hope of the United States ratifying the Kyoto Protocol.

The second major international environmental agreement of the post-Cold War period was the Paris Agreement. As with the Kyoto Protocol, the United States played an active role in the negotiations leading up to, during and after the signing of the Agreement, and its success has come to be seen as one of the most significant accomplishments of the Obama Administration. One key difference between the Paris Agreement and the Kyoto Protocol is that the Paris Agreement was framed as an executive agreement, which negated the requirement for congressional approval – a near certain impossibility in a Congress where both the House and Senate were Republican controlled. Following the election of Donald Trump as the forty-fifth President of the United States (and the maintenance of Republican control of both the House and Senate), it was announced in June of 2017 that the United States would be withdrawing from the Paris Agreement. While the move appeared unprecedented, as we have seen, it was largely in keeping with Republican discourse and behaviours on environmental issues. In the announcement President Trump focused on how the agreement would 'undermine our economy … [and] … hamstring our workers', recycling decades-old Republican rhetoric and assertions regarding the incompatibility of economic growth and environmental protection as also employed in response to the Kyoto Protocol.[39]

What these two cases highlight is the politically subjective nature of what are, and are not, a nation's environmental interests. These interests are not fixed and are continually redefined within the discourses and machinations of the domestic political arena. In this regard, we can see that certain groups have the potential to radically redefine the national environmental interests along lines which more closely reflect their identities than any collective national 'good'. This is not unique to the United States, and the case of Pakistan provides a particularly helpful illustration of this phenomenon in action.

Pakistan, like the United States, is a federal republic. Of its four provinces, Punjab and Sindh are the largest and most economically developed. Geographically, the nation of Pakistan is made possible by the Indus River, which cuts a ribbon of green through the otherwise semiarid region, providing for the lives and livelihoods of those along its banks. The province of Punjab is the upper-riparian and by far the largest province in terms of population, geographic space, economic output and political importance. Sindh is the lower-riparian, and while still an economically and politically important region, it is considerably smaller in both population and economic output than its northern neighbour. This imbalance has led to chronic disputes between the two provinces, with complaints by Sindh that the Punjab is stealing (or trying to divert or store) its water through large-scale dam infrastructure becoming a perennial fixture of Pakistani political discourse.[40] It is beyond the scope of this work to go fully into detail into these dynamics; however, there is one aspect of it which is of importance for this discussion. As a result of the dominant position of the Punjab province within the Federal Government,[41] the close geographic proximity between the Federal Government and Punjab province, and the overall importance of the Punjabi agricultural economy to the Pakistani state as a whole,[42] the Punjabi conceptualizations about what water is (and what it is for) along with the understanding of Punjabi water interests have been largely adopted as the national water interests of Pakistan.[43] In so doing, the Punjabi provincial has become the de facto national scale, at least insofar as it relates to national and international water politics. This case provides clear parallels to the process by which certain groups have been able to redefine American understandings of what the environment is and what American environmental interests are.

An analysis of the framework of political will in the case of US engagement with the Kyoto Protocol and Paris Agreement reveals a few key insights. Beginning with the issue of sufficient sets of decision makers, the Paris and Kyoto cases present two significantly divergent situations. The biggest difference was that in the case of the Paris Agreement, the American negotiating teams did not have to worry about their efforts being contingent upon congressional approval. This allowed them to operate in a more focused manner, and without fear of their work being undone in the Republican controlled Congress. In the case of Kyoto, there was an insufficient number of Senators willing to support the protocol, which effectively curtailed its political possibility.

The second point, that of a 'common understanding of a particular problem', is the first main area in which the importance of identities, interests and the 'hegemonic common-sense' becomes self-evident. What form that 'common understanding' takes is entirely dependent upon the discourses and identities of the major groups involved in its formulation. In both cases we see a clear divergence between the two parties with no consensus or common understanding as to the particular problem. For Democratic policymakers, politicians and some voters, there was a common understanding (which grew stronger by the time of the Paris Agreement) that climate change was a serious threat requiring American global leadership – it was (and is still) argued that this engagement did not endanger the American economy and indeed presented a number of opportunities for new and innovative growth.[44] To Republicans, engagement itself, alongside environmental protections, was the commonly understood problem, presenting an existential threat to the American economy – as illustrated by the Byrd–Hagel Resolution. This dynamic has not changed and still characterizes the interests, discourses and policies of the major parties. With such a clear ideological and ideational divergence, the presence of a sufficient set of decision makers to pursue particular policy outcomes becomes a near impossibility.

The third aspect of political will is a commitment to support. Again, as we have seen, this commitment to support in the case of environmental policy has been largely bifurcated along ideational and political lines. Your likelihood to support certain policies is determined largely by the environmental identity of the party of which you are a member. This aspect is where formal lobbying traditionally takes place, with varied economic and non-state interests petitioning policymakers in the hopes of directly influencing their commitment to support certain policies. However, as we have seen, this commitment to support is largely based upon their common understanding and ideational background, meaning that while lobbying can change the voting intentions of specific actors, it usually cannot change the wider environmental identities of these actors without substantial investment and effort in redefining the environmental identities and interests of the political group as a whole (i.e. the Republican or Democratic parties). Again, in the cases of Kyoto and Paris, the Kyoto Agreement lacked a sufficient set of decision makers who were committed to support the protocol, largely as a result of divergent common understandings. The Paris Agreement differed in that the nature of US participation as derived from executive action meant that ultimately only one decision maker was required to support the President of the United States. This, however, has made the Agreement uniquely vulnerable to administrative shifts.

Finally, the fourth aspect of political will highlighted by Post, Raile and Raile is that there be sufficient support for a 'commonly perceived, potentially effective policy solution'. This involves a fundamental dependence upon ideational and discursive factors in that whether policymakers commonly perceive a policy solution as effective depends entirely upon their understanding of what the problem is. Suffice to say, in neither the Kyoto nor Paris examples was there any cross-party parity or common understanding on either the solution or problem. What this model shows us is that the core element deciding the political will (and political possibility) of environmental policy is the common-sense notions about what (if any) the problem is – notions which are ultimately derived from the environmental identities and perceived environmental interests of the major parties and groups involved. As long as this ideological and ideational gulf remains, true progress on American involvement in global environmental protection and diplomacy will remain elusive. It should be made clear though that the model of political will proposed by Post, Raile and Raile is not a definitive *if that then this* formula as much as it is a conceptual model. It will never be entirely descriptive or predictive and considerable variation is to be expected. That being said, it remains an immensely useful conceptual model for understanding and viewing the politics and ideational factors behind the practice of environmental policy and diplomacy.

Conclusion

Over the course of this chapter, I brought together insights from environmental identity, critical geopolitics and political will to nuance our understanding of the processes by which a state conceptualizes their own environmental interests and determines the appropriate level of engagement with international environmental negotiations and agreements. Focusing my discussion around the pillars of environmental identity, political will and critical geopolitics, I have argued that a state's perception of what its environmental interests are is an inherently emergent phenomenon that is produced within the maelstrom of domestic-level conflicts between competing notions of environmental identity and interests amongst different political and ideological groups. It is by this process that the conditions within which environmental diplomacy can exist and be made politically possible are produced.

In American environmental politics, the two main parties became hosts to two wildly divergent environmental identities and perceptions of national environmental interest. Moreover, despite occasional attempts at engagement with international environmental agreements, the elevation to 'common-sense' of the idea of a zero-sum mentality with environmentalism as antithetical to economic growth is reflective of the general success of Republican discourse in proselytizing environmental identities which are hostile to environmentalism. However, there has been a consistently rising majority support amongst

Americans in support of the Paris Agreement (and varying degrees of action on climate change and pollution) in opinion polling, alongside a majority disapproval of Trump for the unilateral withdrawal.[45] This suggests that we may be seeing a gradual shift away from this traditional line of thinking – though this cannot be said with any degree of certainty and opinion remains highly partisan.

What this – alongside the insights of Linton & Budds and Schmitt et al. – reminds us is that environmental identities, and conceptualizations about what the environment is, are constantly evolving in a co-evolutionary process of identity construction. Looking forward, the emergence of new norms from both within domestic discourse and elsewhere – such as Greta Thunberg and the rise of the Extinction Rebellion movement – will inevitably continue to fundamentally redefine the environmental identities of our political groups, and in the process serve to change environmental interests and what is or is not politically possible. This discursive process of ideational production shifts the space within which diplomacy is conducted and understood; however, only certain ideas and interests can become nationally understood as common sense. For example, while too early to speculate, the evidence at time of writing seems to indicate that SARS-CoV-2 (COVID-19) entered human populations as a result of a combination of over-exploitation of wildlife perceived as resources, poor protections for natural habitats and a disregard for holistic environmental biodiversity. Issues of environmental exploitation, and limited protections, have given rise to most of the epidemics in human history, including HIV/AIDS, and time will tell if the unprecedented disruption caused by COVID-19 galvanizes a shift in environmental discourse and identities towards a renewed interest in environmental protections.[46]

In these pages I have attempted to be as thorough and wide reaching as practicable and desirable. However, this discussion was fairly limited in a few keyways with considerable avenues for expansion and further study. Firstly, while I touch upon an example outside of the United States in the form of Pakistan, a useful future enquiry would be a full comparative study exploring the divergent roles and forms of environmental identities in the environmental diplomacy and policies of a range of cases. Ideally such a discussion would include states with both federal and non-federal, structures. Additionally, due mainly to space constraints, I did not go into detail in these pages into the role of global and international norms in helping to shape domestic-level environmental identities and discourse over environmental issues within and between particular groups. I would suggest that these global and international norms play a role in domestic-level ideational processes; however, further study would be needed to elaborate upon this point. Additionally, greater work on the history of the environmental policies and identities of the main political parties would serve to further enrich any arguments made.

In sum, individual environmental identities are a largely social phenomenon whereby individuals come to understand their identities in relation to those of others. This is a dialectical process which shapes the collective common-sense environmental identities of the group as well. In the case of the United States, the Democratic and Republican parties have diverged wildly in both their environmental identities and derived perceptions of environmental interests – with the opposition of environmental protection and economic growth becoming a hegemonic common-sense notion. This process affected the political possibility of certain policies with considerable implications for US engagement with both the Kyoto Protocol and Paris Agreement. These identities are fluid, and certain actors like Donald Trump, or Extinction Rebellion, can attempt to shift them, but full ideational change on the part of the groups and actors involved is a much slower and unpredictable emergent process.

Notes

1   These, just to name a few. When one also considers other concerns ranging from biodiversity (including disease and the microbial environment), land ownership, to food and water supplies, and the marine and extra-terrestrial environment, it becomes clearly obvious just how truly inseparable humans (and our politics) are from our environment. Indeed, one of the most central questions facing humanity in the twenty-first century is simply, what is the environment, and what is our place within (or without) it? But that is a question for a different day.
2   Stuart Elden, *The Birth of Territory* (Chicago: The University of Chicago Press, 2013).
3   The hydro-social cycle is 'a socio-natural process by which water and society make and remake each other' with human societies and the natural world directly intertwined and engaged in a dialectical process of co-evolution. See Jamie Linton and Jessica Budds, 'The Hydrosocial Cycle: Defining and Mobilizing a Relational-Dialectical Approach to Water', *Geoforum*, Vol. 57 (2014), 170–80.
4   Questions such as how changes in flow patterns affect territory, the allocation of newly emerging land and islands, and who owns dried-up riverbeds. Elden, *The Birth of Territory*, 2013.
5   Thomas Bernauer, 'Climate Change Politics', *Annual Review of Political Science*, Vol. 16 (2013), 421–48, 441.

6   John E. Carroll, *Environmental Diplomacy: An Examination and A Prospective of Canadian – U.S. Transboundary Environmental Relations* (Ann Arbor: University of Michigan Press, 1983).
7   Lawrence E. Susskind, *Environmental Diplomacy: Negotiating More Effective Global Agreements* (Oxford: Oxford University Press, 1994); M. K. Tolba and I. Rummel-Bulska, *Global Environmental Diplomacy: Negotiating Environmental Agreements for the World, 1973–1992* (Cambridge: MIT Press, 1998).
8   Susskind, *Environmental Diplomacy: Negotiating More Effective Global Agreements*, 4.
9   A more detailed breakdown of current and former agreements can be found through the University of Oregon's excellent International Environmental Agreements Database Project.
10 An effective breakdown of the commons can be found in Elinor Ostrom, *Governing the Commons: The Evolution of Institutions for Collective Action* (Cambridge: Cambridge University Press, 1994).
11 This is particularly evident in the example of rivers such as the Indus and Mekong. For more, see the works of C. Fox and C. Sneddon, 'Rethinking Transboundary Waters: A Critical Hydropolitics of the Mekong Basin', *Political Geography*, Vol. 25 (2006), 181–202; E. Swyngedouw, 'Neither Global nor Local: "Glocalization" and the Politics of Scale', *Spaces of Globalization: Reasserting the Power of the Local*, Vol. 32, No. 1 (1997), 137–66; E. Swyngedouw, 'Modernity and Hybridity: Nature, Regeneracionismo, and the Production of the Spanish Waterscape, 1890–1930', *Annals of the Association of American Geographers*, Vol. 89, No. 3 (1999), 443–65; E. Swyngedouw, 'Technonatural Revolutions: The Scalar Politics of Franco's Hydro-Social Dream for Spain, 1939–1975', *Transactions of the Institute of British Geographers*, Vol. 32, No. 1 (2007), 9–28; E. Swyngedouw, 'Globalisation or "Glocalisation"? Networks, Territories and Rescaling', *Cambridge Review of International Affairs*, Vol. 17, No. 1 (2010), 25–48; E. Norman and K. Bakker, 'Transgressing Scales: Water Governance across the Canada–U.S. Borderland', *Annals of the Association of American Geographers*, Vol. 99, No. 1 (2009), 99–117; M. Akhter, 'Infrastructure Nation: State Space, Hegemony, and Hydraulic Regionalism in Pakistan', *Antipode*, Vol. 47, No. 4 (2015), 849–70; M. Akhter, 'The Hydropolitical Cold War: The Indus Waters Treaty and State Formation in Pakistan', *Political Geography*, Vol. 46 (2015), 65–75.
12 For example, see Robert Darst, *Smokestack Diplomacy* (Cambridge: MIT Press, 2001); Marshall Goldman, *The Spoils of Progress: Environmental Misuse in the Soviet Union* (Cambridge: Harvard University Press, 1972); D. Peterson, *Troubled Lands: The Legacy of Soviet Environmental Destruction* (Boulder: Westview Press, 1993); Philip Pryde, *Conservation in the Soviet Union* (Cambridge: Cambridge University Press, 1972); Boris Komarov, *The Destruction of Nature in the Soviet Union* (London: Pluto Press, 1980).

13 Stephen Brain, 'The Appeal of Appearing Green: Soviet-American Ideological Competition and Cold War Environmental Diplomacy', *Cold War History*, Vol. 16, No. 4 (2016), 443–62, 462.
14 L. A. Post, A. N. W. Raile and E. D. Raile, 'Defining Political Will', *Politics & Policy*, Vol. 38, No. 4 (2010), 653–76.
15 J. Agnew, 'The Origins of Critical Geopolitics', in Klaus Dodds, Merje Kuus, and Joanne Sharp (eds), *The Ashgate Research Companion to Critical Geopolitics* (Abingdon: Routledge, 2016); G. Ó Tuathail and J. Agnew, 'Geopolitics and discourse', *Political Geography*, Vol. 11 (1992), 190–204; G. Ó Tuathail, *Critical Geopolitics* (London: Routledge, 1996).
16 Agnew, 'The Origins of Critical Geopolitics', 19.
17 K. Dodds, 'The 1982 Falklands War and a Critical Geopolitical Eye: Steve Bell and the If … Cartoons', *Political Geography*, Vol. 15 (1996), 571–92; J. P. Sharp, *Condensing the Cold War: 'Reader's Digest' and American Identity* (Minneapolis: University of Minnesota Press, 2000); J. Dittmer, 'Captain America's Empire: Reflections on Identity, Popular Culture, and Post-9/11 Geopolitics', *Annals of the Association of American Geographers*, Vol. 95, No. 3 (2005), 626–43; G. Ó Tuathail and J. Agnew, 'Geopolitics and Discourse', *Political Geography*, Vol. 11 (1992), 190–204; S. Dalby, 'Critical Geopolitics: Discourse, Difference, and Dissent', *Environment and Planning D: Society and Space*, Vol. 9, No. 3 (1991), 261–83.
18 S. Dalby, 'Recontextualising Violence, Power, and Nature: The Next Twenty Years of Critical Geopolitics?', *Political Geography*, Vol. 29 (2010), 280–8.
19 J. Linton and J. Budds, 'The Hydrosocial Cycle: Defining and Mobilizing a Relational-dialectical Approach to Water', *Geoforum*, Vol. 57 (2014), 170–80.
20 Though these factors undoubtedly do play a role in shaping wider governance strategies and policy approaches, they are less central to the establishment of individual perceptions of environmental interest.
21 E. Kals et al., 'Emotional Affinity toward Nature as a Motivational Basis to Protect Nature', *Environment and Behavior*, Vol. 31 (1999), 178–202.
22 E. K. Nisbet et al., 'The Nature Relatedness Scale: Linking Individuals' Connection with Nature to Environmental Concern and Behaviour', *Environment and Behaviour*, Vol. 41 (2008), 715–40.
23 P. W. Schultz, 'Inclusion with Nature: The Psychology of Human-nature Relations', in P. Schmuck and P. Schultz (eds), *Psychology of Sustainable Development* (Dordrecht: Kluwer Academic, 2002).
24 F. S. Mayer and C. M. Frantz, 'The Connectedness to Nature Scale: A Measure of Individuals' Feeling in Community with Nature', *Journal of Environmental Psychology*, Vol. 24 (2004), 503–15.
25 Michael T. Schmitt, 'What Predicts Environmental Activism? The Roles of Identification with Nature and Politicized Environmental Identity', *Journal of Environmental Psychology*, Vol. 61 (2019), 20–9, 21.

26 For example, see Wendy Simms and Marie-Claire Shanahan, 'Using Reflection to Support Environmental Identity Development in the Classroom Context', *Environmental Education Research*, Vol. 25, No. 10 (2019), 1454–78; Frans Meijers et al., 'Environmental Identity and Natural Resources: A Dialogical Learning Process', *Resources*, Vol. 5, No. 1 (2016), 11; Linda P. Tugurian and Sarah J. Carrier, 'Children's Environmental Identity and the Elementary Science Classroom', *The Journal of Environmental Education*, Vol. 48, No. 3 (2017), 143–53.

27 D. Holland, 'Multiple Identities in Practice: On the Dilemmas of Being a Hunter and an Environmentalist in the U.S.A.', *Focaal – European Journal of Anthropology*, Vol. 42 (2003), 31–49.

28 Michael T. Schmitt, 'What Predicts Environmental Activism? The Roles of Identification with Nature and Politicized Environmental Identity', *Journal of Environmental Psychology*, Vol. 61 (2019), 20–9, 28.

29 D. Holland, 'Multiple Identities in Practice: On the Dilemmas of Being a Hunter and an Environmentalist in the U.S.A.', *Focaal – European Journal of Anthropology*, Vol. 42 (2003), 31–49, 34.

30 I am only referring specifically to political parties when I say 'groups'. However, in practice groups can include not just parties but also NGOs and advocacy groups, corporations, unions, public organizations or any actor – or group of actors – of a substantial enough size to have an understandable environmental identity.

31 For further details on this, see James M. Turner, 'The Specter of Environmentalism: Wilderness, Environmental Politics, and the Evolution of the New Right', *Journal of American History*, Vol. 96, No. 1 (2009), 123–48; Michael Bruner and Max Oelschlaeger, 'Rhetoric, Environmentalism, and Environmental Ethics', *Environmental Ethics*, Vol. 16, No. 4 (1994), 377–96; Daniel A. Farber, 'The Conservative as Environmentalist: From Goldwater and the Early Reagan to the 21st Century', *Arizona Law Review*, Vol. 59 (2017), 1006–60; R. E. Dunlap, C. Xiao and A. M. McCright, 'Politics and Environment in America: Partisan and Ideological Cleavages in Public Support for Environmentalism', *Environmental Politics*, Vol. 10, No. 4 (2010), 23–48; Peter J. Jacques, Riley E. Dunlap and Mark Freeman, 'The Organisation of Denial: Conservative Think Tanks and Environmental Scepticism', *Environmental Politics*, Vol. 17, No. 3 (2008), 349–85; Craig J. Jenkins, 'Democratic Politics and the Long March on Global Warming: Comments on McCright and Dunlap', *The Sociological Quarterly*, Vol. 52, No. 2 (2011), 211–19; Jared L. Peifer, Simranjit Khalsa and Elaine Howard Ecklund, 'Political Conservatism, Religion, and Environmental Consumption in the United States', *Environmental Politics*, Vol. 25, No. 4 (2016), 661–89.

32 Michael T. Schmitt, 'What Predicts Environmental Activism? The Roles of Identification with Nature and Politicized Environmental Identity', *Journal of Environmental Psychology*, Vol. 61 (2019), 20–9.

33 S. Dessai, N. S. Lacasta, and K. Vincent, 'International Political History of the Kyoto Protocol: From The Hague to Marrakech and Beyond', *IRES*, Vol. 4, No. 2 (2003), 183–205; Sebastian Oberthur and Hermann Ott, *The Kyoto Protocol: International Climate Policy for the 21st Century* (Berlin: Springer-Verlag, 1999).

34 John Peterson and Mark A. Pollack, *Europe, America, Bush: Transatlantic Relations in the Twenty-First Century* (London: Routledge, 2003).

35 *S.Res.98 – A resolution expressing the sense of the Senate regarding the conditions for the United States becoming a signatory to any international agreement on greenhouse gas emissions under the United Nations Framework Convention on Climate Change (Byrd-Hagel Resolution)*, 1997, S. Rept. 105-54, 07/25/1997: vote no. 205.

36 Daniel A. Farber, 'The Conservative as Environmentalist: From Goldwater and the Early Reagan to the 21st Century', *Arizona Law Review*, Vol. 59 (2017), 1006–60.

37 J. Krogstrup and G. T. Svendsen, 'Can the EU Persuade the US to Rejoin the Kyoto Agreement?', *Energy & Environment*, Vol. 15, No. 3 (2004), 427–35, 428.

38 For more on this perceived duality, see Stefano B. Longo and Joseph O. Baker, 'Economy "Versus" Environment: The Influence of Economic Ideology and Political Identity on Perceived Threat of Eco-Catastrophe', *The Sociological Quarterly*, Vol. 55, No. 2 (2016), 341–65.

39 *Statement by President Trump on the Paris Climate Accord*, 1 June 2017, The White House, 3:32 P.M. EDT.

40 For more, see M. Akhter, 'Infrastructure Nation: State Space, Hegemony, and Hydraulic Regionalism in Pakistan', *Antipode*, Vol. 47, No. 4 (2015), 849–70; M. Condon et al., 'Challenge and Response in the Indus Basin', *Water Policy*, Vol. 16 (2014), 58–86; D. Mustafa, 'Social Construction of Hydropolitics: The Geographical Scales of Water and Security in the Indus', *Geographical Review*, Vol. 97, No. 4 (2007), 484–501; D. Mustafa, 'Understanding Pakistan's Water Security Nexus', *Peaceworks*, Vol. 88 (2013), 1–36; D. Mustafa et al., *Contested Waters: Subnational Scale Water Conflict in Pakistan* (Washington, DC: United States Institute of Peace, 2017).

41 See the works of Adeney for an excellent overview of this topic. K. Adeney, 'Comment: The "Necessity" of Asymmetrical Federalism?', *Ethnopolitics*, Vol. 6, No. 1 (2007), 117–20; K. Adeney, 'Democracy and Federalism in Pakistan', in B. He, B. Galligan and T. Inoguchi (eds), *Federalism in Asia* (Cheltenham: Edward Elgar Publishing Limited, 2007), 8–33; K. Adeney, 'Constitutional Centring: Nation Formation and Consociational Federalism in India and Pakistan', *Commonwealth & Comparative Politics*, Vol. 40, No. 3 (2010), 8–33; K. Adeney, 'A Step towards Inclusive Federalism in Pakistan? The Politics of the 18th Amendment', *Publius: The Journal of Federalism*, Vol. 42, No. 4 (2012), 539–65.

42 Further details on the economic role of the Punjab province within Pakistan can be found in the *Pakistan Economic Survey 2017–2018* and *Agricultural Census 2010*.

43 Kuemmerle, H., Mustafa, D., 2020, The IWT and the Scalar Hydropolitics of the Indus Basin, Journal of Water Law, vol. 26, 239–248.
44 The official party platform of the Democratic Party makes this point clear by arguing that 'Democrats reject the notion that we have to choose between protecting our planet and creating good-paying jobs. We can and we will do both'. *2016 Democratic Party Platform*, approved 8–9 July 2016, Democratic Platform Committee, Democratic National Party, Washington, DC.
45 Dina Smeltz et al., 'Growing Support in US for Some Climate Change Action', *The Chicago Council on Global Affairs* (2016).
46 For further on this topic, see David P. Fidler, *SARS, Governance, and the Globalization of Disease* (Basingstoke: Palgrave Macmillan, 2004).

6

Diplomacy and domestic populations

Dr Thomas Colley

'Diplomacy is too important just to leave to diplomats.'[1]

Ever since Robert Putnam suggested that diplomacy is a two-level game involving international and domestic elements, scholars have become increasingly interested in domestic influences on diplomacy.[2] Interest has grown in the Digital Age, in which increasingly widespread internet access and, later, social media have further globalized communication networks.[3] Diplomacy scholars saw this as heralding a 'New Public Diplomacy' through which governments could communicate with citizens.[4] Through this, the traditionally private, elite practice of diplomacy would be enriched by a new class of diplomats engaging more directly with citizens. Public diplomacy would be dialogic and participatory, rather than the top-down projection of press releases from foreign embassies to local publics.[5]

The spread of social media then led to the emergence of Digital Diplomacy.[6] While ostensibly interested in digital media's general utility in diplomacy, research has mostly considered how states might leverage social media to enhance public diplomacy and project soft power.[7] As theorist Corneliu Bjola explains, authors have made grand claims that digital media could grant 'extraordinary powers' to diplomats, enabling them to 'increase their diplomatic clout to levels they might otherwise not be able to reach'.[8] Results have been mixed in reality. It is debatable how much genuine engagement has come from digital diplomacy campaigns. Many have looked more like attempts to be seen to engage with citizens rather than genuine efforts to empower them to shape diplomatic agenda.[9]

The theory that digital connectivity broadens where and how diplomacy can occur has generated interest in the role of 'ordinary' people in diplomatic exchange. Some argue that domestic citizens communicating with foreign publics are participating in public diplomacy.[10] The logic by which digital connectivity means that anyone could become a 'citizen journalist' implies that anyone could become a 'citizen diplomat'.[11]

Some go further. Former diplomat, Tom Fletcher, argues that it is not just the case that citizens *can* be more involved in diplomacy today. For him, citizen diplomacy is necessary in order to build a more just and tolerant global society. As he contends, in 'a time of fake news, sound bites and echo chambers', 'outrage, intolerance' and 'closed minds', diplomacy is 'too important just to leave to diplomats'.[12]

If domestic citizens are – or should be – more prominent in diplomacy, then understanding public perceptions of diplomacy is more important than ever. Yet surprisingly, few studies of diplomacy examine it from the point of view of ordinary citizens. The importance of diplomats considering domestic and international audiences has certainly been recognized.[13] However, such approaches remain focused on what the *diplomat* must consider. Few if any studies of diplomacy begin from the perspective of the everyday citizen and how they interpret diplomacy.

Why citizens' perspectives matter in diplomacy

Citizens' perspectives on diplomacy are important for several reasons. First, if a thriving global society requires diplomatically engaged citizens, then helping citizens understand their role is vital. Developing understanding requires a grasp of how people perceive diplomacy in the first place. Just because researchers see diplomacy as becoming more about dialogue, engagement and participation[14] does not mean that ordinary citizens understand it similarly. Indeed, research suggests that domestic publics continue to see diplomacy as a private, international practice and do not recognize their increasing role in it.[15]

Secondly, citizens' perceptions of diplomacy potentially shape their broader attitudes towards their governments and could influence electoral choices. People observe with whom their leaders choose to negotiate. They may see some negotiations, such as with groups perceived as terrorists, as unjust. This may undermine the government's legitimacy. Citizens observe the outcomes of diplomacy in the form of treaties, trade negotiations, wars and peace. In the process, they develop their own assumptions about the diplomatic ability of their nations and leaders. These perceptions in turn generate expectations about how future events will play out.

As this chapter will show using the case of Britain and Brexit, if assumptions about a state's diplomatic ability are unrealistic, people may overestimate what is possible in a given negotiation. In the case of Brexit, the assumption of British diplomatic superiority, derived from its imperial past, reinforced the claim that Britain could secure more lucrative trade deals than other countries could manage, and much more quickly. At the time of writing, shortly after Britain formally left the EU in January 2020, there is little evidence that Britain can swiftly secure more lucrative trade deals than they had within the EU. Nevertheless, exaggerated claims about what is diplomatically possible can influence electoral choices by making citizens think that a decision will bring their country greater prosperity than is realistic. Consequently, public understandings of how diplomacy works require deeper study.

Theoretical approach

The chapter examines how diplomacy is perceived by domestic populations through studying their narratives about their country's role in the international system. The approach is ground-up and interpretive, focusing not on aggregating public opinion but on understanding the stories and myths told by 'ordinary' people about what diplomacy is and how it works.[16] This approach is similar to 'vernacular' and 'everyday' approaches that are steadily emerging in security studies.[17]

Central to the argument is how *myths*, deeply embedded in culture, can shape *scripts* about how the future will play out. To explain, myths are symbolic stories told by a society that illuminate its key values.[18] They shape what is unquestioned or treated as common sense in a given culture.[19] Myths play an integral role in the construction of national identity. A common example is how states maintain their national identities through the (re-)narration of historic victories and heroic defeats.[20] Myths often appear unquestioned, subject to little critical scrutiny, whether factually accurate or otherwise. They explain generally how things are, how things were or how things tend to be.

As cognitive constructs held by individuals and groups, myths are closely related to scripts.[21] Both are structured in the form of narrative, as they contain a plot – they concern how events play out over time.[22] The difference is that myths typically concern how events played out in the *past*, whereas scripts are stories about how events will play out in *future*.[23] They overlap because the past is the only resource one has to interpret the future. If individuals or collectives internalize a myth about how past events played out, this can be used to create a script for how they anticipate similar events will play out in future. Politicians or media outlets can try and influence the process by using metaphors and analogies to make present events seem comparable to events in the past.[24]

Britain is the focus here, in the context of the Brexit vote to leave the EU. Myths from Britain's history were integral to official narratives during the Brexit campaign because they generated scripts concerning how future negotiations would transpire. The Second World War was prominent, reflecting its long-recognized centrality to British national identity.[25] Pro-Brexit politicians and journalists claimed that Britain was once more 'standing alone' against European tyranny, as it had apparently done in 1940. The myth of Britain standing alone was used to create a script about how Brexit negotiations could succeed: if Britain stood strong, as it did against Hitler, Europe would fold, just as it did then. The idea that the Second World War reflected an exceptional British capacity to cope with challenges was revealed in former Brexit Minister David Davis's suggestion that 'our civil service can cope with World War Two, they can easily cope with this'.[26]

The mythology of Empire was prominent in Leave campaign rhetoric, and the Remain campaign frequently criticized this. Critics blamed 'Brexiteer' delusions that some form of 'Empire 2.0' might be possible if Britain is 'unshackled' from the EU, with some combination of the Commonwealth or Anglosphere enhancing British wealth and prosperity.[27] In contrast, the EU was seen as a drain on British sovereignty.[28]

Another important myth has received very little attention and is the key focus hereafter: the myth of British diplomatic exceptionalism. This myth tells the story of a nation that has developed a unique diplomatic ability and cultural understanding of others. Throughout history, this has enabled it to achieve more than others could in negotiations. This was shown by its ability to run the world's largest empire with only a handful of civil servants and diplomats. As the analysis will show, this myth shaped pro-Brexit politicians' claims that Britain would be able to finalize a range of complex trade negotiations with multiple countries in under two years when individual deals typically take closer to a decade to finalize.[29] As International Trade Secretary Liam Fox claimed in 2017, Britain's trade deal with the EU would be 'one of the easiest in human history'.[30] Such assumptions were partly based on the size of Britain's economy, meaning that other states have strong incentives to give Britain a favourable deal. Pro-Brexit politicians framed this in terms of the Germans wanting to keep selling BMWs or the Italians wanting to secure prosecco sales – claims ridiculed in the pro-Remain press for their naïve oversimplicity.[31] However, these superficial claims were also underpinned by the myth that Britain has always 'punched above its weight' diplomatically, achieving influence other nations could not.[32]

These examples show how official discourse during the Brexit campaign drew on the myth of British diplomatic exceptionalism to generate scripts about how easy future trade negotiations would be. Ordinarily, the nuances of diplomacy and trade negotiations are peripheral concerns to most citizens. Given their prominence in Brexit debates, however, a key question is: how do ordinary people interpret these claims?

Methodology

To address this, this chapter draws on qualitative data from prior research by the author on how British citizens interpret their country's foreign policy and role in the world.[33] In-depth, semi-structured interviews were conducted between October 2014 and January 2015 with a wide range of sixty-seven British citizens resident in England. Returning to this data in the wake of the Brexit vote reveals striking evidence of how people's scripts about how Brexit would proceed contrasted with emerging reality.

Sampling was based on the qualitative principles of range and saturation: interviewing as broad a range of people as possible and doing so until the point of data saturation, whereby no new perspectives were being identified with additional interviews. The resulting sample was highly diverse in terms of age (range eighteen to ninety-two years), gender (n = thirty-four male, thirty-three female) and socioeconomic classification. Resource constraints limited the research to British participants resident in England, although sample diversity is enhanced by numerous Welsh and Scottish participants, as well as British Asians and British Arabs. Nevertheless, future research into national and ethnic variation within the UK would be useful.[34]

After establishing how ordinary people think diplomacy works, these accounts were contrasted with political speeches, policy documents, media articles, blog posts and opinion polls to build a picture of how public perspectives on British diplomatic exceptionalism are reflected in elite discourse on Britain's future outside the EU.

How 'ordinary' people describe how diplomacy works

As many aspects of international diplomacy remain private, it is ripe for myth-making. Theories that one nation has better diplomats than another are essentially unfalsifiable by citizens – it is therefore easy to believe them in the absence of evidence to the contrary.³⁵ Myths can develop around how diplomacy works or who is good at it. They might concern particular individuals accepted as uniquely capable diplomats. Early in his administration, US President Donald Trump tried hard to establish his own mythology as a uniquely artful negotiator, drawing from his business career. Alternatively, myths can develop about the general abilities of nations to achieve their political aims through diplomacy without needing to resort to military force. As will be shown, this is a key element of the myth of British diplomatic exceptionalism.

While participants across the political spectrum agreed that Britain possesses unique diplomatic abilities, their understanding of the diplomatic process itself tends to be basic, with little indication that as citizens they play a role in the process. This does not mean public views are incorrect; indeed, the assumptions of a broad range of participants reflect the concerns of foreign policymakers. Rather, their varied ideas about how Britain exerts diplomatic influence tend to be listed in the form of metaphors and generalities, with little specific detail.

The first assumption of citizens is that the ability to achieve one's aims in diplomatic exchange is largely driven by economic and military power – hard power – which gives countries metaphorical 'weight', 'clout', 'influence' and 'respect'. If a state is powerful enough, it might be at the 'top table' of international affairs. What to do with this status depends on people's political orientation. More nationalist and militarist citizens – that is, those more willing to support the use of military force in pursuit of national interests – may favour military action. Liberal internationalists might aim to mediate conflict and perhaps act as a 'peacemaker', while more pacifistic participants may want to prevent conflict in the first place. Whatever the objective, it is assumed that more material power makes a state more likely to be 'listened to' in diplomatic exchange, because they can 'put their money where their mouth is' and are less likely to be 'pushed around'. As the saying goes, 'You are either at the table, or on the menu'. Some participants were able to list features that grant Britain diplomatic weight and clout, for instance, permanent membership of the UN Security Council, but most generally explained that Britain either was at the top table or should seek to return there.

Beyond this primary focus on hard power, a wide range of participants emphasized British soft power as a major source of influence, even if they did not use the term itself. They explained that institutions such as the BBC, universities, British parliamentary democracy and the English language more generally meant Britain 'punches above its weight' in world affairs. Yet not all citizens agreed that this was sufficient to ensure Britain's influence: Eurosceptic participants in particular saw Britain as having materially declined so far that it was 'insignificant', 'emasculated', with 'not a lot of say' in the world.[36] But however people judged Britain's level of influence, they tended to agree that influence in world politics is exerted through economic and military strength first, and cultural influence second. This generated concern that Britain's relative material decline since imperial times has meant that it is 'no longer listened to', lacks the clout and weight it used to have, and that this is bad for it and the world, even if Britain retains significant cultural influence through its language and institutions.

Comparing ordinary citizens and political elites

Citizens' understanding of the different ways Britain supposedly 'punches above its weight' mirrors closely how British politicians have often framed its foreign policy in recent decades, particularly on the political Right.[37] It is not without criticism: repeated cuts to the armed forces and the Foreign and Commonwealth Office budget reinforce the longstanding argument that Britain 'punching above its weight' is rhetoric, not reality.[38] More recently, the 'Global Britain' campaign, first promoted in 2016 to reassert Britain's global outlook despite the retreat implied by the Brexit vote, has been criticized as a 'superficial branding exercise' that lists existing British activities rather than providing specifics about what would measurably change.[39] Issues such as Britain's lack of trade negotiators, due to the EU having done this centrally, are silenced. More attention is paid to repeating all the ways Britain can be seen as outperforming others. These are used as evidence that Britain would succeed because it has always managed to achieve remarkable feats in international affairs. A 2018 speech to promote the campaign by International Development Secretary Penny Mordaunt exemplifies this in explaining why the world apparently 'needs Britain's leadership':

> We are strong because of our values, we are strong because we are capable. Just think about the incredible response to our diplomatic efforts in the wake of the Salisbury attack. The esteem in which the UK is held as a development superpower. And that our Armed Forces are still the prototype others seek to emulate, and the defence partner of choice. That's what our nation does. And that means our nation is a protector. It's a wealth bringer. A capacity builder. A problem solver. A life-saver. And a peace broker. A commonwealth member. A global 0.7, 2 per cent nation. At a time when the interests of other nations is so diverse. At a time when the world is changing so fast. We are the game changer nation. What other nation has so much to offer to so many?[40]

It is also common for official foreign policy announcements to attribute Britain's disproportionate influence to the superior ingenuity and resilience of its people. MP David Lidington, expounding on how to 'Build a Global Britain' after Brexit, emphasized that it is 'a nation of pioneers, innovators, explorers and creators' with 'cutting edge innovation in every field which is the envy of the world ... and the greatest soft power of any nation on the planet'.[41] Claims that the British people possess superior creativity and resilience can be traced far back through British political history. In imperial times, superior creativity was credited with enabling British technological innovation, which granted economic and military superiority. Superior British character was credited with forging more cultured and principled diplomats and more resilient soldiers than other nations have produced. In British nationalist myth, these characteristics enabled Britain to defend itself and 'freedom' more generally in key moments through history, be it repelling the Roman invasion, the Spanish Armada, the threat of Napoleon or the Battle of Britain.[42] And despite fighting many colonial wars, these characteristics supposedly enabled the British Empire to maintain 'a global peace unmatched before or since'.[43] As Vincent explained (65+, Worcestershire), 'we're a nation full of inventiveness, we're industrious. The ideas socially and industrially, technologically, we really are, we're leaders.'[44]

The mythology of British diplomatic exceptionalism

The idea of British diplomatic exceptionalism thus fits within a broader mythology of British exceptionalism that is a central constituent of national identity, visible in the discourse of political elites and 'ordinary' people. The extent of Britain's greatness today is contested across British citizens, given that they broadly agree that Britain has declined relative to others since the days of Empire.[45] Despite this, people largely agree that Britain possesses unique diplomatic capability. Again, this idea stems from imperial times and the notion that Britain managed to run such a large empire with a remarkably small number of diplomats, civil servants and soldiers, due in part to the superior understanding they developed of other cultures.

The myth of British diplomatic exceptionalism has not sprung up out of nowhere; like most myths it is grounded in some element of truth. Britain did govern approximately a quarter of the world's population and territory at the height of Empire, with what appears to be a remarkably light governmental footprint. For instance, Niall Ferguson estimates that only 900 British civil servants and 70,000 British soldiers managed to govern approximately 250 million Indians.[46] There is present-day evidence too. Britain may only possess a small collection of overseas territories, but it retains one of the most developed diplomatic networks globally. Portland's Soft Power 30 Index placed Britain first globally in 2015, second in 2016 and 2017, and perhaps most surprisingly for some, first again in 2018.[47] The Istanbul Center for Digital Affairs placed it first globally in its new Digital Diplomacy Review Index in 2016 and second in 2017.[48]

Britain's diplomatic exceptionalism has been consistently promoted by British politicians as an area where Britain ought to lead the world.[49] While previously Britain could have 'sent a gunboat' unilaterally and get its way through clever words and the threat of force, today British politicians emphasize Britain's ability to bring countries together to secure collective action. As then Foreign Secretary William Hague explained in a 2011 speech tellingly entitled 'The best diplomatic service in the world':

> There are few if any diplomatic services in the world that can rival Britain in the crafting and negotiating of international agreement as a basis for collective action. Our diplomats excel at finding deft, realistic and workable solutions that bridge the gap between countries with vastly different perspectives.[50]

These sentiments are broadly agreed upon across the British citizens interviewed here. Participants evaluate the British Empire very differently – some see it as a benevolent, free trading enterprise that brought overwhelming benefit to the colonized; others view it as oppressive, exploitative and violent.[51] But at both extremes, citizens agree that ruling so much of the world has given Britain unique understanding of others that it could use to achieve positive diplomatic effect, however they define what that would be:

> Diana (18–24, London): I think people always viewed Britain as the big dog even though it's a small country, but not to be forgotten about because they've always had links with other countries, or allies. And because they have had those colonies, they probably know quite a lot about what's going on in a lot of countries, and we're quite developed so we probably have quite a few links everywhere. So, I think it's quite … we probably have a lot of knowledge of what's going on everywhere.
>
> Kenneth (55–64, Liverpool): [Britain's role in the world] is certainly not subjugating the natives anymore. It should be about … arbitrating things. An expert witness if you like on the way it could be done. I mean we've got

experience of subjugating peoples and ruling empires and things. We should know how different nationalities in different countries work. We should know a bit more than other people I suspect. So, we should be there as mediators in the world perhaps.[52]

How this supposedly superior understanding should be used varies according to people's political perspectives. Kenneth argues that it should be used to 'mediate' world conflict. Similar sentiments were expressed by self-defining liberal participants who suggested that Britain plays a 'patriarchal role' as 'the ones that are consulted when things start to go wrong' in international relations (Faith, 18–24, Cumbria). Conversely, for more nationalist and militarist citizens, possessing superior expertise and understanding is a way of extracting concessions from others to advance narrower national interests. Exerting British influence for either motive is thought possible because 'people look up to us' (Richard, 65+, Worcestershire) and 'come to us' (Terry, 55–64, Worcestershire) to resolve disputes because Britain is seen as 'an honest broker' (Samuel, 65+, Dorset), a 'voice of reason' and even a 'father figure' (Shaun, 55–64, Dorset) which has done 'an awful lot to solve conflict in the past' (Ida, 55–64, Liverpool) and to promote liberal democracy. In this way these ideas underpin assumptions that Britain might be able to use its superior understanding and accumulated goodwill to secure favourable terms during Brexit negotiations.

Perhaps the most intriguing aspect of these accounts is that 'subjugating others' or 'ruling empires' is thought to qualify Britain to mediate world conflict. Myths are forms of common-sense understanding that are often accepted without significant critical thought. Yet there is good reason to suggest that many people, if they reflected on the logic of Kenneth's argument, would reject it outright. After all, the logic that subjugating others qualifies one as an arbiter of international disputes would mean that the greatest despots in human history would be the best people to oversee conflict resolution. That many observers would likely reject this idea instantly suggests a lack of critical thought about British diplomatic expertise that illustrates its mythological nature. A further telling omission is the lack of reflection on whether other countries might see Britain as qualified to play such a role since they may view Britain's imperial past far more negatively. Whether other countries really see Britain as a 'father figure' is doubtful. As for Brexit, international observers such as Japan have described it as a profound act of self-harm. Such judgements presumably disqualify Britain from being a 'voice of reason'.[53]

'Everyone should listen to us just because we're British'

People resolve the apparent contradiction that subjugating others qualifies one as mediator of world conflict through the notion that the British Empire was benevolent overall. Even if Britain did repress, enslave, intern and exploit as an imperial power, Niall Ferguson claims that

> no organization in history has done more to promote the free movement of goods, capital and labour than the British Empire ... and no organization has done more to impose Western norms of law, order and governance around the world.[54]

Or, as Samuel (65+, Dorset) put it, 'I think we could honestly say that we've acted mostly with integrity and mostly with clear objectives, and mostly with giving out excellent signals, give or take the odd massacre.'

While many view the Empire extremely negatively, a YouGov poll in 2014 found that three times as many British citizens are more proud than ashamed of it (59 per cent to 19 per cent). A similar ratio (49 per cent to 15 per cent) felt that the colonized were better off because of it.[55] Apart from illustrating the strength of the myth of imperial benevolence, these views are important because they engender the assumption that Britain's former colonies retain respect for Britain because of this. This imagined residual goodwill is thought to be something Britain can count on when looking to secure favourable terms in future trade deals post-Brexit.

> Samuel (65+, Dorset): Hmm ... well, I would say that we have tremendous ... there remains residual respect for us, because we have been good, generally honest brokers I think, we've been good trading partners for people. ... Because we've got this residual respect, I think there is still a role for us, in diplomacy for instance, and I think also we remain an extremely innovative ... country, full of very innovative people ... We've still got a lot to contribute.
>
> Matt (65+, Wales): The reason Britain was great was largely because we had the Empire ... And since we've lost the Empire I don't think we are, although we still like to think that we've still got a moral responsibility or a moral attitude to life which some people or some of the world still respect.

While British exceptionalism is widely accepted across the political spectrum, it does not go uncontested. A few challenge it:

> Teresa (55–64, Worcs): I think we've got a very inflated view of ourselves actually. ... I sometimes think who on earth do we think we are. We do come across as we know best, and I think sometimes that arrogance is a little bit rich to

be honest. I don't think we do everything better than everybody else, and I think as a nation I think we're lucky, I think we have a fantastic standard of living ... compared to other countries. But I think there's also an underlying view that we can do everything better than everybody else, and everybody should listen to us just because we're British.

When fed into Brexit trade negotiations, it is easy to see how the assumption that 'everybody should listen to us just because we're British' reinforces claims that Britain will be able to achieve deals at a speed others could not, and on more favourable terms.

Views from abroad

The myth of British diplomatic exceptionalism is not just prevalent amongst domestic citizens or British political elites. It also appears in public discourse and popular culture in other countries too.

Family Guy is a satirical American cartoon, set in Quahog, Rhode Island. In one episode, the town's local pub, the 'Drunken Clam', is bought up by a British man, who fills the bar with his friends, all of whom are caricatured as posh English gentlemen. The local protagonist, Peter Griffin, and his friends mount a protest at this, marching into the pub dressed as Minutemen from the Revolutionary War, seeking to kick out the English. With the Americans refusing to leave, the British landlord explains eloquently that 'if you refuse to go peaceably, we will use our superior linguistic skills to convince you to leave'. The scene cuts to the Americans walking out happily, thanking the British and explaining that they 'hadn't seen it that way before', before realizing that they had been deceived by clever words and arguments into accepting the British point of view.[56] In this mock international conflict, the sketch plays on the idea that the British have superior negotiating skills and are able to get their way without resorting to violence.

This can be interpreted as reflecting the myth of British diplomatic exceptionalism: the idea that Britain has developed a unique ability to get its way in negotiations, regardless of its material strength.

The myth of British diplomatic exceptionalism can also be found in commentary from other countries with whom Britain negotiates. On Brexit, while generally critical of Brexit and Britain's level of influence, German commentator Ruth Berschens stated this:

> When the Brexit negotiations began in March 2017, some in the EU feared they could be bamboozled by savvy British diplomats, well-schooled in the country's

imperial tradition. A year later, things look very different. Britain's diplomats are still brilliant, but they have little say in their own country. ... Long after the loss of its colonies, Britain continued to benefit from the Empire's fading aura. But with Brexit, that magic has finally worn off. Left to its own devices, Britain is just a medium-sized state with limited global influence, its Empire long gone.[57]

In a sense such comments suggest that Britain's diplomatic exceptionalism is genuine because influence comes from others believing you are influential. However, Berschens's suggestion that British diplomacy has lost its magic as the Empire recedes into the past implies that much of this was built on the material strength afforded by Empire but not reflected in contemporary reality.

A particular source of criticism of the myth of British diplomatic exceptionalism comes from former colonies themselves. Myths are selective representations of reality. What is striking in the assumptions of the British population and politicians about what makes their country great is the silencing of the perspective of other countries who may not view Britain the same way. Reviving the Commonwealth as an economic bloc has been promoted by pro-Brexit politicians as a renewed source of British prosperity when leaving the EU.[58] Yet, as Tilford notes on India:

> It is notable that so many former British colonies are happy to be members of such a club, but that is perhaps because they see the club differently from many Britons. India is a member, but sees no justification for privileged economic relations with Britain, as illustrated by the Indian government's rather bemused response to Britain's clumsy emphasis on the two countries' shared history as a reason for some kind of special economic relationship. Nor do the Indians, or any other Commonwealth country, see Britain as leading the organisation in the way many British appear to.[59]

Such criticisms are merely the latest in decades of observations that Britain has long harboured delusions of grandeur about its international status. As a country it continues to struggle to find a role in the world to mitigate the sense of decline after the loss of most of its empire.[60] From this perspective, optimism about Britain's global influence after Brexit is misplaced and hubristic. It is the fault of politicians across the political spectrum who have for decades exaggerated British political power and diplomatic influence.[61] There is some irony here. Those who criticize Brexit as the end of an era for British diplomacy have played their part in perpetuating the myth of British diplomatic exceptionalism over decades. In this respect, they have unwittingly reinforced the assumption of Brexit supporters – that British diplomatic superiority will enable post-Brexit Britain to thrive.

Myth versus reality

One way of establishing how strongly a myth is entrenched is through observing its persistence in the face of contradictory reality. In the case of Britain and its prospects in Brexit trade negotiations, the myth of British diplomatic exceptionalism contrasts with its initial lack of experienced trade negotiators, with this having been an EU responsibility for over two decades.[62] Similarly, the EU's position throughout negotiations has been consistent and fairly uncompromising. Prime Minister May's Brexit deal, for instance, contained concessions deemed so unacceptable that it could not be passed by Parliament. The transitional agreement passed by Boris Johnson's government for Britain to leave the EU in January 2020 contained even more concessions. The script that Europe will falter once more if Britain stands strong looks overly optimistic. It does not seem like 1940 again.

These issues appear to contradict the myth of British diplomatic exceptionalism. But rather than undermining it, people resolve the contradiction in two ways. First, pro-Brexit supporters claim that Europe's intransigence is proof of its tyrannical nature, and that they were right all along that Britain should leave. This argument's logic does not require any reference to Britain's diplomatic ability and thus does not undermine the myth of British diplomatic exceptionalism.

Second, people maintain the myth of Britain's unique diplomatic capability by blaming the incompetence of its contemporary politicians rather than its civil service diplomats. Mainstream media reinforced this early in negotiations, where Brexit Secretary David Davis was ridiculed for unpreparedness in bringing no paperwork to initial negotiations compared to EU counterparts armed with a stack of documents.[63] These images reflect longer-term public impressions of a generation of inept, careerist politicians who have no idea how the world works compared to the great leaders of yesteryear:

> Shaun (55–64, Dorset): [Our role is] a bit like a father figure. I think we've got a tremendous history and a tremendous wealth of knowledge. I think we've got some real idiots running the country, but that's different.
>
> Tim (35–44, London): A lot of the political class in the past would have been out to serve the people, they had a sense of duty to serve the people. But now it's a case of … they're careerists, they're out for themselves, and they make decisions which favour their own political career rather than serving the people.
>
> Vincent (65+, Lancashire): We seemed to be led in the past by men of experience and principle. We're now led by little boys.
>
> Willow (25–34, London): As with any massive decision from the government, it's always terrifying how little MP's know.

Matt (65+, Wales): Our politicians, there's nobody that strikes me as having character. When I look back I think of the character of people like Churchill and Lloyd George.

Mabel (55–64, Scotland): We don't seem to have statesmen at the moment.

Daisy (65+, Worcs): I think Margaret Thatcher was very strong. I think she was what the country needed. She spoke her mind. She wasn't always right, but she was a leader with conviction … I don't think we have the strength in the politicians anymore.

Blaming contemporary politicians only partially undermines the myth of diplomatic exceptionalism. The assumption remains relatively unchallenged that behind the scenes British diplomats retain the expertise to secure more favourable terms and still possess superior understanding of others. It is seen as common sense that Britain retains the ability to achieve things in a timeframe others could not, but efforts are merely being scuppered by the politicians of the day. Indeed, criticism of politicians charged with negotiating Brexit has often come from British diplomats themselves, excoriating the government for 'ill-founded arguments', 'muddled thinking' and for ignoring established expertise on Europe.[64]

In the end the strongest reinforcement of the idea that Britain retained exceptional diplomatic influence during Brexit negotiations came not from Brexit itself but from the 'Skripal Affair', where Britain secured a significant diplomatic victory in getting over twenty countries to join it in expelling Russian diplomats in the wake of the Novichok nerve agent attack on Sergei Skripal and his daughter in Salisbury in March 2018. For many commentators, this confirmed that Britain retains diplomatic capabilities that would not be diminished by Brexit and would ensure success after it.[65]

Conclusion

This chapter has sought to shed light on an under-researched aspect of diplomacy research: how diplomacy is perceived by ordinary citizens. Since the turn of the millennium, interest has turned to the field of 'New Public Diplomacy', focusing on how digital connectivity was making diplomacy more open and dialogic. Sub-fields of Digital Diplomacy and Citizen Diplomacy developed in turn, examining how diplomats could use social media to engage with citizens and how citizens could use social media to engage with diplomats and international audiences. Despite these growing fields, few have stepped back to ask how citizens understand diplomacy in the first place. Few have asked whether ordinary citizens perceive these changes in a similar way. Trying to maximize diplomatic effect through utilizing one's own citizens is likely to be less effective if they do not view their communications as potentially contributing to beneficial diplomatic effects.

This is important because public perceptions of how diplomacy works and what is diplomatically possible can shape support for policies that rely on it. If domestic populations believe that the aim of diplomacy is completely unrealistic, they may be less likely to support it and may prefer alternatives. In Britain, one assumption underpinning the economic logic of Brexit was that Britain's historically superior diplomatic capability would enable it to secure favourable trade deals far faster than other nations typically can. This may transpire. However, it looks unlikely at the time of writing. Even if a deal is agreed relatively swiftly, it is unlikely to be favourable, given the considerable concessions the Johnson government has already made to secure a transitional agreement with the EU to leave in January 2020.[66] As this chapter has shown, publics do not simply passively absorb and repeat statements from political leaders about how diplomatic efforts are likely to proceed. They bring with them deeply held narratives and myths of their country's roles in the world that shape their assumptions about what is and is not realistic or possible in a given diplomatic scenario. In the case of Brexit, the discourse advocating that Britain should 'Leave' was partly informed by the mythological assumption that Britain's imperial achievements were because of the inherent superiority of British diplomacy and that this would guarantee its future success outside the bloc. The reality of Britain lacking a cadre of trained trade negotiators, or that the decision to leave would erode Britain's influence with those it had just spurned, was marginalized compared to the mythological narrative that a key reason 'Britannia ruled the waves' was because of the transhistorical superiority of the British diplomat.

British citizens, at least, appear to have little sense of their role in diplomacy because they still see it as an elite, private activity. There is a widespread assumption that when a British diplomat walks into a room, compared to others they possess superior experience, skill and character, or at least they should. The politicians providing the outward face of private diplomacy are characterized as incompetent, but there remains belief that in the secret negotiations that the public cannot see, Britain retains unique capability.

In the absence of knowing exactly how diplomacy takes place and who is good at it, citizens fall back on historical myths which they use to create scripts about how future negotiations will occur. Nations that folded before are assumed to do so again. Historical influence is thought to be retained, but there is little evidence that everyday citizens see themselves as diplomats, digital or otherwise. It seems important to acknowledge that this may partly be the product of the general audience this research targeted. Were one to ask participants of the Erasmus student exchange scheme or attendees at China's Confucius Institutes whether they saw themselves as participants in public diplomacy, answers might be different. Yet it is still significant that across a broad cross-section of the British population, the overriding impression of diplomacy is a traditional one – secret, private, and something Britain excels at.

Britain is a particularly useful case, not just because of recent events, but because diplomatic excellence is one of the established myths on which British national identity is based. Other countries' citizens' perspectives are important too, and would benefit from further research. In the United States, for example, the belief that President Trump could secure more favourable deals by re-negotiating existing agreements was part of the basis of his support, at least initially. Foreign policy analysts may lament that his 'disruptive' approach to diplomacy has undermined American exceptionalism. Citizens observing Trump's diplomacy may have had different perspectives, admiring his appearance of strength while lacking sufficiently detailed knowledge to tell whether his deals really have been better than previous ones, as he has claimed. Admiration for Russian President Vladimir Putin – considered the world's most powerful man by Forbes from 2013 to 2016 – reflects respect for those who manage to get their way through realpolitik.[67] Citizens' understandings of diplomacy matter.

All of this suggests that future efforts to harness digital or citizen diplomacy would benefit from paying closer attention to the way everyday citizens understand diplomacy and their role in it. Academics and politicians see diplomacy as transforming in the Digital Age, but it would be helpful to understand first the perspectives of potential citizen diplomats if they wish to bring them along in the process. If they do, governments may be better able to legitimize foreign policy, help citizens make more informed democratic decisions, and improve relationships between their citizens and international society.

Notes

1 Tom Fletcher, *The Naked Diplomat* (London: HarperCollins, 2016), xxiv.
2 Robert D. Putnam, 'Diplomacy and Domestic Politics: The Logic of Two-Level Games', *International Organization*, Vol. 42, No. 3 (1988), 427–60.

3   For discussion of these trends, see Brian Hocking and Jan Mellissen, 'Diplomacy in the Digital Age', Clingendael, Netherlands Institute of International Relations, 2015, https://www.clingendael.org/sites/default/files/pdfs/Digital_Diplomacy_in_the_Digital%20Age_Clingendael_July2015.pdf, last accessed 9 December 2019.
4   Jan Melissen (ed.), *The New Public Diplomacy: Soft Power in International Relations* (Basingstoke: Palgrave, 2005); James Pamment, *New Public Diplomacy in the 21st Century: A Comparative Study of Policy and Practice* (London: Routledge, 2012).
5   Ellen Huijgh, 'Public Diplomacy', in Costas Constantinou, Pauline Kerr and Paul Sharp (eds), *The SAGE Handbook of Diplomacy* (London: Sage, 2016), 437–50.
6   See Corneliu Bjola, *Digital Diplomacy: Theory and Practice* (London: Routledge, 2015).
7   Joseph Nye Jr., *Soft Power: The Means to Success in World Politics* (New York: Public Affairs, 2005); James Pamment, *British Public Diplomacy and Soft Power: Diplomatic Influence and the Digital Revolution* (New York: Springer, 2016).
8   Corneliu Bjola, 'Digital Diplomacy Myths', https://uscpublicdiplomacy.org/blog/digital-diplomacy-myths, last accessed 28 August 2018.
9   Ronit Kampf, Ilan Manor and Elad Segev, 'Digital Diplomacy 2.0? A Cross-National Comparison of Public Engagement in Facebook and Twitter', *The Hague Journal of Diplomacy*, Vol. 10, No. 4 (2015), 331–62.
10 Melissa C. Tyler and Craig Beyernick, 'Citizen Diplomacy', in Costas Constantinou, Pauline Kerr and Paul Sharp (eds), *The SAGE Handbook of Diplomacy* (London: Sage, 2016), 521–9.
11 Ibid.; Stuart Allan and Einar Thorsen (eds), *Citizen Journalism: Global Perspectives* (New York: Peter Lang Publishing, 2009).
12 Fletcher, *The Naked Diplomat*, xxiv.
13 Putnam, 'Diplomacy'.
14 Huijgh, 'Public Diplomacy'.
15 Ellen Huijgh, 'Changing Tunes for Public Diplomacy: Exploring the Domestic Dimension', *Exchange: Journal of Public Diplomacy*, Vol. 2, No. 1 (2011), 62–73.
16 Here, 'ordinary' people describes those not directly involved in political decision making.
17 Nils Bubandt, 'Vernacular Security: The Politics of Feeling Safe in Global, National and Local Worlds', *Security Dialogue*, Vol. 36, No. 3 (2005), 275–96; Stuart Croft and Nick Vaughan-Williams, 'Fit for Purpose? Fitting Ontological Security Studies "into" the Discipline of International Relations: Towards a Vernacular Turn', *Cooperation and Conflict*, Vol. 52, No. 1 (2017), 12–30.
18 Nicholas O'Shaughnessy, *Politics and Propaganda: Weapons of Mass Seduction* (Manchester: Manchester University Press, 2000), 88–9.
19 William T. Cavanaugh, *The Myth of Religious Violence: Secular Ideology and the Roots of Modern Conflict* (Oxford: Oxford University Press, 2009).

20 Felix Berenskoetter, 'Parameters of a National Biography', *European Journal of International Relations*, Vol. 20, No. 1 (2014), 262–88.
21 Lawrence Freedman, *Strategy: A History* (Oxford: Oxford University Press, 2013); Roger C. Schank, *Tell Me a Story: Narrative and Intelligence* (Evanston, IL: Northwestern University Press, 1996).
22 Schank, *Tell Me a Story*.
23 Ibid., 7.
24 Yuen Foong Khong, *Analogies at War: Korea, Munich, Dien Bien Phu, and the Vietnam Decisions of 1965* (Princeton, NJ: Princeton University Press, 1992).
25 David Reynolds, 'Britain, the Two World Wars, and the Problem of Narrative', *The Historical Journal*, Vol. 60, No. 1 (2017), 197–231.
26 Peg Murray-Evans, 'Brexit and the Commonwealth: Fantasy Meets Reality', in Patrick Diamond, Peter Nedergaard and Ben Rosamond (eds), *Routledge Handbook of the Politics of Brexit* (Abingdon, Oxon: Routledge, 2018), 197–207; James Tapsfield, '"If We Can Cope with World War Two, We'll Cope with This": David Davis Dismisses Fears Government Is Not Ready for Brexit Showdown with the EU', *Daily Mail*, 18 January 2017, http://www.dailymail.co.uk/news/article-4131160/MPs-block-Brexit-don-t-like-final-deal-David-Davis.html, last accessed 29 August 2018.
27 See, for example, James Blitz, 'Post-Brexit Delusions about Empire 2.0', *Financial Times*, 7 March 2017, https://www.ft.com/content/bc29987e-034e-11e7-ace0-1ce02ef0def9, last accessed 2 September 2018.
28 Ibid.
29 Murray-Evans, 'Brexit'.
30 Paul McClean, 'Liam Fox: EU-UK Trade Deal Should Be One of "Easiest in Human History"', https://www.ft.com/content/f6904138-e90d-30f4-b3b7-23f3755d8b86, last accessed 10 December 2019.
31 See David Davis, 'Brexit: What Would It Look Like?', http://www.daviddavismp.com/david-davis-speech-on-brexit-at-the-institute-of-chartered-engineers, last accessed 3 September 2018; Rowena Mason, Peter Walker and Patrick Wintour, 'Boris Johnson Ridiculed by European Ministers after Prosecco Claim', *Guardian*, 17 November 2016, https://www.theguardian.com/politics/2016/nov/16/european-ministers-boris-johnson-prosecco-claim-brexit, last accessed 3 September 2018.
32 Ben Wellings, 'Brexit and British Identity', in Patrick Diamond, Peter Nedergaard and Ben Rosamond (eds), *Routledge Handbook of the Politics of Brexit* (Abingdon, Oxon: Routledge, 2018), 147–56.
33 For more details on the study's methodology, see Thomas Colley, *Always at War: British Public Narratives of War* (Ann Arbor: University of Michigan Press, 2019); Thomas Colley, 'Is Britain a Force for Good? Investigating British Citizens' Narrative Understanding of War', *Defence Studies*, Vol. 17, No. 1 (2017a), 1–22;

Thomas Colley, 'Britain's Public War Stories: Punching Above Its Weight or Vanishing Force?' *Defence Strategic Communications*, Vol. 2 (2017b), 162–90.

34 See ibid. for further details.
35 O'Shaughnessy, *Politics and Propaganda*.
36 For a more detailed outline of the different stories narrated by British citizens about foreign policy, see Colley, 'Britain's Public War Stories'.
37 See Elke Krahmann, 'United Kingdom: Punching above Its Weight', in Emil Kirchner and James Sperling (eds), *Global Security Governance: Competing Perceptions of Security in the Twenty-First Century* (New York: Routledge, 2007), 93–112.
38 Stuart Ward (ed.), *British Culture and the End of Empire* (Manchester: Manchester University Press, 2001).
39 House of Commons Foreign Affairs Committee, 'Global Britain: Sixth Report of Session 2017–19', https://publications.parliament.uk/pa/cm201719/cmselect/cmfaff/780/780.pdf, last accessed 31 August 2018.
40 Mordaunt, Penny, 'The Great Partnership: Delivering Global Britain', https://www.gov.uk/government/speeches/the-great-partnership-delivering-global-britain, last accessed 30 August 2018. The '0.7. 2 per cent nation' presumably reflects Britain's commitment to devote 0.7 and 2 per cent of its GDP to development and defence spending respectively, thus meeting international obligations in comparison to many other countries who do not.
41 David Lidlington, 'Building a Global Britain', https://www.gov.uk/government/speeches/building-a-global-britain, last accessed 30 August 2018.
42 Lawrence James, *Warrior Race: A History of the British at War* (London: Abacus, 2010).
43 Niall Ferguson, *Empire: How Britain Made the Modern World* (London: Penguin, 2004), 366.
44 See Colley, 'Always at War', 104.
45 Colley, 'Britain's Public War Stories'.
46 Ferguson, *Empire*, 163.
47 'The Soft Power 30', https://softpower30.com, accessed 3 September 2018.
48 'Digital Diplomacy Review 2017 #DDR17 Global Ranking', http://digital.diplomacy.live/ddr17/, accessed 28 August 2018.
49 Pamment, *British Public Diplomacy*.
50 William Hague, 'The Best Diplomatic Service in the World: Strengthening the Foreign and Commonwealth Office as an Institution', https://www.gov.uk/government/speeches/the-best-diplomatic-service-in-the-world-strengthening-the-foreign-and-commonwealth-office-as-an-institution, accessed 28 August 2018.
51 Colley, 'Always at War'.
52 Ibid., 115.
53 David Warren, 'The UK–Japan Relationship in an Age of Populism', in *Anglo-Japanese Cooperation in an Era of Growing Nationalism and Weakening*

Globalization. London: Chatham House, 2018, https://www.chathamhouse.org/sites/default/files/publications/research/2018-02-13-anglo-japanese-cooperation-growing-nationalism-conference.pdf, last accessed 30 August 2018.

54 Ferguson, *Empire*, xxii.
55 Will Dahlgreen, 'The British Empire Is "Something to be Proud of"', https://yougov.co.uk/news/2014/07/26/britain-proud-its-empire, last accessed 30 August 2018.
56 Family Guy, Season 3, Episode 4. 'One If By Clam, Two If by Sea'. Written by Jim Bernstein, Michael Shipley. Directed by Dan Povenmire. Twentieth Century Fox, 2002.
57 Ruth Berschens, 'Brits Are in Denial about Their Diminishing Importance', https://global.handelsblatt.com/opinion/germany-brits-are-in-denial-brexit-905941, last accessed 30 August 2018.
58 Simon Tilford, 'The British and Their Exceptionalism', Center for European Reform, 3 May 2017, https://www.cer.eu/insights/british-and-their-exceptionalism, last accessed 3 September 2018.
59 Ibid., 2.
60 For instance, see Bernard Porter, *Britain, Europe and the World, 1850–1982: Delusions of Grandeur* (London: HarperCollins, 1983).
61 Tilford, 'The British'.
62 Jed Odermatt, 'Brexit and British Trade Policy', in Patrick Diamond, Peter Nedergaard and Ben Rosamond (eds), *Routledge Handbook of the Politics of Brexit* (Abingdon, Oxon: Routledge, 2018), 80–91.
63 Jennifer Rankin, 'Day Two of Brexit Talks – and the UK Looks as Underprepared as Ever', *Guardian*, 17 July 2017, https://www.theguardian.com/politics/2017/jul/17/brexit-talks-uk-underprepared-david-davis-michel-barnier-eu, last accessed 31 August 2018.
64 Jon Stone, 'UK Does Not Have the Skills to Negotiate a Good Brexit Deal, Former Downing Street Trade Envoy Warns', *Independent*, 5 January 2017, https://www.independent.co.uk/news/uk/politics/brexit-deal-negotiations-lord-marland-theresa-may-whitehall-skills-boris-johnson-david-davis-a7510576.html, last accessed 31 August 2018.
65 For a critique of this view, see Mary Dejevsky, 'The UK Overestimates Its Diplomatic Clout – Post-Brexit, It Will Be a Small Player on the International Stage', *Independent*, 28 March 2017, https://www.independent.co.uk/voices/brexit-foreign-policy-diplomacy-russia-small-player-a8278411.html, last accessed 3 September 2018.
66 James Blitz, 'Boris Johnson's Deal Is Bad for the UK Economy', *Financial Times*, 16 October 2019, https://www.ft.com/content/22c38654-f00e-11e9-ad1e-4367d8281195, last accessed 24 March 2020.
67 Forbes, 'Vladimir Putin', https://www.forbes.com/sites/davidewalt/2018/05/08/the-worlds-most-powerful-people-2018/, last accessed 10 December 2019.

7

'Information War' – The Russian strategy that blends diplomacy and war

Dr Ofer Fridman

The contemporary understanding of the relationship between politics and war has been long shaped by the famous Clausewitzian dictum – 'War is merely the continuation of policy by other means.'[1] While this thesis subordinates war to politics, it also suggests a definitive division between two different types of international politics. The first is war – 'an act of force to compel our enemy to do our will.'[2] And since war is a 'policy conducted by fighting battles rather than by sending diplomatic notes,'[3] the second type of international relations, implied by the Clausewitzian dictum, is diplomacy that involves sending these 'diplomatic notes' instead of fighting. While Clausewitz neither clearly defined the nature of diplomacy, nor elaborated on its role, his understanding of the relations between war and diplomacy is implied several times in his writing. They both share the same goal of compelling the enemy to do our will. While war achieves this through violence, diplomacy does it by non-violent means.[4] In other words, diplomacy can be defined as the non-violent means, such as 'correspondence, private talks, exchanges of views, lobbying, visits, threats and other related activities', by which states 'articulate, coordinate and secure particular or wider interests'.[5]

In addition to this distinction between war (violent) and diplomacy (non-violent) as different forms of politics, Clausewitz suggested another important characteristic of the relations between them. Since 'Clausewitz saw peaceful diplomacy as the normal mode of promoting the goals of states'[6] and war as something that states have to resort to when diplomacy fails, the natural state of relations between states is characterized by diplomacy (i.e. peaceful relations) punctuated by periods of war.

This chapter is part of a research project generously supported by the Gerda Henkel Foundation.

This interpretation of Clausewitz's distinction between war and peace rests at the heart of Western understanding of the relationship between war and diplomacy. It is rooted so deeply in the Western (especially American) approach to war that, according to some scholars, war should be considered not as a continuation of political discourse, but as 'a symptom of its failure'.[7] It therefore seems right to argue that in the Western understanding, there is a clear distinction between diplomacy (a strategic way to achieve political goals through non-violent means) and war (a strategic way to achieve political goals through violent means).

While this may be the case in the West, Russian political–military thought seems to conceptualize the relationship between war and diplomacy differently. During the last decade, many Western experts on Russia have been arguing that the Kremlin's contemporary strategy attempts to blur the line between war and peace.[8] Following this observation, the purpose of this chapter is twofold. First, it will explore the roots of the Russian approach to war and diplomacy, arguing that in Russia the line between war and peace has never been so distinctive as it has been in the West. The second aim of this chapter is to explore how in contemporary Russia the idea of 'Information War' has become the new strategic way to achieve desired political goals by blending military and non-military means.

To demonstrate how Russia blends military and non-military means to achieve its political goals, the chapter will analyse two different cases: the Kremlin's decision to introduce economic counter-sanctions (a non-military mean) and its intervention in the Syrian conflict in 2015 (a military means). It will conclude by arguing that while these are seemingly unconnected, in fact, they constitute Russia's strategic way of conduct in international relations – 'Information War' – that blends war and diplomacy.

War and peace in the Russian strategic thought

In analysing Russian strategic thinking, it is impossible to miss that Clausewitz's idea to submit war to politics has been embraced from the very beginning. For example, already in 1869, Genrikh Leer, one of the most prominent Russian strategists of the nineteenth century, praised Clausewitz's 'On War' as a good example of strategic literature, opening his book with a paraphrase: 'War is one of the tools in the hands of politics, the most extreme tool to achieve state's goals'.[9] From Leer and until contemporary Russian strategists, such as Vasilii Mikryukov, Alexander Vladimirov Andrey Kokoshin, this idea has generally remained undisputed.[10] Yet, the Russian interpretation of the relationship between war and peace has been entirely different to the Western view. While in the West, war has been seen as an unfortunate and temporary event that punctuates the default sate of peace between states, in Russia, war is considered as a more natural state of affairs.

According to Ivan Ilyin, one of the famous Russian political philosophers of the early twentieth century, in the Russian mind, Russian history is 'the history of defence, struggle and sacrifice: from the first attacks of nomads on Kiev in 1037 until today'.[11] This state of a constant fight for survival has been described best by another famous Russian philosopher Ivan Solonevich as the major reason behind the Russian cultural predisposition towards strong and decisive authority, rather than democracy.[12] An additional outcome of this state has been the increased importance of war in the Russian mentality:

> The whole history of the Russian state is an extreme struggle for its security against external and internal threats, a struggle that has left a recognisable trace on the consciousness of the Russian people.[13]

This understanding of war as a permanent struggle has played influential roles in the Russian cultural context throughout all of its history. Events of the twentieth century contributed to this phenomenon even more than any other period in Russian history. After all, the ideology enforced by the Soviet leadership glorified the idea of class conflict,[14] leading to the absence of conceptual-philosophical and practical development of the ideas of non-violence and peacemaking.[15]

The very same understanding of war as the default state of international affairs can be traced across Russian strategic thought. For example, the 1899 Imperial Nicholas Military Academy (The General Staff Academy) manual on strategy stated: 'A war is a struggle for existence … [it] is this special way, by which one culture, the stronger one, overwhelms the other weaker one.'[16] This line of thought was echoed by contemporary strategist Major General Alexander Vladimirov, the author of the imperative monograph titled *Fundamentals of General Theory of War*, according to whom: 'an eternal war – this is what the history of humanity offers instead of eternal peace, which philosophers and moralists have dreamt about'.[17]

Many contemporary Western experts on Russia accuse the Kremlin of an attempt to blur the line between war and peace.[18] Yet, it seems that in Russia's political–military thought this dividing line has never passed in the same place at it was in the West. While the Western mind perceives war as a temporary and unfortunate phenomenon and, therefore, separates between diplomacy (politics in times of peace) and war (politics in times of war), Russians subordinate both (war and diplomacy) to the state of 'eternal' war between nations. This idea of eternal war has always been present in the Russian political–military discourse. In the late nineteenth century, Evgeny Martynov, an influential Russian Imperial strategist, argued that if a state has 'nothing to desire and fight for, then we can be sure that this state has already fulfilled its role in the history, it is in a decline, living through its period of degeneration'.[19] In the Soviet Union it was the Marxist idea of the permanent class struggle that shaped the understanding of blended relationship between war and peace.[20] And in post-Soviet Russia, the concept of 'Information War' has been defining the Russian strategic way to understand and conduct international relations.

For the last two decades, Russian professional and academic discourse has been flooded by books, articles, speeches and official documents that focus on the role of the struggle in information dimension in general, and on what Russians call 'Information War' in particular. According to Russian conceptualizations of this phenomenon, Information War is a combination of military and non-military means intended to influence the information-psychological space of a targeted audience in an attempt to achieve certain clearly defined political goals. In other words, the contemporary Russian understanding of international relations is conceptualized as an Information War, a strategic way that encompasses the blend of diplomacy and war.

'Information War' as a default state of international relations

In the eyes of many Russians, the dissolution of the Soviet Union was a painful event in Russia's modern history, which most of them have regretted since the moment of the collapse until today.[21] Russian people struggle to agree[22] on the main reasons for what many Russian scholars and political leaders, including their President, call 'the greatest geopolitical catastrophe of the century'.[23] However, according to many Russian political scientists, who analysed the long process that had led to the collapse of the Soviet Union, it did not occur overnight. According to them, it was an outcome of a very long confrontation designed to politically and economically undermine the Soviet Union from inside, rather to win in an open confrontation. Following their analyses of the Cold War and the causes of the Soviet defeat in it, Russian contemporary strategists and political scientists have emphasized two main aspects of international relations in the era of the Informational Revolution: (1) the aim to break the spirit of the adversary's nation by a gradual erosion of its culture, values and self-esteem and (2) an emphasis on diplomatic (i.e. political, informational and economic) instruments, rather than on kinetic military force.[24] This analysis has led them to conclude that contemporary international relations can be best characterized by 'Information War'.

One of the first and the main advocates of this approach to international relations is Professor Igor Panarin, who has been publishing on Information War since the early 1990s. According to him, Information War is

> a type of confrontation between parties, represented by the use of special (political, economic, diplomatic, military and other) methods [based on different] ways and means that influence the informational environment of the opposing party [while] protecting their own [environment], in order to achieve clearly defined goals. [Therefore] The major dimensions for waging informational-psychological confrontations [are] political, diplomatic, financial-economic, [and] military.[25]

While Panarin was the first to promote the concept of Information War in the Russian political-academic discourse, he was definitely not the last. For example, Yuri Grigor'yev offers a very similar definition:

> Non-violent actions directed to alter or destroy the unified informational domain of the adversary state. The purpose of information war is not the destruction of people, but an alteration of certain fragmented variables that dominate the informational domain of a considerable part of the citizens to a degree when these variables fall out of the unified informational domain of the native country, thus forcing these citizens to start organising themselves in different opposing structures.[26]

Another example is given by Professors Vladimir Lisichkin and Leonid Shelepin, who state that information wars are waged 'by a direct influence on the public consciousness, on the souls of people. The main purpose is to coerce masses to act in a desired direction, even against their own general interests, and in the adversary camp to split people and force them to rise one against another.'[27]

It is important to note that, when Russian scholars talk about different dimensions of Information War, they refer not only to direct political, diplomatic, financial-economic or military activities, but also, and most importantly, to the informational impact that these activities generate on the targeted audiences in order to gain clearly defined political benefits. According to them, this influence can be achieved by information manipulation, disinformation, fabrication of information, lobbying, blackmail or any other possible way of extracting the desired information, or simply by the mere denial of information originating from the adversary. For example, according to Panarin, when one state wages an Information War against another, it 'aims to interrupt the balance of power and achieve superiority in the global informational dimension' by targeting 'the decision-making processes of the adversary' via the manipulation of international and domestic public opinion.[28]

In other words, it seems right to argue that while in the West the use of words, actions and images to achieve certain political goals in peacetime is called diplomacy, in Russia the same practice is conceptualized as a part of Information War. The usage of the term 'war', however, in this context has to be taken with two main clarifications. First, as stated above, in the Russian cultural mindset, war is understood quite differently from the West. In addition to being a default state of international relations, war is also understood by the Russian mindset as an inherently defensive affair. Without any doubt, not all Russian wars were defensive or even can be justified as such. In the Russian mind, however, Russian history is a history of defensive wars, in which Russia has always been seen as 'a kind of "sweet booty" for the nomadic East, as well as for the settled West'.[29] As famous Russian philosopher Ivan Solonevich put it: 'While a Westerner fights to better the world, a Russian fights to survive.'[30]

The second clarification is the difference in the meaning of the term 'Information War', as it is used by the Russian military and political/academic communities. According to the Russian military, Information War is

> an open and violent collision between states in which the enemy's resistance is suppressed by the use of means of harmful influence on his information sphere, destruction or disruption of the normal functioning of his information and telecommunication systems, [undermining] the security of his information resources [and] obtaining unauthorised access to them, as well as [employing] massive information and psychological influence on the Armed Forces' personal and the population of the enemy in order to destabilise society and the state.[31]

In other words, Information War is understood by the Russian military as an information dimension of war that supports the main kinetic effort of the military. As Professor Adnrey Kokoshin, one of the most influential contemporary Russian strategists, put it: 'Information – psychological influence [and] special propaganda are intended first and foremost to serve the task of suppressing the enemy's will to resist [and] the disruption of control at all major links, but by other means – without direct physical influence on the enemy's personnel.'[32] Therefore, this military understanding of Information War is more akin to PSYOPs as they are defined by the US Department of Defence.[33]

In contrast to this military interpretation of Information War, the Russian political and academic community interprets it as a much broader political phenomenon that occurs not as a part of an armed conflict, but instead of it. In the Russian eyes it does not necessarily characterize a supporting dimension of kinetic confrontation, but the overall state of international relations. When describing the Western reaction to Russia's actions in Crimea, Vladimir Putin claimed that 'we face a growing barrage of information attacks unleashed against Russia by some of our so-called partners', and Sergey Lavrov stated that 'we are faced with the large-scale information war'; they did not mean the Information War, as defined by the Russian military, as there was no kinetic confrontation between Russia and the West. Instead, they refer to what Panarin defines as information-psychological influence, which is 'a purposeful creation and distribution of specially created information, intended to directly influence (positively or negatively) the information-psychological environment that determines the behaviour and development of a society'.[34]

Following this understanding, Russian literature divides all possible actions in Information War into two main groups. The first consists of 'non-military means' – economic, diplomatic and other non-military actions intended to achieve certain information-psychological impact on target audience. The second includes different 'military means' – kinetic actions (as a part of armed conflict or not) conducted by the military more for their information-psychological effect, rather than for purely military goals.

'Non-military means' in Information War

Discussing the role of information in the twenty-first century, Aleksandr Dugin, one of the most extreme Russian thinkers in this field, stated that

> [Today] reality is secondary in relation to virtual. The image is much more important than reality. Reality itself becomes real only after reports about it appear in the informational dimension, and therefore, the major factor is control of the informational dimension. The one who controls the informational dimension, controls everything.[35]

While Dugin's and Panarin's writings present quite extreme views on the role of the Information War in international relations, they are definitely not the only ones. Inspired by their work, the Russian academic and political discourse relating to Information War has been flourishing. Since the 2000s, a vast number of books and articles had been published analysing international relations through the conceptual prism of Information War; PhD dissertations have been defended and even a special journal titled *Informatsionnyye Voyny* (*Informational Wars*) was established under the supervision of famous General Makhmut Gareev as head of the scientific-editorial council.[36]

Therefore, according to the Russian understanding of Information War, the effectiveness of actions in international relations is measured not by their impact in the real world, but by their influence on the information dimension. It is important to note that in relations between a real action and its impact on the information dimension, the latter comes first. In other words, in Information War, the desired informational-psychological effects on target audiences should be decided, and then most suitable real actions for achieving these effects should be selected – a type of 'Propaganda of the Deed', but on a much more sophisticated, multifaceted and hyperbolic level.

The term 'non-military means' first penetrated the Russian political discourse already in the late 1990s. The 1997 National Security Concept stated that international cooperation 'significantly increases the potential of non-military means in ensuring Russia's of national security by legal, political, economic and other means'.[37] The 2000 Military Doctrine also used this term, stating that Russia 'prioritises political, diplomatic and other non-military means to prevent, localise and neutralise military threats on regional and global levels'.[38] Since none of these documents gave a definition for 'non-military means', it is not surprising that Vladimir Serebryanikov and Alexander Kapko, a retired lieutenant general and a former high-level diplomat, who were among the first to write on this topic, argued in 2000:

> Today, even in the highest echelons of the state leadership, it is difficult to find an expert who is professionally engaged with the problems of the use of non-military means … In the past 10–15 years, only a few popular articles appeared in this field. Neither aims, nor subjects of the study are defined. Domestic and foreign experiences are not summarised. There are no scientists who specialise in this field.[39]

According to them, 'non-military means' constitute 'a cluster of social institutions (organisations), legal norms, spiritual values, information and communication systems, used by a state to influence internal and external relations in order to strengthen national security'.[40]

On the one hand, the idea of 'non-military means' in international relations seems to offer very little conceptual novelty, as the eight 'families' of non-military means suggested by Serebryanikov and Kapko – political–diplomatic, legal, economic, ideologic-psychological, informational, humanitarian, intelligence and public (non-governmental) actions – have been used as political tools for many decades, if not centuries. On the other, a combination of this conceptualization of different non-military political tools with the concept of Information War in the Russian discourse seems to produce if not something entirely novel, then at least something very innovative (especially taking into consideration the Information Revolution of the late twentieth to early twenty-first centuries). In other words, in the times of Information War (and according to many Russian scholars this is a natural state of affairs in international relations, rather than a restricted in time event),[41] 'non-military means' should be valued not only for the their intended effect in the real world, but also (and more importantly) for their potential to achieve desired goals in the information dimension. For example, coming back to the 'diplomatic notes' that Clausewitz was writing about,[42] and which are considered in the West as a political tool in times of peace (i.e. diplomacy), in the Russian interpretation of international relations, they constitute non-military means of Information War. Moreover, their real value is not in what they say, promise or try to negotiate, but in the ability to achieve the desired information-psychological impact on targeted audience of the decision makers.

One of the best examples of the Kremlin's employment of 'non-military means' for their informational, rather than real, value was the set of counter-sanctions introduced by the Kremlin in its reaction to the Western sanctions imposed on Russia following Russia's takeover of Crimea. Since the beginning of the Ukrainian Crisis in 2014, the United States, the European Union and other countries and international organizations have imposed a series of sanctions against Russia.[43] On 6 August 2014, in a response to the increasing sanctions imposed by the West, Putin signed a decree mandating an effective embargo on imports of the agricultural products originating in countries that had either 'adopted the decision to introduce economic sanctions against Russian legal and (or) physical entities, or joined such decision'.[44]

While economic sanctions are usually considered as an economic tool to achieve political goals, one might argue that in the case of the Russian counter-sanctions it was a political tool to achieve economic aims by stimulating domestic manufacturers and decreasing Russia's dependence on the international market.[45] On the one hand, it seems that the Kremlin's policy of 'import substitution' has been relatively successful in 'stimulating the growth of the industries shielded by the protectionist barriers'.[46] On the other, a deeper analysis of the outcomes of this policy suggests that while counter-sanctions had certain short-term political and economic benefits, they also had a very negative impact on an already distressed (by Western sanctions and low oil prices) Russian economy, failing to create any long-term positive changes. This understanding raises a question about the true purpose of the counter-sanctions: whether their goal was political: 'to prepare conditions for negotiation about ... [and] the removal of restrictions that are sensitive to the Russian economy'; economic: 'to create conditions for growth of industries selected for protectionist shield';[47] or something entirely different.

While there is little doubt that Russian counter-sanctions had their political and economic effects, it seems that their main intended impacts have been on the domestic and international information domains. For the last decade, the Kremlin has been positioning itself as 'a counterbalance [to the West] in international affairs and the development of global civilization'.[48] Therefore, the introduction of counter-sanctions intended not only to inflict certain damage to the Western economies and strengthen the Russian economy (even if only for a very short term), but also to be a perfect action that would reinforce the Kremlin message to international political actors, unhappy with the Western policies. In other words, in addition to being short-term economic and political measures, Russian counter-sanctions seem to be a very good employment of 'non-military means' on the international informational battlefield between Russia and the West for the hearts and minds of non-aligned political actors. After all, there is no better way to communicate 'counterbalance' to Western sanctions, than to state that they 'are counterproductive and meaningless, especially with regard to a country like Russia'[49] and introduce counter measures.

The intended message of the counter-sanctions for domestic audiences is more complicated. Due to the Western sanctions and low prices of oil, the Russian economy was already in a bad shape; therefore, the introduction of counter-sanctions that would ultimately worsen the situation could be a hard sell to the Russian people. Especially taking into consideration the fact that while Western sanctions targeted big companies and industries, Russian counter-sanctions negatively impacted the everyday life of common citizens.[50] The logic of the Kremlin's decision, however, becomes clear in the context of the Russian political culture that is based on the cult of personality. From a historical perspective, this culture has proved itself as the most efficient way to rule Russia, due to 'the specifics of the Russian mentality, bureaucratic apparatus, and the sacralization of the leader's personality, guarded by the mass media and trustworthy thinking intellectuals'.[51]

It is important to note that the strength of political leadership in the Russian political-cultural context focuses not only on how strong, decisive and important a leader is, but also on how good that leader is in overcoming and concealing Russia's weaknesses. As Dimitri Trenin put it, 'Even if the odds are against Russia, [a strong leader] is punching above the country's weight rather than submitting himself to the will of the others.' Putin had learned from the history of both Nikolas II (the last Tsar) and Mikhail Gorbachev (the last Soviet leader) that the most important thing is 'never to be weak, and never appear weak',[52] and his decision to decisively countermeasure the West was perceived by the Russian domestic audience as a message of political determination and strength. Historically, led by a strong leader, the Russian people demonstrate levels of endurance and sacrifice that cannot be grasped by the Western mind. But, without powerful leadership, the same people, who had successfully defended their Fatherland against the all-powerful Napoleon and Hitler, managed to bring down their own state twice within a single century: in 1917 and again in 1991.[53] Therefore, it is not surprising that the vast majority of Russian people approve and support the counter-sanctions introduced by the Kremlin, regardless of their economic drawbacks.[54] In other words, in addition to their role in the international Information War, counter-sanctions have been very important tools ('non-military means') shaping and influencing the perception of the Russian people about the strength of Putin's leadership.

'Military means' in Information War

In analysing Russian conceptual discourse on the role of the military in the twenty-first century, it is difficult not to notice that in addition to its traditional (kinetic power) role, Russian military professionals and scholars assign to the Russian military a task of an informational 'non-military' nature. In other words, in addition to their traditional purpose of winning wars and conflicts, armed forces might be used as a tool that supports political–diplomatic, economic, information and other non-military actions simply by their presence or by the demonstration of military potential.[55] As Aleksandr Dugin put it:

> Informational support of war stops being a secondary supporting factor (as classic propaganda was), but becomes the *raison d'etre* of war. In essence, a war has become informational, [where] military operations have only a secondary supporting role.[56]

One of the best examples of how the Kremlin has been using 'military means' to achieve its goals in the information dimension was the Russian intervention in Syria in 2015. Since the very beginning of the Syrian crisis, Russia was one of a very few major international actors that proactively supported the regime of Syrian President Bashar al-Assad. While on the diplomatic front the Kremlin was not alone in averting the attempts of Western countries to impose significant sanctions on Syria,[57] it was the only power that continued to provide military assistance to the Syrian military. From 2011 to 2015, Moscow delivered to Syria an estimated $983 million in weapons and military equipment.[58] Defending its actions against vast international criticism, Russian officials alluded briefly to the fact that all deliveries had been done 'in accordance with international law, in compliance with the procedures and within the framework of existing contracts'.[59]

Despite the fact that President Putin's decision to deploy forces in September 2015 surprised many Western politicians and political analysts, those who closely monitored Russian affairs could see the upcoming signs. On the tactical level, the transfer of military hardware and troops from Russia to Syria had begun already in August, and was well reported by different media outlets and social networks.[60] But on the strategic level, Moscow's desire to play a greater role in the international affairs was well signalled to the West since the early 2000s. While many experts refer to the famous 2007 President Putin's Speech at the Munich Security Conference,[61] a better example of how this desire had been communicated by Moscow can be seen in a comparative analysis of Russian self-perception in the sequential Foreign Policy Concepts.[62] While the 2000 Concept gingerly stated that 'the Russian Federation has a real potential for ensuring itself a worthy place in the world',[63] the 2008 Concept proclaimed Russia as 'the largest Euro-Asian power ... one of the leading States of the world and a permanent member of the UN Security Council'.[64] The 2013 Concept clearly stated that 'Russia's foreign policy ... reflects the unique role our country has been playing over centuries as a counterbalance in international affairs and the development of global civilisation'.[65]

Almost six months later, while many were still conjecturing that the Kremlin's real reasons for intervention differed substantially from the officially stated goals of 'stabilising the legitimate power in Syria and creating the conditions for political compromise',[66] Putin declared that the goal has been 'generally accomplished' and ordered the start of the withdrawal of Russian forces.[67] On the one hand, there is no doubt that the positions of al-Assad have significantly improved due to the Russian military intervention. On the other, it seems too simplistic and naïve to argue that helping al-Assad was the only goal that the Kremlin had been trying to achieve by deploying its military outside of the post-Soviet sphere for the first time since the end of the Cold War.

From the beginning of the Russian deployment in Syria, many Western experts argued that Moscow's decision to send its troops to Syria was driven by the fact that Damascus is 'effectively the only ally which Russia has in the region' and 'it is very important [to Russia] to preserve this platsdarm [bridgehead] in the region'.[68] Nonetheless, a closer analysis of Russo-Syrian relations in general, and Russian strategic interests in Syria in particular, suggests several major flaws in this assumption. Since the end of the Cold War, Russian foreign policy has lost the ideological elements that previously fuelled its approach to the Middle East. While Syria continued to acquire Russian military equipment, Damascus had lost its status as a strategic partner, becoming just another client and, eventually, not the most reliable at paying its bills. Moreover, building Syria as a bridgehead for the potential expansion of influence in the Middle East suits more the ideological policies of the Soviet Union than pragmatic approaches of the Kremlin in the twenty-first century which, first, and foremost, thinks about Russia's national interests.

It seems right to suggest that the Kremlin's goal to stabilize al-Assad's power in Syria was not the major aim, after all. Without significant political self-interest to intervene, Moscow could continue with its indirect support providing general protection against unfavourable resolutions in the UN Security Council and military hardware via Iran. Even though al-Assad has been the main beneficiary of the Russian intervention, it seems correct to surmise that Moscow was driven more by its own interests than by a bold support of the ill-fated Syrian president.

Comparing Russian intervention in Syria to the military operations deployed by the Western countries against the Islamic State, the Kremlin was much more successful in the informational domain than its Western counterparts. From Putin's rhetorical call to arms during his speech to the UN General Assembly just days before the 'surprising' deployment of Russian forces in Syria, up until the truly unexpected announcement of 'mission accomplished' almost six months later, the statements, as well as actions, of the Russian leadership have resembled more a well-staged play than a simple attempt to help al-Assad or build a bridgehead in the Middle East. After all, Russia was involved in the Syrian conflict before September 2015, and it is still deeply involved even after the official withdrawal in March 2016. If the true goal of this intervention was rescuing al-Assad, building a political–economic–military bridgehead in the Middle East, Moscow could have done so without all the theatrical performance that accompanied its actions.

As discussed above, Russian strategic thought during the past two decades has been paying an increasing attention to the importance of informational struggle – 'Information War' – as a way to conceptualize and understand international relations. Thus, it seems right to assume that the role of the Russian military in Syria was more to fight the battle for hearts and minds of domestic and international audiences than eliminating terrorists on the ground or saving al-Assad from the opposition. In other words, the task of the military was more to conduct a decisive and carefully staged performance of silver rockets, brave soldiers, shiny hardware and fast (and almost easy) achievements to influence the political behaviour of domestic and international audiences, rather than just save al-Assad's regime.

It is not surprising that, domestically, Putin's approval ratings were record high (88 per cent) in mid-October 2015 due to the Russian military intervention in Syria. While during the following years these approval rates decreased, they stayed well above 80 per cent for the three consecutive years and went down only in the middle of 2018 due to several domestic issues, rather than Russia's involvement in Syria.[69] It is more surprising that the Russian military deployment had a more or less similar effect on Western public opinion. In light of the West's general stalemate in its fight against the Islamic State in 2015, the Kremlin's dramatic call for an international coalition, combined with the no less theatrical (and effective) immediate actions of its military, was overwhelmingly approved by the Western public. For example, 77 per cent of British people supported forming a common front involving Russia to fight the Islamic State,[70] whereas 53 per cent of the US public thought that Russia had the upper hand in Syria.[71] It was probably the first time in modern history that a deployment of Russian armed forces enjoyed such vast public support in the West.

Therefore, it seems that the Russian intervention in Syria was not only a military operation, it was also a well-staged manoeuvre in the information space intended to shape the public opinion inside and outside of Russia. For a domestic audience, this intervention was presented as a decisive action to fight 'between five to seven thousand fighters from Russia and CIS countries', who joined the Islamic State, thus preventing them from bringing 'the experience from Syria back at our home'.[72] Such interpretation not only perfectly suited the Russian traditional interpretation of war as a defensive affair, but also supported Putin's narrative of a strong leader, the importance of which in the Russian political culture has been discussed above. For the international audience, in addition to the Western audience, the Kremlin's military intervention was an important message 'to recruit geographically distant nations as partners in constructing a new multipolar, anti-U.S. world order' – something that already can be seen in Russian relations with Venezuela.[73] Moreover, this intervention sends an important message all across the Middle East, boosting the Kremlin's relations with all sides of the region's bitter rivalries: Iran and Israel, the Kurds and Turkey, Qatar and Saudi Arabia.[74] In other words, it seems that Russia's use of its military in Syria was successful in fulfilling its goals and aims in the information domain (domestically and internationally) to the same (if not higher) degree of success, as it was achieving its more conventional military goals of this intervention.

Moreover, as a part of the Kremlin's aspiration to counterbalance the West in international affairs, the intervention in Syria created a feasible alternative to the Western diplomatic efforts, bestowing on Russia the title of a peacemaker. Since 2012, the Kremlin had made attempts to promote itself as a peace negotiator in Syria,[75] something that could ultimately increase its status on the global arena. However, as fighting intensified and the West took diplomatic initiatives on its own (e.g. the 2012 and 2014 Geneva Conferences), Moscow started to feel that it missed the opportunity. Military intervention brought the Kremlin back onto the map. It allowed them to initiate an alternative peace process in Astana (2016–18) and later in Sochi (in 2018), demonstrating to the rest of the world that Russia was back in the geopolitical game as a peacemaker. In other words, the kinetic operation in Syria was merely a tool (an example of the use of 'military means'), employed not so much to help al-Assad, but to shape the diplomatic image of the Kremlin.

Conclusion

On the one hand, the Western instrumental approach to war as a temporary and unfortunate kinetic struggle of political will between states helps to bring much clarity into international affairs, allowing a clear cognitive division between the times of peace and the times of war. On the other, since the diplomacy (politics in the times of peace) has to be based on 'diplomatic notes' and not on 'fighting battles',[76] this approach creates certain restrictions on the means available to diplomacy. As discussed above, the Russian approach to this distinction is that the whole of international relations is nothing less than one eternal war. While this approach frees the hands of diplomacy from any restrictions, allowing the use of any (military or non-military) available tool, it also has its own disadvantages, when the most significant disadvantage is the risk of misunderstanding.

The Russian contemporary conceptualization of international relations as Information War is a very dangerous, slippery slope, not so much because of the Kremlin's intention to use all available means for psychological-informational influence on international and domestic audiences, but because it is defined as a war. Firstly, 'there are no wars in history that were won by non-military means, or by the use of information, alone'.[77] And secondly, without using military force, such confrontations are not wars, and to call them as such is 'a dangerous misuse of the word "war"'.[78] Even General Makmut Gareev, one of the most respected Russian contemporary strategists put it, 'An over-free employment of such a word as "war" devalues the severe [nature of this] concept and dulls its adequate perception in society.'[79]

The West should approach Russia's conceptualization of international relations as Information War with caution for two main reasons. First, the fact that Russia declares that they are in the midst of Information War against the West[80] does not mean Russia seeks a kinetic war with the West. The second and more important reason is that the Kremlin's actions should be analysed through the prism of their conceptualization of international relations and not through the Western one. The counter-sanctions introduced by the Kremlin were not only a reactive continuation of politics between Russian and the West, but also a powerful diplomatic tool in the relations between Russia and the rest of the world. The intervention in Syria was not only the continuation of politics between the Kremlin and Damascus, but also a continuation of Russia's diplomacy with the West, as well as with different non-aligned international political actors. In other words, in the Russian view, diplomacy entails influencing the behaviour of foreign governments and officials not only through different non-violent means, but through a blend of all means available.

Moreover, in its quest to parry Russia's strategic way that blurs the lines between war and diplomacy, the West should remember two important lessons. The first is that this way is neither new, nor particularly Russian. For example, France employed this strategic mix during the American Revolution by military supporting the American colonies whilst simultaneously maintaining peace with Britain,[81] and the Cold War was not a real war, but a period of very hostile international relations between the West and the USSR that mixed direct diplomacy with a large number of indirect proxy wars. This leads to the second lesson. Sun Tzu's famous maxim asserts that 'if you know the enemy and know yourself, you need not fear the result of a hundred battles'. While the topic of 'knowing yourself' should be discussed separately, 'knowing the enemy' is the very message of this chapter. To truly understand Russia, the West should stop looking east through the prism of the Western worldview. The sacred line between war-making and diplomacy, the clear division between achieving political goals by peaceful means and by the means of force, is nothing more than a Western understanding of international relations. And, according to the previously mentioned historical examples, it is a very contemporary one. This chapter showed not only that Russia does not necessarily subscribe to this view, but also that it never has done. The sooner the West realizes and accepts it, the sooner it will be able to craft its strategic approach (either diplomatic, or military or both) towards Russia effectively.

Notes

1. Carl Von Clausewitz, *On War*, ed. and trans. Michael Howard and Peter Paret (Oxford: Oxford University Press, 2008), 28.
2. Ibid., 13.
3. Ibid., 255.
4. Hugh Smith, 'The Womb of War: Clausewitz and International Relations', *Review of International Studies*, Vol. 16, No. 1 (1990), 39–58.
5. Ronald Barston, *Modern Diplomacy*, 4th ed. (Oxon: Routledge, 2019), 1.
6. Smith, 'The Womb of War', 46.
7. Benjamin Buley, *The New American Way of War: Military Culture and the Political Utility of Force* (New York: Routledge, 2008), 2.
8. For example: Oscar Jonsson, *The Russian Understanding of War: Blurring the Lines between War and Peace* (Washington, DC: Georgetown University Press, 2019); Dave Johnson, 'Russia's Approach to Conflict – Implication for NATO's Deterrence and Defence', Research Paper No. 111, NATO Defence College, Rome, 2015; Costinel Anuta, 'Old and New in Hybrid Warfare', in Niculae Iancu, Andrei Fortuna, Cristian Barna and Mihaela Teodor (eds), *Countering Hybrid Threats: Lessons Learned from Ukraine* (Amsterdam: IOS Press BV, 2016).
9. Genrikh Leer, *Opyt kritiko-istoricheskogo issledovaniya zakonov vedeniya voyny (polozhitel'naya strategiya)* [A Historical-Critical Research of the Laws of Military Art (Positive Strategy)] (Saint Petersburg: Pechyatnya V. Golovina, 1869), 1, 36.
10. Vasilii Mikryukov, *Voyna: nauka i iskusstvo* [War: Science and Art], Vol. 1 (Moscow: Rusayins, 2006); Alexander Vladimirov, *Osnovy Obshchey Teorii Voyny* [Fundamentals of General Theory of War], Vol. 1 (Moscow: Moskovskiy Finansovo-Promyshlennyy Universitet 'Sinergiya', 2013); Andrey Kokoshin, *Politologia i sotziologia voyennoy strategii* [The Politics and Sociology of Military Strategy] (Moscow: Lenand, 2016).
11. Ivan Ilyin, *Sushchnost' i svoyeobraziye Russkoy kul'tury* [The Essence and Peculiarity of Russian culture] (Moscow: Russkaya Kniga-XXI Vek, 2007), 110.
12. Ivan Solonevich, 'Tak chto zhe yest' demokratiya?' [So, What Is Democracy?], *Nasha Strana*, No. 35 (1950), 1–2, No. 36 (1950), 1–2, No. 38 (1950), 1–2; Ivan Solonevich, 'Doklad o mezhdunarodnom polozhenii' [Report about the International Situation], *Nasha Strana*, No. 60 (1950), 1–2.

13   V. Gubanov, *Russkiy natsional'nyy kharakter v kontekste politicheskoy zhizni Rossiii* [Russian National Character in the Context of the Russian Political Life] (Saint Petersburg: Izdatel'skiy Tsentr SPbGMGU, 1999), 147.
14   Vladimir Lenin, *Sotsializm i voyna* [Socialism and War] (Moscow: Partizdat TsK VKPb, 1937).
15   E. Rudnitskaya and N. Lisovoi, 'Mirotvorcheskaya Paradigma Russkoy Mysli' [The Peacemaking Paradigm of the Russian Thought], in E. Rudnitskaya (ed.), *Mirotvorchestvo v Rossii – Tserkov', Politika, Mysliteli, ot rannego srednevekov'ya do rubezha XIX-XX stoletiy* [Peacemaking in Russia: The Church, Politics, Thinkers: From the Early Middle Ages to the Boundary between the Nineteenth and Twentieth Centuries] (Moscow: Nauka, 2003), 4.
16   P. Izmest'yev and A. Messner, *Konspekt strategii* [The Abstract of Strategy] (Saint Petersburg: Tipo-Litografiya A.E. Landau, 1899).
17   Vladimirov, *Osnovy Obshchey Teorii Voyny* [Fundamentals of General Theory of War], 163.
18   For example: Andrew Monaghan, 'Putin's Way of War: The "War" in Russia's "Hybrid Warfare"', *Parameters*, Vol. 45, No. 4 (2015–16), 65–74; Jonsson, *The Russian Understanding of War*.
19   Evgeny Martynov, *Obyazannosti politiki po otnosheniyu k strategii* [The Responsibilities of Politics in Its Relations with Strategy] (Saint Petersburg: Tipografiya Glavnogo Upravleniya Udelov, 1899), 1.
20   V. Solov'ev and A. Dremkov, 'Yeshche raz o predmete i strukture voyennoy nauki' [One More Time on the Subject and Structure of Military Science] *Voyennaya Mysl'*, No. 9 (1994), 34–5.
21   Levada Centre, 'Nostalgiya po SSSR' [Nostalgiya for the USSR], 19 December 2018, https://www.levada.ru/2018/12/19/nostalgiya-po-sssr-2/, last accessed 30 August 2020.
22   Levada Centre, 'Raspad SSSR: pritchiny I nostal'giya' [The Dissolution of the USSR: Causes and Nostalgia], 5 December 2016, https://www.levada.ru/2016/12/05/raspad-sssr-prichiny-i-nostalgiya/, last accessed 30 August 2020.
23   Putin, Vladimir, 'Speech to the Federal Assembly', 25 April 2005, Moscow (Russian), http://kremlin.ru/events/president/transcripts/22931, last accessed 30 August 2020.
24   For example: Alexander Vladimirov, 'Gosudarstvo, voyna i natsional'naya bezopasnost' Rossii' [State, War and the National Security of Russia], *Prostranstvo i Vremya*, Vol. 1, No. 3 (2011), 26–38; Pavel Zolotoryev, 'Global'noe izmerenie voyny: novye podhody v XXI veke' [The Global Dimension of War: New Approaches in the Twenty-First Century], *Rossiya v Global'noy Politike*, Vol. 8, No. 1 (2010), 45–58; Igor Panarin, *Pervaya mirovaya informatsionnaya voyna: razval SSSR* [The First World Information War: The Dissolution of the USSR] (Saint Petersburg: Piter, 2010).
25   Igor Panarin and Lyubov' Panarina, *Informatsionnaya voyna i mir* [Information War and the World] (Moscow: OLMA-PRESS, 2003), 1–20.

26 Yuri Grigor'yev, 'Antirossiyskiye Informatsionnyye Voyny' [Anti-Russian Information Wars], *Informatsionnye voyny*, Vol. 4, No. 36 (2015), 6.
27 Vladimir Lisichkin and Leonid Shelepin, *Tret'ya mirovaya informatsionno – psikhologicheskaya voyna* [The Third World Information – Psychological War] (Moscow: Eskimo-Algoritm, 2003), 17.
28 Panarin, *Pervaya mirovaya informatsionnaya voyna* [The First World Information War], 24.
29 Ilyin, *Sushchnost' i svoyeobraziye Russkoy kul'tury* [The Essence and Peculiarity of Russian Culture], 110.
30 Ivan Solonevich, *Zagadka i razgadka Rossii* [The Riddle and the Key of Russia] (Moscow: 'FondIV', 2008), 295.
31 The Ministry of Defence of the Russian Federation, *Military Encyclopaedic Dictionary*, http://encyclopedia.mil.ru/encyclopedia/dictionary/details.htm?id=5211@morfDictionary, last accessed 30 August 2020.
32 Kokoshin, *Politologia i sotziologia voyennoy strategii* [The Politics and Sociology of Military Strategy], 502–3.
33 James Farwell, *Persuasion and Power: The Art of Strategic Communication* (Washington: Georgetown University Press, 2012), Chapter 1.
34 Igor Panarin, *Informatzionnaya voyna, PR i mirovaya politika*, [Information War, PR and World Politics] (Moscow: Goryachaya Liniya – Telecom, 2006), 180.
35 Aleksandr Dugin, 'Teoreticheskiye osnovy setevykh voyn' [The Theoretical Grounds of Network Wars], *Informatsionnye voyny*, Vol. 1, No. 5 (2008), 4.
36 As stated on the Journal's website: http://www.iwars.su/redkol (Russian), last accessed 30 August 2020.
37 Presidential Decree No 1300, 'The Concept of the National Security of the Russian Federation', Moscow, 17 December 1997 (Russian).
38 Presidential Decree No 706, 'The Military Doctrine of the Russian Federation', Moscow, 21 April 2000 (Russian).
39 Vladimir Serebryanikov and Alexander Kapko, 'Nevoyennyye sredstva oboronnoy bezopasnosti Rossii' [The Non-Military Means of the Defence Security of Russia], *Dialog*, No. 2 (2000), 29–30.
40 Ibid., 21–2.
41 For example: Nikolay Volkovsky, *Istroiya informatzionnykh voyn* [The History of Information Wars], in Vols. 2 (Saint Petersburg: Poligon, 2013); Sergey Tkachenko, *Informatsionnaya voyna protiv Rossii* [Information War against Russia] (Saint Petersburg: Piter, 2011); Vladimir Novikov, *Informatsionnoye oruzhiye: oruzhiye sovremennykh i budushchikh voyn* [Information-Weapon: The Weapon of Contemporary and Future Wars] (Moscow: Goryachaya Liniya-Telekom, 2011); Dmitry Belyayev, *Razrukha v golovakh: Informatsionnaya voyna protiv Rossii* [The Destruction in the Heads: Information War against Russia] (Saint Petersburg: Piter, 2015); Panarin, *Informatzionnaya voyna* [Information War]; Lisichkin and

Shelepin, *Tret'ya mirovaya informatsionno-psikhologicheskaya voyna* [The Third World Information – Psychological War].

42 Von Clausewitz, *On War*, 255.

43 Steve Holland and Jeff Mason, 'Obama Warns on Crimea, Orders Sanctions over Russian Moves in Ukraine', *Routers*, 6 March 2014, https://www.reuters.com/article/ukraine-crisis-obama/update-4-obama-warns-on-crimea-orders-sanctions-over-russian-moves-in-ukraine-idUSL1N0M30XQ20140306, last accessed 30 August 2020.

44 Presidential Decree No 560, 'On the Use of Specific Economic Measures Aimed to Ensure the Security of the Russian Federation', Moscow, 6 August 2014 (Russian).

45 For a good review of different literature about this argument, see Aleksandr Lyakin and Mikhail Rogov, 'Sanktsii i kontrsanktsii: ispol'zovaniye politicheskikh instrumentov dlya realizatsii ekonomicheskikh tseley' [Sanctions and Counter-Sanctions: The Use of Political Tools for Economic Purposes], *Natsional'nyye interesy: prioritety i bezopasnost'*, Vol. 3, No. 8 (2017), 1396–414.

46 Ibid., 1406.

47 Ibid.

48 Ministry of Foreign Affairs of the Russian Federation, *The Foreign Policy Concept of the Russian Federation-2016*, Moscow, 2016 (Russian).

49 Vladimir Putin quoted in 'Putin nazval novyye sanktsii SSHA bessmyslennymi' [Putin Called the New US Sanctions as Meaningless], *RiaNovosti*, 22 August 2018, https://ria.ru/20180822/1527039375.html, last accessed 30 August 2020.

50 Lyakin and Rogov, 'Sanktsii i kontrsanktsii' [Sanctions and Counter-Sanctions].

51 Vyacheslav Viktorov, 'Proshloe, nastoyqschee i buduyuschee kul'ta lichnosti v Rosii' [Past, Present and Future of the Cult of Personality in Russia], *Gumanitarnye Nauki*, Vol. 1, No. 5 (2012), 40.

52 Dimitri Trenin, *Should We Fear Russia?* (Cambridge: Polity Press, 2016), 27.

53 Dimitri Trenin, 'Putin's Biggest Challenge Is Public Support', *Carnegie Moscow Center*, 15 January 2015, http://carnegie.ru/2015/01/15/putin-s-biggest-challenge-is-public-support/hzl5, last accessed 30 August 2020.

54 Levada Centre, 'Sanksii i kontrsanktsii' [Sanctions and Counter-Sanctions], 15 May 2017, https://www.levada.ru/2017/05/15/sanktsii-i-kontrsanktsii-3/, last accessed 30 August 2020.

55 For example: Sergey Chekinov and Sergey Bogdanov, 'Strategicheskoe sderzhivanie i nazhional'naya bezopasnost' Rossii na soveremennom etape' [The Strategic Deterrence and National Security of Russia in the Modern Age], *Voennaya Mysl'*, No. 3 (2012), 16.

56 Dugin, 'Teoreticheskiye osnovy setevykh voyn' [The Theoretical Grounds of Network Wars], 4.

57 Neil MacFarquhar, 'U.N. Resolution on Syria Blocked by Russia and China', *The New York Times*, 4 October 2011, https://www.nytimes.com/2011/10/05/world/

middleeast/russia-and-china-block-united-nations-resolution-on-syria.html, last accessed 30 August 2020.
58 Stockholm International Peace Research Institute, *SIPRI Arms Transfers Database*, http://www.sipri.org/databases/armstransfers, last accessed 30 August 2020.
59 Maria Efrimomva, Ivan Safronov and Elena Chernenko, 'Rossiya ukrepila Bashara Asada granatometami i beteerami' [Russia Reinforced Bashar Assad with Grenade Launchers and APCs], *Kommersant*, 9 September 2015, http://www.kommersant.ru/doc/2806541, last accessed 30 August 2020.
60 Alec Luhn, 'Russia Sends Artillery and Tanks to Syria as Part of Continued Military Buildup', *The Guardian*, 14 September 2015, http://www.theguardian.com/world/2015/sep/14/russia-sends-artillery-and-tanks-to-syria-as-part-of-continued-military-buildup, last accessed 30 August 2020; 'Russian Rroops "Fighting alongside Assad's Army against Syrian Rebels"', *The Telegraph*, 2 September 2015, http://www.telegraph.co.uk/news/worldnews/middleeast/syria/11840713/Russian-troops-fighting-alongside-Assads-army-against-Syrian-rebels.html, last accessed 30 August 2020.
61 Vladimir Putin, 2007 *Speech at the Munich Security Conference* (Russian), http://www.stringer-news.com/publication.mhtml?Part=50&PubID=7070, last accessed 30 August 2020.
62 A. Smirnov, 'Kontseptsii vneshney politiki Rossiyskoy Federatsii: sravnitel'nyy analiz [The Foreign Policy Concept of the Russian Federation – Comparative Analysis]', in S. Smul'skii, O. Abramova and V. Buyanov (eds), *Vneshnyaya politika Rossii: teoriya i praktika* [The Foreign Policy of Russia: Theory and Practice] (Moscow: Kniga i Biznes, 2013), 58–83.
63 Ministry of Foreign Affairs of the Russian Federation, *The Foreign Policy Concept of the Russian Federation-2000*, Moscow, 2000 (Russian).
64 Ministry of Foreign Affairs of the Russian Federation, *The Foreign Policy Concept of the Russian Federation-2008*, Moscow, 2008 (Russian).
65 Ministry of Foreign Affairs of the Russian Federation, *The Foreign Policy Concept of the Russian Federation-2013*, Moscow, 2013 (Russian).
66 Vladimir Putin quoted in 'Putin nazval osnovnuyu zadachu rossiyskikh voyennykh v Sirii' [Putin Declared the Main Task of the Russian Military in Syria], *Inerfax*, 11 October 2015, http://www.interfax.ru/russia/472593, last accessed 30 August 2020.
67 Vladimir Putin quoted on Official Website of the President of the Russian Federation, 'Vstrecha s Sergeyem Lavrovym i Sergeyem Shoygu' [Meeting with Sergey Lavrov and Sergey Shoygu], Moscow, 14 March 2016, http://kremlin.ru/events/president/news/51511, last accessed 30 August 2020.
68 Igor Sutyagin, 'RUSI Experts Igor Sutyagin and Michael Stephens Assess the Reasons and Prospects of Russia's Military Campaign against Daesh/ISIS' (Video), https://www.facebook.com/RUSI.org/videos/10153607933636718/, last accessed 30 August 2020; see also Payam Mohseni (ed.), *Disrupting the Chessboard Perspectives*

on the Russian Intervention in Syria (Cambridge, MA: Harvard Kennedy School, Belfer Center for Science and International Affairs, 2015).

69 Levada Centre, 'Odobreniye institutov vlasti' [Approval of the Institutions of Power], https://www.levada.ru/indikatory/odobrenie-organov-vlasti/, last accessed 30 August 2020.

70 Milan Dinic, 'Public: West Should Join with Russia in Fight against ISIS', *YouGov*, 29 September 2015, https://yougov.co.uk/news/2015/09/29/public-west-should-join-russia-fight-against-isis/, last accessed 30 August 2020.

71 Dana Blanton, 'Fox News Poll: Voters Say Obama Has No Syria Plan, Putin "Strong and Shrewd"', *Fox News*, 20 December 2015, http://www.foxnews.com/politics/2015/10/14/fox-news-poll-voters-say-obama-has-no-syria-plan-putin-strong-and-shrewd.html, last accessed 30 August 2020.

72 Vladimir Putin, 'Zasedaniye Soveta glav gosudarstv SNG' [Meeting of the CIS Council of the Heads of States], Borovoe, 16 October 2015, http://www.kremlin.ru/events/president/news/50515, last accessed 30 August 2020.

73 Vladimir Rouvinsk, 'Russian-Venezuelan Relations at a Crossroads', Woodrow Wilson International Centre for Scholars, Latin American Program, February 2019, 1.

74 'Vladimir Putin's Road to Damascus: Russia's Military Gamble in Syria Is Paying off Handsomely', *The Economist*, 12 May 2009, https://www.economist.com/middle-east-and-africa/2019/05/16/russias-military-gamble-in-syria-is-paying-off-handsomely, last accessed 30 August 2020.

75 Julian Borger and Bastien Inzaurralde 'West "Ignored Russian Offer in 2012 to Have Syria's Assad Step Aside"', *The Guardian*, 15 September 2015, https://www.theguardian.com/world/2015/sep/15/west-ignored-russian-offer-in-2012-to-have-syrias-assad-step-aside, last accessed 30 August 2020.

76 Von Clausewitz, *On War*, 255.

77 Bettina Renz and Hanna Smith, 'PART 2: A Dangerous Misuse of the Word "War"? "Hybrid Warfare" as a Quasi-Theory of Russian Foreign Policy', in Bettina Renz and Hanna Smith (eds), 'Russia and Hybrid Warfare – Gong Beyond the Label', *Papers Aleksanteri*, no. 1, 2016, 11.

78 Samuel Charap, 'The Ghost of Hybrid War', *Survival*, Vol. 57, No. 6 (2015/16), 52.

79 Makhmut Gareev, 'Struktura I osnovnoe soderzhanie novoy voennoy doktriny [The Structure and the Content of the New Military Doctrine]', *Voenno-Promyshlennyy Kur'er*, no. 3 (2007), http://www.vpk-news.ru/sites/default/files/pdf/issue_169.pdf, last accessed 30 August 2020.

80 Ofer Fridman, *Russian 'Hybrid Warfare': Resurgence and Politicisation* (New York: Oxford University Press, 2018), Chapter 7.

81 Jonathan Dull, *A Diplomatic History of the American Revolution* (New Haven: Yale University Press, 1985).

8

Social movements, diplomacy and relationships of trust

Dr Francesca Granelli

Social movements and traditional diplomacy have always interacted. This chapter asks how the relationship – sometimes complementary, often conflicting – changed in the twenty-first century. Academia has typically approached the subject through theories of social movements,[1] international relations and global politics without integrating them fully. This is understandable but inadequate: a new, interdisciplinary approach is required to explore the intersection of social movements and diplomacy. Since trust is familiar to both fields, it offers an excellent way to do this.

Although the ability of social movements to influence domestic politics is hardly new, contemporary developments have seen them exercise growing power internally, over the policies of their own government, and externally, over the policies of other states. Consider, by way of illustration, the Arab Spring; climate change demonstrations; anti-austerity, anti-authoritarian and anti-corruption protests; Brexit and anti-Brexit; and other independence movements. Technological changes are partly responsible for such empowerment through 'the diversification of involvement, the sustenance of participation, the association-based spread and solidification of influence, and the anticoagulation and refinement of control'.[2] However, while researchers have argued social media spread democratic ideas across international borders and shaped political debates,[3] with online revolutionary conversations often preceding major events, the Arab Spring was not in fact a 'Twitter Uprising' or a 'Facebook Revolution'.[4] This chapter argues that technology is a less fruitful lens than trust.

Trust has always been at the centre of national governance and international order.[5] We are blessed with numerous case studies that demonstrate how trust creates value and allows for win-win outcomes – by, for instance, enabling statesmen to circumvent traditional routes of interstate negotiations or to overcome obstacles in the way of Pareto optimal outcomes.[6] Yet trust is also vital to social movements – a fact often obscured by researchers subsuming the concept into notions of solidarity and collectivism so that it becomes one facet of many; consequently, there has been scant exploration of the different relationships of trust and how they interact.

A possible explanation is that trust remains a difficult concept to assimilate across cultural lines and to deploy in practice. Academics do not help, often presenting the concept as multifaceted, complex and abstract. Consequently, trust remains difficult to identify, let alone quantify. It should be distinguished from similar concepts, such as reliance and cooperation, and is certainly distinct from more distant notions, including belief, ideology, solidarity and social capital. Even with a ground clearing exercise, multiple types of trust remain (from personal to impersonal trust, general to systems trust) and rightly so: it would do violence to our understanding to smooth out its crooked timber. However, all kinds of trust involve the following: *an acceptance of vulnerability in the expectation of certain outcome or behaviours in a specific situation and at a specific time.*

From this, we can derive personal trust (between individuals), impersonal trust (between an individual and an institution), general trust (the norms in society and how closely they are observed), systems trust (between an individual and a system) and many more. We also need to be clear that distrust is the opposite, not the absence, of trust; moreover, it should not be confused with mistrust, which is shorthand for misplaced trust.

This chapter seeks to address that lacuna. First, it sets out the backdrop that underpins the changing relationship between diplomacy and social movements in the twenty-first century. Second, it looks briefly at each of the two fields in the twenty-first century. Third, it explains how both are underpinned by trust and its changing relationships. Fourth, it harnesses the latter to explain the perception and practice of contemporary diplomacy. The chapter concludes by summarizing the current trends and setting out the focus of future research.

The backdrop: Uncertain contemporary futures and digital connectivity

The place to start is with the changing relationship between diplomacy and social movements, which is dependent on two key features of our world today: uncertainty and connectivity.[7]

Historians are right to remind us that many generations have faced massive uncertainty and, of course, even more thought they did. Provided that remains front of mind, we should not ignore the abundant evidence of contemporary political, social and economic flux. For it surely indicates that we are entering another period of significant uncertainty: mass migration creates huge stress and major social divisions;[8] religious fundamentalism paves the way for terrorism; non-state actors and the 'benefit scramble' challenge the state from above and below;[9] the rise of China shifts the axis of global influence; the re-emergence of Iran upsets the regional equilibrium; Russian posturing and aggression threaten European security; globalization exacerbates the divide between rich and poor; and ongoing debt crises undermine growth and stability.

At root, these are the outcomes of globalization. As with uncertainty, this is hardly the first wave of globalization but it is nonetheless profound in scale, rate and consequence. Patrick, for instance, writes that 'we are now living in a new, fast-evolving multipolar world economy in which some developing countries are emerging as economic powers, others are moving towards becoming additional poles of growth, and some are struggling to attain their potential within this new system'.[10]

The upshot is that states are fast losing their pre-eminence: the international order is increasingly being challenged by *transnational* networks, *supranational* unions and *global* corporations. Equally, national identity and provincial values continue to be 'eroded by the impact of global cultural industries and multinational media'.[11] This is not to say that there is a one-way cultural tide from America or even the West; recent studies dispute claims of an American century and instead point to an exchange of ideas, values and identities.[12] Moreover, there has been a marked backlash – reflected in the Brexit referendum, Trump's inauguration and the popularity of the far right across Europe – that has further contributed to instability.

What is unique to the contemporary situation, of course, is digital connectivity, which has kindled a number of powerful tensions: the order of the state versus the disorder of personal networks; the globalization of the economy versus the fragmentation of society; and the increased connectivity of people versus the atomization of urban communities.

The digital mediascape has an impact on everything we do: 'the matrix is everywhere'[13] or, as countless Hollywood screenwriters have it, we are never 'off the grid'. Our new environment is defined by the unprecedented speed, range, volume and utility of information. With this evolution in communication technology and its applications, many researchers are investigating 'a pattern common to all life' today: the emergence of networked communities that are casually formed yet highly cohesive and which pursue social and/or political change.[14] As Lash points out, these information and communication structures are replacing traditional social hierarchies.[15]

We are connected not just through the sharing of ideas but, perhaps more significantly, through the *idea* of sharing in the wake of digital connectivity.[16] However, we should not allow a technological or materialist explanation to displace the role of trust.[17] For the key *explicans* is the ability of people to actively participate and the potential for a new global hegemony based on individuals, rather than states. Where Anderson rightly foregrounded the idea of nations as 'imagined communities',[18] we should now also talk about 'virtual communities' – each of which links terrain, frames thinking and shapes identity – even though the latter is increasingly fluid to accommodate the co-existence of multiple identities (e.g. European, British, English, Pakistani and Londoner).[19]

Although access to digital resources remains uneven, the consequence is that social graphs are increasingly self-generated collections of individuals connected by personal trust. Furthermore, the competing forms and networks of trust all have the potential to divide as much as unite and they yield turbulent relationships that threaten the status quo.[20]

This is the environment in which social movements find themselves – and they are in pole position. Given the way they organize, they are well placed to embrace digital media in contrast to regimes that, despite attempts to catch up, still face structural handicaps. A major challenge, for instance, in a world that is becoming more and more interconnected is simply to be heard through the noise; to capture attention among many diversions; and retain interest in the face of competing attractions. Lewis's *AIDA* model, which seems consumers progressing through Awareness, Interest, Desire and Action, is relevant once more.

The two fields: Diplomacy and social movements

While the theory of diplomacy is unchanged, its praxis has been challenged by innumerable structural and situational factors. The former includes a shift from a state centric international system towards a global political and economic order, from formal centralization to informal networks, and from structure to fragmentation. The latter span the end of the Cold War, international terrorism, the rise of China, the revolution of internet-based global communication, the problems of legitimacy faced by liberal democracy and growing public sensitivity to foreign policies.[21] As a result – whether viewed as art, craft or both – diplomats now require greater knowledge, deep understanding of the communications environment and wider experience to meet the novel demands of international politics.

Most relevant is the dramatic encroachment of non-state actors on their turf. The aim of these actors is to influence discourse, shape values and define norms to an extent previously unimaginable.[22] This is particularly evident in the digital space.[23] Put simply, as the chairman of the Coca-Cola Company said: 'We will change the world because we can and we must!'[24] Empowered by technological innovation in a new media landscape, social movements have demonstrated an ability to disrupt traditional diplomacy – from Trump's many cancelled visits to the Brexit negotiations between the UK and EU, and Greta Thunberg's address at Davos. While this is not unique, the speed, scale and never-ending onslaught is redefining diplomacy such that it is no longer private, dictated by protocols, or carried out by defined actors. At the same time, conventional practice has to deal with the blurring of public and private, domestic and foreign, citizen and state alongside an exponential increase in dis-, mis-, mal- and non-information.[25] These changes have shifted, by degrees, the emphasis from traditional diplomacy to public diplomacy. With a focus on dialogue and negotiation, *traditional diplomacy* refers primarily to 'a peaceful approach to the management of international relations, the aim of which is the pursuit of national interests and values, and the promotion of a country's economic and political place in the world'.[26] Such delivery draws upon a state's toolkit of hard, soft, smart and sharp power.[27] Although a definition is yet to be agreed, *public diplomacy* is best understood as a state's 'direct communication with foreign peoples, with the aim of affecting their thinking and, ultimately, that of their governments'.[28] Both are concerned with the implementation, rather than development, of foreign policy.

It is important to understand this process of change. On the one hand, diplomacy is diversifying its influence. The UN Climate Change Conference 2017, for instance, represents the largest multilateral discussion beyond the foreign policy realm that was, at the same time, increasingly sensitive to publics challenging various national interests. Citizens are using digitally savvy social movements to make more demands on diplomacy, from topics as diverse as whaling to refugees. Such 'negotiations' are taking place in the full glare of the media and public scrutiny – meaning that social movements and other non-state actors not only challenge how diplomacy is perceived but question its legitimacy and effectiveness.

One component behind the shift is the engagement of contemporary social movements in issues hitherto considered to be the prerogative of government. Private citizens can have a substantial impact on international relations and legislation such as the Logan Act is powerless to stop them.[29] From terrorist atrocities to protest movements, individual agency has become more powerful, forcing states and their representatives to be increasingly agile in their response – often at the expense of more strategic objectives. This inevitably reconfigures well-established diplomatic roadmaps.

So where, precisely, do social movements fit in the new world order of the twenty-first century? The TL;DR[30] answer is: everywhere. They underpin waves of populism, protest and democracy.[31] Whether as part of the Colour Revolutions and the Arab Spring; climate change demonstrations; anti-austerity, anti-authoritarian and anti-corruption protests; Brexit and anti-Brexit; and other independence movements, *voces populi* have captured the world's attention as never before.[32]

Four broad themes emerge from the diversity. First, confidence in traditional mechanisms of public decision making has declined and led to calls for 'real democracy', such as the Occupy Wall Street (OWS) movement. Second, there is strong demand for a participatory and deliberative culture, with more inclusive forms of democracy at multiple territorial levels; Catalonia's vote for independence is exemplary. Third, protests that favour participation, openness, publicity and equality have flourished in place of mobilization through networks of associations; here, the recent plastics campaign is illustrative. Fourth, there is – despite attempts by some politicians, such as Trump and the alt right, to appeal to nativist instincts – an increasingly cosmopolitan vision that recognizes the need for global solutions to global problems on issues such as migration, identity politics, the internet and climate change.

The evolution of social movements can be seen as part of a transition in citizenship, which is adapting to new styles of governance and democracy in societies facing transnational exchanges of goods, services, capital, people and information. Social movements – with their ability to respond quickly, innovatively and virally – have succeeded, in many cases, in becoming channels for activist citizenship.[33] This has not only facilitated intervention in favour of groups excluded from established norms of citizenship, but disrupted accepted orders, practices, roles and statutes, and even questioned the immutability of a particular body politic.

Naturally, this is not to say that all social movements have succeeded; some have not even survived.[34] For example, despite OWS's global notoriety, it has yet to achieve policy changes, while movements on gun violence prevention and carbon emissions reduction continue to struggle to gain ground – and many others form, break, and reform in an ever-changing political and social landscape. #BlackLivesMatter, for instance, can be understood as a new iteration of the civil rights movement. Yet the fact remains that, while social movements have always had the potential to shape the debate, in the twenty-first century they have the increasing ability to quickly and visibly impact diplomacy in many more ways.

First, they influence state actors. Consider the shift in policy to allow unaccompanied minors into the UK after the closure of the Calais 'Jungle'. The Dubs amendment, premised on a universal politics of childhood that seeks to protect their innocence, raised awareness and the resulting pressure 'forced' the British and French governments to negotiate a solution.[35] The wider campaign fronted by UK Help Refugees[36] (which started life as a hashtag) and supported by over 100 celebrities underlaid the 'child first, migrant second' approach advocated by humanitarian organizations and was a key argument in the 'Dubs amendment'.

Second, they sway international actors. An example is the Convention on the Prohibition of the Use, Stockpiling, Production and Transfer of Anti-Personnel Mines and on Their Destruction (or 'Mine Ban Convention'). Adopted in 1997, over 150 countries have now joined the treaty following the advocacy work of the Red Cross and MAG (with Diana, Princess of Wales) as part of the International Campaign to Ban Landmines.[37]

Third, they disrupt negotiations between these actors. Popular protests are said to have led Trump to cancel his visit to open the new US embassy in London in January 2018. Confirmation came via Twitter, with Trump claiming 'Bad deal. Wanted me to cut ribbon-NO!', whereas the 'Trump blimp' was a more likely cause than any commercial arrangements. Although diplomatic relations were maintained throughout, popular protests interdicted diplomatic process. However, it is not clear how long they will continue: while protests undoubtedly retain the power to disrupt, their success rate in bringing about systemic politic change has plummeted from 70 per cent twenty years ago to 30 per cent today.[38]

Fourth, they change the forums in which such negotiations take place. In the early 1990s UNICEF only spent 100,000 USD/year on an issue affecting over 100 million girls. There was a concerted effort by Equality Now, an NGO that has grown exponentially over the last twenty-five years, to launch a global campaign to raise awareness of Female Genital Mutilation (FGM) and place it high on the UN agenda. Moreover, they stepped in subsequently to harness the legitimacy of the international forum in order to bring about change on the ground by working with a regional network of END FMG activists.³⁹

Fifth, they provide extra-diplomatic space for negotiation. Consider the ongoing global plastics campaign which operates in every available space (public and private), across every medium (from television to education), and through public and traditional diplomacy. The ongoing debate is simultaneously shaping domestic and foreign policies, offering opportunities and complicating discussions. It reflects the widening content (e.g. oil-, resources-, logistics- and humanitarian-diplomacy) and concomitant shift in spaces of diplomacy.⁴⁰

Sixth, they provide a voice to the marginalized. Research has shown that, the more disadvantaged a group is, the more important civil society representation becomes to their substantive representation in policymaking.⁴¹ Examples range from identity-based movements (such as LGBTQ+, ethnicity, disability, youth or gender movements) to issue-based political protest (from climate change, anti-austerity, human rights, to surveillance and policing). Yet despite the hugely positive potential of marginalized voices appearing in democratic spaces, there is also a risk that such movements can create their own mechanisms of exclusion and hence a danger of fragmentation as the voices are told 'you cannot represent us'.⁴²

Seventh, they create new transnational voices. This is illustrated by the loosely allied anti-austerity, OWS and LGBTQ+ movements. All comprise networks of activists coming together to coordinate international cross border campaigns. They seek to leverage their transnational voice to achieve their stated objectives against international actors, other states or international institutions.⁴³ However, while the 'globalness and massiveness' of these protests attract attention for their newness and the potential for political impact, their grassroots activities and mobilization should not be overlooked.⁴⁴ They provide a feedback mechanism to implement change at local level.

Eighth, they respond more quickly than diplomatic actors. Social movements, especially those harnessing social media, can rapidly apply pressure and bring about change. For example, the Arab Spring swiftly toppled dictators (Tunisian President Zine El Abidine Ben Ali in twenty-eight days and Egyptian Hosni President Mubarak in eighteen days) while Trump's hugely unpopular zero-tolerance immigration policy, introduced on 6 April 2018, was reversed on 20 June 2018. However, while digital technology enables social movements to quickly build connections and coalitions, mobilize participants and resources, and amplify alternative narratives at little to no cost, it creates weak ties that often lack resilience.⁴⁵

Four elements underpin their success. Social movements have (i) produced networks that are orthogonal to the diplomatic; (ii) created efficient feedback loops between populations and diplomats; (iii) increased transparency and thereby held diplomats to account; and (iv) activated publics that demand action or forbearance on the part of (inter)governmental actors. Moreover, a single phenomenon is key to explaining all four: the changing nature of trust and its relationships.

Changing relationships of trust

This chapter has already offered a partial explanation for how this came about: the uncertain contemporary futures and digital connectivity. This led to a movement *between* impersonal and personal trust and also by flux *within* both impersonal trust (towards expectation and reliance) and personal trust (between 'weak' and 'strong' ties).[46]

Consider the movement from personal to impersonal trust. The state has, to varying degrees, become an important component of solidarity and identity in Western nations; it is 'an instrument of generalised trust' that increases the confidence of citizens while reducing risk and uncertainty.[47] Furthermore, the modern state has trampled 'the closely knit and cliquish local bodies which had made collective provision in the past and replaced them with overarching, more impersonal institutions on a city-wide or even national scale'.[48] Yet a structure well suited to a fiscal-military state of the eighteenth century is no longer fit for purpose in the twenty-first century.[49] The addition of 'low' as well as 'high' politics to its responsibilities has meant that the nature of trust evolved as citizens became confident that bureaucracy delivers reliability, consistency and universality alongside checks and balances that reduce uncertainty and risk.

However, there is a complication: on the one hand, states are criticized for encouraging citizens to be dependent on the state while, on the other, the trust enjoyed by government is low and falling.[50] An increasing reliance on the state had a profound and counterintuitive implication for impersonal trust: rather than invest more time and effort on the relationship, we instead fall back on rules and sanctions, checks and balances, laws and bureaucracy. With no room for uncertainty, we simply rely on them to work. This has led to an expectation among the citizenry of *no risk* rather than low risk and, consequently, an even weaker form of impersonal trust: non-betrayal. When mistakes come to light or an institution fails, this is not met with a sense of unease, caution or distrust but the more destructive feeling of betrayal.

This increasing reliance on the state has a profound and counterintuitive implication for impersonal trust: rather than invest more time and effort in the relationship, we instead fall back on rules and sanctions, checks and balances, laws and bureaucracy. With no room for uncertainty or risk, we simply rely on them to work. It has led to the expectation of *no* risk rather than *low* risk. The result is an even weaker form of impersonal trust: non-betrayal. When mistakes come to light or an institution fails, this is met not with a growing sense of unease, caution and distrust, but with the more destructive notion of betrayal.

Non-betrayal is also harder to manage, since the absence of values or emotions within this weak form of impersonal trust means that few institutions can differentiate themselves and thereby produce goodwill. This is reminiscent of debates over the decline in social capital in Western states[51] and the need to create social capital *ex nihilo* in the former communist states during the 1990s.[52] Instead, modern 'industrial nations are being forced to redefine and articulate new collective values and aspirations' to ensure and sustain social cohesion,[53] by shifting trust from a passive, impersonal role to an active, re-personalized one – in short, from a model of compliance to cooperation.[54] The modern state desires to replicate, and thereby benefit from, the collaborative relationships that develop in social movements; progress, it is argued, is better achieved with a cooperative model built on values rather than an instrumental model based on interest.[55] Confidence, judgement, behaviour and character replace risk, vulnerability, rationality, rules and sanctions.

As Jackson and Gau explain, obligation is a reaction to current authority while trust is an enabler of future action.[56] The latter has three important advantages. First, trust encourages the citizenry actively to participate, such that an individual is more vested in the process and outcome. Second, it enables both state and society to adapt more quickly to a rapidly changing situation than if they were built on more rigid values. Third, it increases the discretion of the state, since authority has the latitude to act within an agreed perimeter. These models aim to migrate the benefits of personal trust to impersonal relationships of trust – that is, to re-personalize them. This cannot help but energize and empower social movements.

For this reason, although many regimes – particularly, but not exclusively, in the Western, liberal democratic tradition – recognize the benefit of such a move, this is not true of all governments. Arguably, this has profound implications for diplomacy, since the choice of approach itself can divide states and encourage public diplomacy at the expense of traditional democracy.

A related argument sees the state as 'hollowed-out' and irrelevant because of external factors, rather than its own doing.[57] It posits challenges from, on the one hand, international organizations fulfilling the role of the state and, on the one other, global corporations exerting greater influence on the individual – whether distant bureaucracies such as the European Union, social media platforms such as Facebook, or lifestyle brands such as Apple. While the first sounds like the most potent threat – after all, territorial governments are characterized as outdated, intermediary authorities in an ever more internationalized system – an alternative to the state has still to be found; indeed, the conjunction of nation and state ensures that 'international' means 'interstate'. Equally, governments have come to acknowledge the need for international alliances to challenge the power of global corporations, leading to new notions of territorial sovereignty and the pursuit of mutual interests at the expense of national interests. This echoes previous recognition of the need to tackle issues such as migration, climate change and terrorism at a global level.[58]

A better account regards the two challengers – international organization and global corporations – as adding to, rather than displacing, layers – thereby increasing the potential for tension and conflict in this complex artificial landscape.[59] Whatever the model, however, it must provide space for individual agency – a significant task, given the remarkably complex and fluid nature of one's relationships, interactions and networks. We now form communities of like-minded individuals that stretch around the world. Empowered by digital technology, which reconceptualizes time and space, the state faces a pincer movement, intentional or otherwise, from these networks; this is compounded by the permeability of the state noted above.[60]

Yet again, the real driver is personal trust: this is what builds, sustains, breaks and reconstructs our relationships, interactions and networks – and, crucially, now enables them to transcend politically and territorially defined spaces.[61] Personal trust has typically existed between individuals who enjoy a face-to-face relationship and, while technology has always expanded the domain of personal trust, it typically did no more than facilitate such relationships. By contrast, digital communication has brought with it a qualitative change: the proliferation of weaker ties between more individuals. This has many implications, including the lowering of barriers to entry to activism (so-called 'clicktivism'); the consequent amplification of minor, transitory attitudes; the dissolution of geographic barriers and facilitation of the transnational; the diffusion of information and, with it, transparency; and the activation of publics through the Spartacus Effect.[62]

Global social movements, such as Occupy Wall Street, have succeeded in grabbing the headlines.[63] Yet despite their stated intention to bring about progressive social change through the reinvention of politics, their impact has been limited to date.[64] Such movements have been more concerned with freedom of expression, active participation, and ethical and moral values than the *revolution* they espouse. They are a response to the growing size of the state; to its increasing bureaucratization;[65] the backlash against globalization; and the failed promises of New Capitalism.[66] The focus has been more on the idea itself: large-scale involvement in social change and the spirit of resistance, which provides a space for the politically marginalized and those hopeful of together creating a new utopia.

The movement has relied, and continues to rely, heavily on individuals trusting the online platforms that unite this transnational movement – and this despite concerns over government oversight and the recent scandal of the use made by Cambridge Analytica and Facebook of trust in digital technology. The movement itself is built on weak ties which time and again fade quickly when the next 'issue' takes priority or achieving their policy goals is slow. These movements struggle to maintain their popularity, driven by media attention, in the face of individual and institutional short termism.[67] Yet that is not to dismiss the fact that the transnational activities of Occupy and Anti-austerity movements challenge diplomacy globally. They have proven incredibly successful at creating networks of networks which circumvent traditional pathways and institutions to increase awareness, educate the public and gain their support.

Described as the prototype for twenty-first-century citizen activism, the Arab Spring offers a case study on the public and traditional diplomacy of Western states.[68] 'On one side are the government thugs firing bullets ... [and] on the other side are young protesters firing "tweets".'[69] The British government's varied responses to the popular uprisings of the 'Arab Spring' have been criticized for being inconsistent and/or selective; in the United States, public support and traditional diplomacy are seen to be in stark conflict.

Despite the headlines, the Arab Spring sets a changing approach to diplomacy against the perceived evolution of social movements. It provides a vivid example not only of the growing tensions within diplomacy but of the misperception of social movements. Obama's powerful Cairo speech on 4 June 2009 was a masterful display of public diplomacy that bypassed tradition institutional structures to speak directly to Middle Eastern publics. Two years later, however, the Arab Spring was only cautiously welcomed. This was quickly replaced by a combination of fear and pragmatism, and a return to traditional 'back room' diplomacy that resulted in an Egyptian military coup. National interest trumped Western ideals of democracy. At the same time, the media heralded the age of social media revolution, despite the fact that these so-called leaderless revolutions were in fact the result of planning and long-term coalition building. While social media was undoubtedly a useful tactical tool, it did not replace face-to-face relationships built over time within and between identity or issue-based collectives, such as the Muslim Brotherhood trade union movements, and sport clubs.

Finally, consider insurgent groups, such as Daesh and Al Qaeda (grown out of social movements). Where the former strives for a new state with territorial boundaries, the latter pursues the idea of *thawrah alamiyyah* (complete and comprehensive world revolution)[70] that echoes the debates in secular Marxism[71] about global ambitions and the appropriate pathway to revolution.[72] Working beyond the confines of a state to create a new global caliphate governed by *Sharia* law, this breed of revolutionary seeks to reshape the social structure and to redraw the world order. With an uncompromising worldview, it is reminiscent of past religious wars – which, in itself, has profound implications for states, individuals and trust. Although both are proficient at using *propaganda of the deed*,[73] they also communicate diplomatically with both individuals and states.

Social movement theory can be used to explain the behaviour of terrorist groups, without suggesting that they can be equated with groups that adhere to non-violent, constitutional methods.[74] These groups seek to undermine the trust placed by citizens in their governments, while simultaneously encouraging blind trust in their organizations that is typically augmented by draconian controls. Building relationships of trust was used to alter an individual's worldview, making any communication and diplomacy between the groups and state extremely challenging. This situation has been further complicated by the disruption of social movements into the discussions. The public has voiced its disgust of the terrorist groups and their deadly conduct, while also raising concerns about human rights, drone killings, and women and children held in camps.

Diplomacy in the twenty-first century

Accordingly, diplomacy is no longer confined to governing elites in the corridors of power:[75] anyone with a smartphone can instantly reach a global audience in order to share content, voice opinions and encourage action.[76] Technologically empowered individuals now have an unprecedented ability to disrupt the political process locally, nationally and internationally – thereby, some have suggested, hammering the final nail in the coffin of 'Ferrero Rocher' and 'Kodak' diplomacy.[77]

What began with Woodrow Wilson's 'new diplomacy' after the First World War, which exposed diplomacy to the fourth estate and public opinion,[78] has now reached its logical conclusion. In a world where information and communication are increasingly democratized, diplomacy must adapt and innovate as diplomacy has shifted from the traditional, bilateral and ambassadorial diplomacy to the novel, multilateral and public. It must now engage not only with other states, supranational unions, religious organizations, non-governmental organizations, multi- and trans-national corporations, and charitable foundations but also, crucially, with individuals who are ultimately affected by the decisions being made. Diplomacy must balance vertical and horizontal, formal and informal, tactical and strategic – and, moreover, do so in a space where secrecy is far from guaranteed.

By way of illustration, we need to only consider the effect on the credibility of diplomats and the authority of the foreign service when Wikileaks published secret cables exposing the mechanics of State Department decision making to the world. Similarly, the ongoing Brexit negotiations comprise a particularly difficult set of negotiations, which involve traditional and public diplomacy – all taking place against a backdrop of competing social movements such as The People's Vote, For Our Future's Sake and Open Britain.[79]

This has necessitated a radical change in the tools, actors and province of diplomacy. There has been a conceptual shift away from *club diplomacy* to *network diplomacy*[80] – from traditional, hierarchical, closed communities engaging in private, conventional, written dialogue to fresh, chaotic, open alliances that conduct public, contemporary, multimedia discourse. As a result, in a world where time and space have collapsed, it has become increasingly difficult for states to lead rather than follow to proact rather than react.

Nonetheless, it is premature to sound the death knell of traditional diplomacy; the need for *good* diplomacy is greater than it has ever been. For while states 'incontrovertibly share the global stage with public and private entities, with whom they must also share the mechanisms of global politics',[81] they remain the most significant actors in the international system: they confer legitimacy on diplomats that non-state actors cannot match, set national interest objectives rather than argue single issue positions, and represent the nation as a whole rather than specific interest groups. Furthermore, the shifting political landscape has led to a diffusion of power and authority that is reminiscent of the diplomatic arena. Diplomats are well placed to capitalize on their experience (many of whom are now being recruited from the private sector) operating in complex environments and negotiating with multiple interested parties.

Conclusion

Contemporary diplomacy is subject to unprecedented opportunity and constraint, with the expansion of multi-lateral diplomacy (e.g. the UN climate change conference in 2017) and withdrawal from some areas of international relations and policymaking (such as Trump's bilateral or 'mano a mano' diplomacy). The result is an increasing involvement of other parties in the diplomatic space and the accelerated iteration of moves. This has led, in turn, to the impression that professional diplomacy is overshadowed by the activities of traditionally non-diplomatic actors who have more impact on public moods and thereby on growing inter- and intra-state politics. Nonetheless, to paraphrase Mark Twain, 'the rumours of the death of diplomacy have been greatly exaggerated'.

It is actually in rude health.[82] Its *raison d'etre* – to represent, communicate and negotiate – is more important than ever as the space of diplomatic negotiations contracts and expands; public and private, domestic and foreign, tactical and strategic are increasingly blurred; and the relationship between citizens on the local, regional, national, international and transnational levels evolves. Furthermore, as transnational organizations have waxed and state delivery of policy has waned, traditional diplomacy has expanded beyond the confines of 'high politics' to encompass the 'low politics' of health, environment, development, science and technology, education, law and the arts.

Key to understanding these phenomena are the changing relationships of trust, which have shifted the emphasis from traditional diplomacy to public diplomacy, from club diplomacy to network diplomacy. Three dominant themes have emerged. First, the evolving nature of trust has significantly affected not only the understanding but, crucially, the practice of diplomacy and social movements. Second, networks of personal and impersonal trust have increased exponentially, many driven by advances in digital technology, to produce a dizzying array of weak and strong ties. Third, while trust underpins intra- as much as inter-group trust, thereby supporting division as much as unity, the former is now exacerbated by growing individualism and the fragmentation of a once unifying framework of trust.

There has always been an intersection of social movements and diplomacy, but the confluence of several factors in the twenty-first century has seen an 'explosion' of this – sometimes complementary often conflicting – relationship. Academia typically studies these phenomena with insufficient attention given to social movement, international relations and political theory. This chapter has done no more than introduce the topic in the hope of sparking further debate and shifting the focus of study. We need a new, interdisciplinary approach to explore the intersection of social movements and diplomacy, with trust a key analytical lens from both perspectives.

Notes

1. Classic theories include collective behaviour, mass social theories and relative deprivation to contemporary theories structural approaches – political opportunity, resources mobilization and social movement theory to social constructivist approaches with new social movements.
2. Carmen Leong, Shan L. Pan, Shamshul Bahri and Ali Fauzi, 'Social Media Empowerment in Social Movements: Power Activation and Power Accrual in Digital Activism', *European Journal of Information Systems*, Vol. 28, No. 2 (2019), 173–204.
3. Extracts from the *Project on Information Technology and Political Islam* (http://pitpi.org/?p=1051). The week before Egyptian President Hosni Mubarak's resignation tweets about political change in that country ballooned from 2,300/day to 230,000/day while videos featuring protest and political commentary went viral – the top twenty-three videos received nearly 5.5 million views – online content by opposition groups increased dramatically. In Tunisia, conversations about liberty, democracy and revolution on blogs and on Twitter often immediately preceded mass protests. Twenty per cent of blogs were evaluating Ben Ali's leadership the day he resigned, up from just 5 per cent the month before, while the primary topic for Tunisian blogs was 'revolution' until the old regimes relinquish power.
4. Philip N. Howard, Aiden Duffy, Deen Freelon, M. M. Hussain, Will Mari and Marwa Maziad, 'Opening Closed Regimes: What Was the Role of Social Media During the Arab Spring?' *SSRN* (2011). Available at: Opening Closed Regimes: What Was the Role of Social Media during the Arab Spring? (2011), https://ssrn.com/abstract=2595096. Examples include: the Spanish Los Indignados, OWS and the Umbrella Revolution in Hong Kong.
5. Francesca Granelli, *Trust, Politics and Revolution: A European History* (London: I.B. Tauris, 2019).

6   Brian C. Rathbun, 'Trust in International Relations', in E. M. Uslaner (ed.), *The Oxford Handbook of Social and Political Trust* (Oxford: Oxford University Press, 2018). See Nicholas J. Wheeler, 'Trust-Building in International Relations', *Peace Prints: South Asian Journal of Peacebuilding*, Vol. 4, No. 2 (2012), 21.
7   'The accessibility of information, normalisation of digital media technologies in international politics, the growing citizens' engagement with foreign policy issues and the acknowledgement that they have been given a voice have altered international communication flows opening up the possibility to target publics from all over the globe'. Paweł Surowiec and Ilan Manor, *Public Diplomacy and the Politics of Uncertainty* (London: Palgrave, 2021), Introduction.
8   'As of the end of 2014, 38 million people around the world had been forced to flee their homes through conflict and violence' – iDMC, 2015, www.internal-displacement.org/publications/2016/annual-report-2015, 9 October 2016.
9   Beer, SH., 1982, Britain against itself: the political contradictions of collectivism (NY:WW Norton & company).
10 Stewart P. Patrick, *The G20 and the United States: Opportunities for More Effective Multilateralism* (New York: Century Foundation, 2010).
11 Mark Kirby, *Sociology in Perspective* (Portsmouth, NH: Heinemann, 2000), 407–8.
12 Mel van Elteren, *Cultural Globalization and Transnational Flows of Things American* (INTECH Open Access Publisher, 2011).
13 Manuel Castells, 'Informationalism, Networks, and the Network Society: A Blueprint', in Manuel Castells (ed.), *The Network Society: A Cross-Cultural Perspective* (Northampton, MA: Edward Elgar, 2004), 1–73.
14 Fritjof Capra, *The Hidden Connections: Integrating the Biological, Cognitive, and Social Dimensions of Life into a Science of Sustainability* (New York: Doubleday Books, 2002).
15 Scott Lash, *Critique of Information* (London: Sage, 2002).
16 Referred to as the 'Access' or 'Sharing Economy'. Jeremy Rifkin, *The Age of Access: The New Culture of Hypercapitalism* (New York: Penguin Random House, 2001).
17 Around 63 per cent of the world population is mobile phone users. Forty per cent have an internet connection: nearly 3.5 billion as at 29 July 2016. Extracted from Statista's mobile phone user penetration as a percentage of the population worldwide from 2013 to 2019 (www.statista.com/statistics/470018/, 22 October 2016) and Internet Live Stats' statistics report (www.internetlivestats.com/internet-users/, 24 October 2016).
18 Lisa Anderson, 'Searching Where the Light Shines: Studying Democratization in the Middle East', *Annual Review of Political Science*, Vol. 9 (2006), 189–214.
19 Peter Steiner's 'On the Internet, Nobody Knows You're a Dog', *The Washington Post*, 5 July 1993.
20 John Lukacs, *A Short History of the Twentieth Century* (Cambridge, MA: Harvard University Press, 2013).

21 Andrew F. Cooper, Jorge Heine and Ramesh Thakur, 'Introduction: The Challenges of 21st-Century Diplomacy', in A. F. Cooper et al. (ed.), *The Oxford Handbook of Modern Diplomacy* (Oxford: Oxford University Press, 2013).
22 The transnational movement Open Russia provides a case study. Anna Popkova, 'Non-state Diplomacy Challenges to Authoritarian States: The Open Russia Movement, *The Hague Journal of Diplomacy*', Vol. 14, No. 3 (2019), 250–71.
23 This trend has result in a shift from public to corporate diplomacy. W. Bolewski, Corporate Diplomacy as Symbiotic Transnational Governance, Working Paper Project 'Diplomacy in the 21st Century' No. 17, September 2017.
24 Enric Ordeix-Rigo and João Duarte, 'From Public Diplomacy to Corporate Diplomacy: Increasing Corporation's Legitimacy and Influence', *American Behavioral Scientist*, Vol. 53, No. 4 (2009), 549–64.
25 Disinformation is defined as 'the manipulation of information that purposefully aims to mislead or deceive', while misinformation is defined as 'inaccurate information that is the result of an honest mistake or of negligence'. Jente Althius and Leonie Haiden (eds), 'Fake News: A Roadmap' (Riga: The NATO StratCom Centre of Excellence, 2018). Meanwhile, the Ethical Journalism Network defines mal-information as 'information that is based on reality, that is used to inflict harm on a person, organisation or country'. Meanwhile, non-information is usually understood to be the absence or lack of information, but it can also refer to something that does not contain or constitute useful information.
26 Lawrence-Camille Richard, *Diplomacy in the Twenty-First century: Change and Evolution, Research paper* (Ottawa: Ottawa University, 2011).
27 Joseph Nye, 'How Sharp Power Threatens Soft Power', *Foreign Affairs*, 24 January 2018.
28 Gifford D. Malone, 'Managing Public Diplomacy', *The Washington Quarterly*, Vol. 8 (Summer 1985), 199.
29 The 1799 law prohibits ordinary citizens from negotiating with foreign powers having a dispute with the United States. President Trump recently suggested Secretary of State John F. Kerry broke this law 'conversations' with Iran.
30 *Too Long; Didn't Read*.
31 Social movements are defined as 'collectives of individuals and groups who share a common cognitive praxis and who use unconventional forms of action and structures at least some of the time to bring social change'. Sandra Grey, 'Can We Measure the Influence of Social Movements?' Political Science, RSSS, ANU Political Science Program Seminar – 18 September 2002.
32 Paul Almeida, *Social Movements: The Structure of Collective Mobilization* (Berkeley, CA: University of California Press, 2019).
33 Going beyond their civic duties and responsibilities they 'make claims to justice … break habitus and act in a way that disrupts already defined orders, practices and

statuses'. Engin F. Isin, 'Citizenship in Flux: The Figure of the Activist Citizen', *Subjectivity*, Vol. 29 (2009), 384.

34 Leslie R. Crutchfield, *How Change Happens: Why Some Social Movements Succeed While Others Don't* (Hoboken, NJ: Wiley, 2018).

35 Carly McLaughlin 'They Don't Look Like Children': Child Asylum-Seekers, the Dubs Amendment and the Politics of Childhood, *Journal of Ethnic and Migration Studies*, Vol. 44, No. 11 (2018), 1757–73.

36 https://helprefugees.org.

37 Jim L. Nelson, 'Global Movement to Ban Landmines: A Case Study in Transformative Politics', in Janie Leatherman and Julie Webber (eds), *Charting Transnational Democracy* (New York: Palgrave Macmillan, 2005).

38 As *New York Times* journalists Max Fisher and Amanda Taub concluded in a column exploring the roots of the current wave of discontent.

39 Noha Shawki, 'Political Opportunity Structures and the Outcomes of Transnational Campaigns: A Comparison of Two Transnational Advocacy Networks', *Peace & Change*, Vol. 35 (2010), 381–411.

40 R. P. Barston, *Modern Diplomacy*, 5th ed. (London: Routledge, 2019).

41 Laurel Weldon, *When Protest Makes Policy: How Social Movements Represent Disadvantaged Groups* (Ann Arbor: University of Michigan Press, 2011).

42 Dario Azzellini and Marina Sitrin, *They Can't Represent Us!: Reinventing Democracy from Greece to Occupy* (London: Verso Books, 2014).

43 Dontella Della Porta et al. (eds), *Social Movements in a Globalizing World*, 2nd ed. (New York: Palgrave Macmillan, 2009).

44 Kim Voss and Michelle Williams. 'The Local in the Global: Rethinking Social Movements in the New Millennium'. IRLE Working Paper No. 177-09 (2009).

45 Marcia Mundt, Karen Ross and Charla M. Burnett. 'Scaling Social Movements Through Social Media: The Case of Black Lives Matter', *Social Media + Society* (November 2018).

46 Mark Granovetter's (1973) strong and weak ties. Compare Robert Putnam's (2000) 'thick and thin trust' and refer to the Malcolm Gladwell versus Clay Shirky debate in 2010–11.

47 Geoffrey Hosking, *Trust: A History* (Oxford: Oxford University Press, 2014), 174.

48 Hosking, *Trust*, 175.

49 The West has 'inherited a nineteenth-century bureaucracy which for all its modifications and refinements remains ill-suited to the task of translating political wishes into practical reality'. Peter Hennessey, cited in M. Bevir and R. A. W. Rhodes, *Interpreting British Governance* (London: Routledge, 2003), 150.

50 See Edelman (2018) Trust *Barometer Global Report* (London), https://www.edelman.com/trust-barometer

51 Miller (1974), Citrin (1974), Lipset & Schneider (1987), Craig (1996) and Miller & Borelli (1991) have charted the extraordinary collapse of trust.

52 Robert D. Putnam, *Bowling Alone: The Collapse and Revival of American Community* (New York: Simon & Schuster, 2000).
53 Barbara A. Misztal, *Trust in Modern Societies: The Search for the Bases of Social Order* (Cambridge: Polity Press, 1996), 4.
54 Trust, in influential definitions, is assumed to be an integral element of legitimacy. Tom R. Tyler, 'Psychological Perspectives on Legitimacy and Legitimation', *Annual Review of Psychology*, Vol. 57 (2006), 375–400.
55 Jonathan Jackson and Jacinta M. Gau, 'Carving Up Concepts? Differentiating between Trust and Legitimacy in Public Attitudes towards Legal Authority', in B. Shockley et al. (eds), *Interdisciplinary Perspectives on Trust: Towards Theoretical and Methodological Integration* (New York: Springer, 2016), 1–19. Tom R. Tyler. 'Trust in the Twenty-First Century', in E. Shockley et al. (eds), *Interdisciplinary Perspective of Trust: Towards Theoretical and Methodological Integration* (New York: Springer International Publishing, 2016), 203–15.
56 Jackson and Gau, 'Carving Up Concepts'.
57 Arnoud Lagendijk et al., 'Shifts in Governmentality, Territoriality and Governance: An Introduction', in Bas Arts, Arnoud Lagendij and Henk J. van Houtum (eds), *The Disoriented State: Shifts in Governmentality, Territoriality and Governance* (Netherlands: Springer, 2009), 3–12 argue it has neither retreated nor been hollowed out but is disorientated.
58 Anne-Marie Slaughter, 'America's Edge', *Foreign Affairs*, Vol. 88, No. 1 (2009), 94–113.
59 Serge Sur, 'The State between Fragmentation and Globalization', *European Journal of International Law*, Vol. 3 (1997), 422.
60 'Mediat[ing] time and space', 'problematising the multi-layered significance of how they are experienced'. Panayiota Tsatsou, 'Reconceptualising "Time" and "Space" in the Era of Electronic Media and Communications', *PLATFORM: Journal of Media and Communication*, Vol. 1 (2009), 11.
61 Sven Beckert et al., 'AHR Conversation: On Transnational History', *The American Historical Review*, Vol. 111, No. 5 (2006), 1459. Their list is not comprehensive, but includes religious sects, trade diasporas, craft associations, patron–client ties, credit networks, kinship groups and mutual aid societies.
62 Meirion J. Trow, *Spartacus: The Myth and the Man*. Stroud (Stroud. United Kingdom: Sutton Publishing, 2006).
63 Buck Sexton, *Occupy: American Spring: The Making of a Revolution* (Washington, DC: Mercury Link, 2012).
64 Social theorists have long studied revolution within the field of 'contentious politics', starting with social psychological theories of group/mass action before branching off into three approaches: structural (Offe (1985) and Tarrow (1994)); rational choice (McAdam (1982), McCarthy & Zald (1977)); and cultural (Thompson (1966), Anderson (1990)). Each approaches their study from a different

perspective on theorists of revolution, focusing a different lens on the origin, social base, organization and dynamics of the movement. They often stress agency, rather than outcome. The result is quite different terminology and a disjunction between the fields of study.

65 Ronald Inglehart and Renata Siemienska, 'Political Values and Dissatisfaction in Poland and the West: A Comparative Analysis', *Government and Opposition*, Vol. 24 (1988), 440–57.
66 Richard Sennett (2006) describes how corporations become more diffuse and decentred under 'New Capitalism', in contrast with Max Weber's (2009) 'iron cage' bureaucracy.
67 Richard Fischer, 'The Peril of Short-Termism: Civilisation's Greatest Threat', *BBC Future*, 2019, www.bbc.com/future/article/20190109-the-perils-of-short-termism-civilisations-greatest-threat
68 First seen in George Packer's *Dreaming of Democracy* (2003), an intense debate surrounds the label 'Arab Spring', due to the orientalist connotations and its notion of being a spectacle for the West. Zuleyka Zevallos, The Egyptian Revolution as a Spectacle for the West, *Other Sociologist.com* (2012).
69 Nicolas D. Kristof, 'Tear Down This Cyberwall!', *The New York Times*, 17 June 2009. www.nytimes.com/2009/06/18/opinion/18kristof.html.
70 Sayyid Qutb quoted in Bassam Tibi, 'Islamism and Violence: The New World Disorder', in *Islamism and Islam* (New Haven, CT: Yale University Press, 2012), 145.
71 The objective was to achieve world socialism and then stateless communism. Nikolai I. Bukharin, 'The Theory of Proletarian Dictatorship and Scientific Communism', in Karl Marx (ed.), *Teaching and Its Historical Importance* (Marxist. org online, 1933).
72 Contrast, on the one hand, the different vision of, and methods for creating, a global caliphate as exemplified by Bin Laden (2005) and the Islamic State and, on the other, successive interpretations of 'international' communism by Russian leaders. Abul A'la Maududi, quoted in Roy Jackson, *Jihad and Just War Theory, What Is Islamic Philosophy?* (London: Routledge, 1995), 144.
73 Neville Bolt, *The Violent Image: Insurgent Propaganda and the New Revolutionaries* (London: Hurst & Co. publishers, 2012).
74 See Asef Bayat, 'Islamism and Social Movement Theory', *Third World Quarterly*, Vol. 26, No. 6 (2005), 891–908 and Charles Kurzman, 'Social Movement Theory and Islamic Studies', in *Quintan Wiktorowicz Islamic Activism: A Social Movement Theory Approach* (Bloomington: Indiana University Press, 2003), 289–303.
75 Traditional diplomacy was highly formal, institutional, interpersonal, slow and usually protected by secrecy. See Geoff Berridge, *Diplomacy: Theory and Practice* (Hertfordshire: Prentice Hall/Harvester Wheatsheaf, 1995).

76 Tom Fletcher, 'Diplomacy in a Changing World', *Overseas Development Institute Talk*, 24 March 2017, www.odi.org/events/4462-diplomacy-changing-world

77 Ferrero Rocher diplomacy is used to describe the language, etiquette and conventions which built up around traditional diplomatic practices, while kodak diplomacy refers to the summits and breakthrough diplomacy of Cold War era. Tom Fletcher, *Naked Diplomacy: Power and Statecraft in the Digital Age* (London: William Collins, 2016).

78 Ernest R. May, 'The News Media and Diplomacy', in G. A. Craig and F. L. Loewenheim (eds), *The Diplomats, 1939–1979* (Princeton: Princeton University Press, 1994).

79 Anti-Brexit protests were primarily played out on online @ScientistsforEU, @the3Million, @Vets4EU, @RemainerNow, @Remain_eu and countless others.

80 Slaughter, *America's Edge*.

81 Richard Langhorne, 'The Diplomacy of Non-State Actors', *Diplomacy and Statecraft*, Vol. 16 (2006), 331–9.

82 Roger Cohen, 'Diplomacy Is Dead', *The New York Times*, 21 January 2013, www.nytimes.com/2013/01/22/opinion/global/roger-cohen-diplomacy-is-dead.html

9

Embody, empower and relate: Emotions in international leadership

Dr Philippe Beauregard

For the last few days, each time Obama had a media availability, there was a mini-intervention beforehand as people tried to help him find the right tone on ISIL. Show more anger. Speak to people's fears. 'As a mother', Susan Rice told him in one of these sessions, 'I can see why people are afraid. You have to meet them where they are.' 'I get that. But more people die slipping in the bathtub than from terrorist attacks', Obama said.[1]

International Relations (IR) scholars have traditionally been sceptical of emotions, focusing instead on how actors pursue their interests and make cost–benefit calculations. Emotions were merely epiphenomenal; they come to justify policy that has been decided for other, more essential, reasons. Policymakers, advisers, diplomats and other practitioners have similarly rejected emotional arguments as dangerous and argued for a level-headed foreign policy. In her book, journalist and former US ambassador to the United Nations (UN) Samantha Power explains how US officials brand as 'emotional' the policies they want to denigrate, as opposed to the cold language of interests.[2] The opening quote of this chapter shows how President Obama was frustrated that he had to calibrate his message to resonate with the public's emotions in contrast to the small likelihood of a terrorist attack.

In innovative new research, international emotion scholars have challenged the traditional view. They found that statesmen provoked anger in order to influence another country's public and elites' foreign policy.[3] Policymakers and diplomats coordinated their response to manage impressions and project specific emotions.[4] Scholars have studied how the cognitive and emotional process of empathy has the capacity to radically transform political situations.[5]

Empathy impacts escalation in security dilemmas[6] and contributes to bridging the gap between belligerents in peace negotiations.[7] Diplomats used emotions to assess their counterparts' intentions in face-to-face encounters,[8] and the interpretation of signals in diplomatic exchanges often depends on fear or anger.[9] Between close allies, signals expressed frustration and led to relational repair,[10] just like trauma might bring a national or international community closer together.[11] Students of coercive diplomacy need to consider the emotions felt by targets as these emotions influence whether these efforts succeed or fail.[12] Emotions not only motivate policymakers to act on their beliefs,[13] it is a key part of the norms and ties that connect them to one another,[14] paving the way for cooperation. Emotions travel quickly and stick to various objects, imbuing them with significance.[15]

This chapter addresses the role of emotions in international leadership at the level of foreign policymaking elites. Leaders take the initiative and inspire others to rally behind their positions. They respond to the ever-changing political environment and try to anticipate potential followers' responses in order to remain representative of the community they seek to lead. Three processes in particular highlight how emotions shape power within cooperation. Leaders *embody* an international position: in their advocacy they represent the community or group that they want to lead. They then *empower* themselves and potential followers, increasing the motivation to act through processes of emotional labour. Finally, they *relate* to followers and relevant audiences – remaining sensitive to how emotionally imbued objects and events resonate. Emotions play a crucial role in establishing how a leader feels representative of a community, in motivating leader and followers to act on their beliefs and helping policymakers coordinate their responses.

The new perspective outlined in this chapter integrates many existing approaches to emotions in international politics, concurrently considering the causal and strategic aspects of emotions to understand what pulls policymakers together. The potential of this approach is illustrated through the Obama administration's efforts in conducting air strikes and making the case for an international coalition to eliminate the threat of ISIS. From the moment the Islamic State in Iraq and Syria (ISIS or ISIL) took over Mosul in June 2014, policymakers in the Obama administration expressed intense emotions. They crafted a rhetoric for domestic audiences and international partners to empower their lead. Obama and his team felt intense emotions when confronted to ISIS as they took decisive unilateral action and built a broad coalition to 'degrade and destroy' the group. They sought to bring people together through shared emotions and emotionally resonant ideas. In doing so, they drew on their own humanity, personal emotions and experiences – for example, 'as a mother' – and their understanding of others' emotions to inform their strategic choices.

Integrating leadership and emotions to rethink cooperation

International cooperation occurs when state policymakers align their foreign policy positions. One path to cooperation is leadership, where a policymaker advocates for a position and followers converge on the same stance. Leadership does not emerge from the sole willingness of one actor, nor does it merely depend on the international structure of capabilities or norms. For example, in the transatlantic security community, French and German policymakers opposed the American superpower's attempts to lead the intervention in Iraq in 2003,[16] while French and British policymakers have taken the diplomatic lead in the case of the NATO intervention against Gaddafi in Libya.[17]

Leadership depends on the broader causal complex including how actors interact with one another, anticipate one another's responses, respond and constantly adjust to both their domestic and international environments. A causal complex explains a key aspect of a phenomenon of interest through the combination of causal mechanisms, which are unobservable processes accounting for change in the social world.[18] These mechanisms aggregate into broader processes, engendering linked sets of events that produce change through time.[19] For example, persuasion is a basic mechanism that explains how one actor convinces another to change his or her beliefs, which can be part of explaining a broader process of policy change.

Research on international cooperation has attempted to simultaneously reconcile the harmonious coordination of various actors and understand their struggle for influence and power. Integrating emotional mechanisms to the leadership process is a step forward to transcend traditional dichotomies.

Power within cooperation

Diplomacy involves both the contest for influence in who will establish leadership and shape the common agreed-upon position, and the willing coordination of various actors on such a position; the power in defining shared positions and the power to act together on them.

IR scholars have focused more on power over others, or structural power where the dominant sets the terms imposed on the subordinates. Barnett and Duvall, for instance, define power as 'the production, in and through social relations, of effects on actors that shape their capacity to control their fate'.[20] They exclude from their definition of power social relations where an actor willingly alters his or her beliefs. They do so because they contend that power concerns how relations work to the advantage of some actors and disadvantage of others, and that power implies that actors' capacities have differential effects in social relations. Yet, a leader might influence people to feel certain emotions, change their beliefs and adopt a given position, gaining power through his or her status as leader, but still obtain willing cooperation from followers. Even when followers willingly follow the leader, this leadership affects actors' capacity to control their fate, and it has advantages for some actors and disadvantages for others.

Recent studies on diplomatic practices have similarly struggled to conceptualize power within cooperation. For example, Adler-Nissen and Pouliot, in their study of cooperation at the UN during the 2011 intervention in Libya, argue that power involves a socially recognized competence which is inseparable from influence, that is, power without apparent coercion.[21] Thus, they contend that in the process of competence contestation, 'other players acknowledge or challenge the skillfulness of a player's move as part of an ongoing struggle'.[22]

This constitutive effect of competence on influence and influence on competence is circular: how can we tell why one actor has more power and successfully obtain recognition for competence claims when others do not? The authors are right that power is not separable from the process through which it comes about, but they leave ambiguous and undertheorized how this power works. A diplomatic practice, like a competence claim, can be resisted, changed or pitted against another practice which would direct cooperation in different directions.[23] A recent illustration is how US President Donald Trump's behaviour of antagonizing close US allies and lashing out at them on Twitter revealed how unconstrained he was by established norms in the transatlantic community. Though incompetence may be an explanation, his behaviour also stemmed from a willingness to transgress common practices to challenge the global order.[24]

Studying leader–follower relationships allows scholars to consider the causal mechanisms moving cooperation forwards as well as their strategic dimension where power struggles enter into the equation. Emotion research provides important insights on this subject.

The diplomacy of emotions

Emotion scholars have built their theories of international cooperation on existing constructivist approaches.[25] Constructivists have emphasized how powerful actors shape international normative structures,[26] or how these structures socialize actors.[27] However, other scholars criticized constructivism for neglecting agency and often assuming that norms and identities directly determine behaviour.[28] In the process of cooperation, actors must decide which norms apply to what cases, whether they should modify or resist existing norms, and how these are to be implemented.[29]

There is a crucial missing link in the explanation from the structure of norms and identities to how actors interact with one another in actual cases. This chapter brings attention to how actors cooperate through time *within* such a structure. Emotion scholars have often imported some of these limits into their own accounts that emphasize notions of emotion-laden communities, norms and identities. Nonetheless, they provide opportunities to go beyond the constructivist conception and its shortcomings.

Affective communities are 'constituted and bound by socially embedded feeling structures that attribute emotional meaning and values'.[30] Emotion norms in these communities prescribe appropriate behaviour and emotions depending on the circumstances. For example, Lucile Eznack has shown how violation of norms of consultation among transatlantic allies during the Suez crisis led to what were considered as legitimate expressions of anger from American policymakers.[31] Emotion norms and their acceptance contribute 'to establishing and maintaining social ties and stability among members of a particular group'.[32] Emotions thus help structure the social world.[33] Emotional discourse constitutes and constantly reproduces norms and communities. Security communities are thus held together by this 'we-feeling'.[34]

Nevertheless, even inside an affective community, there is a wide variety of possible identities, norms and emotional representations that member can use in the cooperation process. Scholars need to study how a 'we-feeling' becomes an actual shared stance on a specific issue in a contested process of coordination. Going further than how emotions constitute normative structures, emotion research provides the opportunity to understand how these crucial factors of cooperation are selectively used, reproduced or transformed through actors' interstate and interpersonal interactions within the leadership process.

A second strand of research, mobilizing *foreign policy analysis*, has focused instead on the strategic use of emotions. Whether individually or as part of groups, political actors intentionally express emotions as powerful 'statecraft tools' in order to influence other actors and achieve their goals. Todd Hall argues in his book *Emotional Diplomacy* that state actors coordinate their responses in a team performance in order to display emotions for strategic reasons. A broad range of official actors representing the state synchronize their behaviour to project anger, guilt or sympathy through 'their language, symbolic gestures, and substantive actions'.[35] In that sense, states can be said to have feelings, to be a group where emotional responses converge.[36] In other works, Hall argues that skilful policymakers like Bismarck are able to use emotion to their advantage through a strategy of provocation.[37] Bismarck provoked anger among French leaders so that they would declare the war that he wanted to fight without declaring it himself. This allowed the Prussian minister to bring German states together in a shared feeling against a common enemy, leading to German unity.

These contributions are essential in bringing strategy and emotion back into diplomacy. Unfortunately, foreign policy analysts tend to focus on state-specific factors and assume that cooperation is an aggregation of states' foreign policies. Policymakers carefully consider outside events as they react to them and continuously interact with other policymakers, especially during international crises.

Moreover, if all states calculate their responses carefully and use emotional diplomacy to project certain emotions, why would any state be provoked by emotion-based strategies? Why was Bismarck able to manipulate French leaders and people's emotions while they appear as passive prey to their feelings? Did German states willingly join Prussia or were they emotionally manipulated? The story of how emotions are strategically employed is incomplete without a careful explanation as to how emotions can also be causal in the international realm. Hall recognizes that 'it is precisely because emotions play such an important role in our everyday lived social existence that displaying emotions on the international stage has value'.[38] In a similar vein, Crawford has argued that 'even the manipulator believes that others think emotions are important and is constrained by emotion to a certain extent'.[39]

A third major research programme in international politics has considered emotions as causal, especially how discrete emotional biases orient foreign policy decisions. Dolan, for instance, argues that frustration and surveillance are two different systems, which have different consequences for how policymakers use information.[40] Markwica develops an emotional choice theory that focuses on appraisal and actions tendencies, cognitive predispositions to appraise the environment and take certain actions based on emotional impulses.[41] Several other authors have studied how emotions motivate policymakers to act.[42]

Not only do these authors focus almost exclusively on conflict dynamics, but by emphasizing individual or small group emotions they bring in similar problems as the strategic perspective. Constituted emotion norms, individual drives and strategies come to life in a broader process that cannot be easily separated. A move towards causal mechanisms and relational processes allows scholars to analytically segment these dynamics while recognizing their interdependence and specific realization in concrete instances.

A few authors have begun to consider causal mechanisms and the complexity of emotional interactions. Hall and Ross discussed mechanisms such as emotional waves and horizontal affective transmission,[43] while Ross emphasized the complexity of how emotions become contagious or stick to various objects and transform themselves in processes of expressing them.[44] In a recent special issue of *Political Psychology* on emotions in diplomacy and security, Lynggaard argues that we need to understand the various positions on emotions as a continuum, and that there is a continuum in emotion research between unintentional, uncontrolled emotions on one side, and emotion as a strategic resource on the other.[45] In the same issue, Keys and Yorke show how a diplomat's personal emotions can leak into politically relevant issues and influence diplomatic relations, in a way that is intensely personal, political and related to interactions with specific counterparts.[46]

This chapter argues that causal and strategic aspects of emotion require one another to work their effect. Emotion-based strategies require emotions to be effective causes of actors' behaviour in order to influence targeted actors. However, if everyone could perfectly control their emotions and manipulate them, emotions would not become strategic. It would be useless to manipulate others' emotions in a world of master manipulators with complete self-control. This would mean going back to the traditional belief in rational actors that are unaffected by their emotions.

Prospective leaders use emotional language in order to directly influence political elites in other states, and indirectly influence them though these elites' domestic audiences who can then put pressure on them. In this process, leaders amplify and transform their own emotions, as well as the emotions of their own constituents, in sometimes unpredictable ways. Leadership is thus a careful balancing act in embodying the leading position, empowering others to follow and act on it, increasing cohesion and relations between members inside the group, but also managing one's own emotion and motivation.

International emotional leadership

In this section, I detail the mechanisms of representativeness, emotional labour and emotional resonance, and provide examples of their relevance during the 2014–15 case of the American-led campaign against ISIS.

Representativeness: Embodying shared feelings

The person who emerges as leader is able to present himself or herself as representative of a broader community, and to be sensitive to potential followers' emotions, all while inspiring them to share the leader's emotional beliefs.

Social identity theory (SIT) argues that members who identify with their group tie their self to the group, and come to see themselves as any member of the group. This matters for who can emerge as the leader of a group. A large body of research now confirms that group leaders emerge and gain more influence by becoming prototypical of the group.[47] A prototype is an ideal representation of something, in that case, it means that leaders present themselves as a representation of what the group should be, of how its members should decide and act. The consequence is that the leader cannot stray too far from what is acceptable to community members and what they are willing to see as representative of themselves. This is why the absence of a 'we-feeling' of community can make cooperation very difficult: no actor is willing to see the other as representative of what they, together, should do.

While some aspects of a situation may enhance the leadership potential of one actor over another, leaders are not just at the mercy of history in this regard. Actors strategically claim leadership, they attempt to anticipate what other members will accept as representative of their community, and they frame issues to best make their case. They emphasize accepted norms and perspectives within the group to increase their chances of bringing followers on board. Leaders are 'entrepreneurs of identity' who promote their own conception of which identities matter and (re)construct identities' boundaries.[48]

One of the key strategies is for group leaders to attack and vilify an outside group in order to cement cooperation against it.[49] This enhances representativeness by increasing the contrast between outgroup members and the features that bind ingroup members together. Of course, groups can also make this outgrouping against themselves easier by their own actions and rhetoric.

In the course of international interactions, leaders must often consider several groups, which may hold different conceptions of their prototypical leaders.

Positioning oneself to be a representative leader can thus be a difficult balancing game. Top policymakers must keep in mind their allies on the international scene, but also their standing in their national arena. Often, diplomats simultaneously belong to several and partly overlapping international communities, including several formal organizations and informal networks.

How policymakers work themselves up to feel certain emotions, what emotions they express and the discourses transmitting these emotions are all important for their chances to lead and rally followers. Group-level emotions are crucial to enhance the member's identification with the group,[50] and a cohesive group will produce members who actively seek agreement with one another in processes of mutual influence.[51] Leaders gain influence within the group through their displays of emotion: displaying the right emotion in the right context, and in a way that resonates with their fellow group members.[52] Marion Eberly and Christina Fong showed that followers share their leaders' emotions, attribute sincerity to their leaders in displaying their emotions, and how followers' perception that the leader is effective depends foremost on that emotional connection.[53]

Obama's emotional case for intervention

President Obama and his advisers were confronted with a complicated balancing game when defending their unilateral air campaign, and later broader coalition to counter ISIS. Key constituencies at home and several close transatlantic partners remembered the Iraq war as a foreign policy blunder that destabilized the region on false premises of removing the threat of Iraq's Weapons of Mass Destruction (WMD). At the same time, in a post 9/11 world, the dramatic surge of an extreme Islamist group, which suddenly controlled a large territory and resources, could not be ignored. It undermined Obama's promises to extricate the United States from the Middle East, and disrupted his plans to pivot American foreign policy towards Asia. The US administration made their case against ISIS by aiming for representativeness.

First, American policymakers justified their intervention through universal humanitarian principles. American action was essential to rescue the endangered Yezidi populations before ISIS could exterminate them. The President emphasized ISIS's barbaric actions, how they were 'rounding up families, conducting mass executions, and enslaving Yezidi women'.[54] Without help, even if the Yezidis escaped ISIS, they would likely die of thirst or hunger in the mountains. Obama stated, 'When we have the unique capabilities to help avert a massacre, then I believe the United States of America cannot turn a blind eye.'[55] US intervention was emotionally justified in light of this suffering and imminent danger, represented in a way that could be universally understood.

Second, US officials did not attempt to reassure Americans and Europeans that the situation was under control. Despite intelligence at the time showing clearly that ISIS was focused on consolidating its local gain and not a threat to Western countries,[56] the Administration depicted ISIS as dangerous, evil and uncivilized monsters. Secretary of State John Kerry emphasized ISIS as 'an organization that rapes and brutalizes women and sells even young girls as brides'.[57] The labels emphasized ISIS as a monster or a cancer spreading in the region, for instance, the President spoke of the 'tentacles of radical extreme Islam'.[58] Rallying followers benefitted from an outside enemy, enhancing ingroup solidarity and ingroup–outgroup difference.

Third, American policymakers tailored their rhetoric to potential followers. They made the argument that foreign fighters who joined insurgents in Iraq and Syria could come back and commit attacks in their country of origin. In the words of Secretary of State Kerry, terrorists in Iraq and Syria are 'thinking about how they can hurt people in London or Paris or Berlin or even the United States'.[59] This frame directly involved European states' interests, but also provided arguments that European policymakers themselves could use and would expect to resonate with their own population.

These elements positioned US leaders as representative leaders in the transatlantic community as they were fighting terrorists dangerous to all Westerners, and standing up to help people in need. It also positioned them as leader in their domestic sphere, as protecting the homeland and heroically standing up against evil. This leadership was driven and amplified by American policymakers' emotional labour, and benefitted from emotionally resonant events that occurred during the crisis.

Emotional labour

Arlie Hochschild's seminal book *The Managed Heart* first proposed the concept of emotional labour. She argues that many jobs now require the effective management of one's own emotions and that this work has psychological consequences for the workers. Emotional labour is thus 'the management of a feeling to create a publicly observable facial and bodily display'.[60] The concept of emotional labour is highly relevant for policymakers who are closely scrutinized and must announce their foreign policies in a convincing manner to their domestic audience and international allies.

In order to manage their emotions, actors may engage in surface acting, where they pretend to feel the emotion that they think is the best in the current situation. Surface acting, however, has many drawbacks. It is more likely that such a performance will fail and be seen as fabricated. Moreover, surface acting creates emotional dissonance; the actor feels inauthentic as his or her behaviour does not align with his or her actual emotional beliefs.[61] This increases stress and psychological discomfort, other issues that can affect the performance. For example, studies on service employees show that surface actors are rated lower in their performance, are less satisfied with their job and are more likely to feel emotional exhaustion when compared with workers who are deep acting.[62]

Deep acting is to actually convince – or fool – oneself in order to make faking unnecessary. Many techniques, such as focusing on some emotional memories, or ruminating over an emotion or an idea over and over again, can bring an actor to actually feel a given emotion. Deep acting is less costly in the long run as actors are not required to constantly feign an emotional response, but have brought their own emotions in line with the appropriate emotions in the situation.

A 2013 study shows that CEOs constantly employ emotional labour. They need to make sure to display the right emotion in the appropriate context.[63] This is certainly also the case for political leaders. Deep acting becomes useful in that context for the leader to work himself or herself up to the right emotion. Deep acting also implies that it is not so easy, once a policymaker has felt and expressed certain emotions, to separate himself or herself from them. Psychological research has found that our behaviour crucially informs ourselves on how we feel, and so deep emotional work becomes part of someone's identity and understanding of themselves.[64] Emotional labour is thus partly strategic and adapted to the political situation, but it also influences policymakers beyond their own control as emotions colour their own perception. What is a strategic power to enhance one's influence easily becomes a bias.

Working themselves up

While sceptics see politicians as manipulating emotions for their own power, there is evidence that Obama and his circle were not merely using emotions strategically, but had intense emotions themselves. Moreover, as illustrated by the quote opening this chapter, they worked to feel the emotions they felt were appropriate.

This determination to make a difference can be seen in the administration's actions. The President engaged important resources in Iraq, a region where he had wanted to withdraw, not go back in. President Obama could have limited US intervention to specific air strikes combined with support for Iraqi and Kurd forces. Instead, after an initially limited effort that was successful in a matter of days in driving ISIS back from Erbil and rescuing the Yezidis trapped on the Sinjar mountains, Obama dramatically increased the stakes with the ambitious mission to 'degrade and destroy' ISIS.

US officials felt genuine emotions regarding people's suffering during the conflict. Members of the Yezidi community in the United States met officials at the White House and the Statement Department to share their stories. Obama's closest adviser, Benjamin Rhodes, was brought to tears in such a meeting and promised the Yezidi that the United States would do something to help them.[65] National Security Advisor Susan Rice writes that the assassination of Americans was 'personally painful', especially journalist James Foley. She met and got to know Foley's mother, and writes that she was 'crushed' when the attempt to rescue him failed.[66]

President Obama often quickly understood the power of emotions in order to provide legitimacy for his foreign policy. According to him, ISIS had made a 'strategic mistake' by killing journalists because it allowed him to mobilize the American public's anger against them.[67] He told Rhodes, 'I see how the Iraq War happened. (…) People are scared right now. (…) It'd be easy for me as president to get on that wave and do whatever I want.'[68] Nevertheless, the President also said in private that he was haunted by the failed attempt to rescue American hostages in Iraq, and compared ISIS with the joker in *The Dark Knight* movie, as agents of chaos who need to be stopped for moral reasons.[69] He considered them as a serious threat despite the fact that he knew, rationally, that they killed 'less than falls in bathubs' do. Emotions therefore crossed the line beyond public expression into private meetings and the decision-making process where they provided the motivation for international leadership.

Emotional resonance

Emotions travel from actor to actor and spread in a way that influences states' foreign policies. While international scholars have mostly focused on emotional contagion, an unintentional mechanism where emotions leap from one body to another,[70] I focus on emotional resonance. Emotions resonate deeply with actors by connecting with their emotional beliefs, personal experiences and socialized identities. Actors thus emotionally respond in a way that is beyond their control. However, because what resonates depends on how issues are framed and dominant norms within a community, policymakers can partially anticipate what will and will not resonate, and thus harness the power of resonance in a more deliberate way.

The concept of resonance has a long history in sociology,[71] where frames of interpretation resonate with potential participants and mobilize them to cooperate for a common cause. Social psychological research has shown how emotions become embodied experience, and past memories and associations are reactivated when people are confronted with new stimuli, including in language.[72] Appraisal theorists have recently suggested that frames interact with personal dispositions in order to produce resonance.[73] Resonance can be both personal and collective: a group of people sharing common values, norms and beliefs may experience similar emotions when confronted to the same stimuli. Combined with contagion, resonance can create 'affective waves' where intense emotions quickly travel from one actor to the other, completely redefining the situation.[74]

Policymakers are not the only actors involved in this game which can lead to an emotional echo chamber amplifying a given emotion: lower-level diplomats, the media, interest groups and international organizations can also add to this resonance.

Coming together

> I think one thing to think about, ISIS in a way was easy, it was easy to generate cooperation. The most important reason is that these guys were so comically evil, so bad in the worst possible ways. It was easy to get support against them. They are burning people alive, beheading Westerners, throwing homosexuals off buildings, killed Iraqi recruits in mass graves. It made our job easier.[75]

The US Administration did the groundwork for their coalition in private communications with other policymakers, including at two conferences, on 5 September at the Wales NATO Summit and on 15 September during the Paris summit. In Wales, Secretary of Defense Hagel organized meetings on the sidelines and prepared what they announced as the 'core coalition' which included the UK, France, Australia, Canada, Germany, Turkey, Italy, Poland and Denmark.[76] Secretary of State Kerry then went to a meeting in Saudi Arabia to rally Arab partners around the Administration's mission.[77] Finally, Kerry travelled to Paris to participate in a summit specifically on the issue of ISIS. Several elements of the US administration's leadership strategy are worth mentioning.

This diplomatic effort intensified at the end of August and the beginning of September. The Administration decided on building a coalition to eliminate ISIS after the emotional resonant assassination of US journalists. The events outraged policymakers and Western publics, and made them receptive to American leaders' message. ISIS helped the case against themselves with their publicized acts of terror, which made opposing the group easier as emotions of fear and anger resonated widely. There is evidence that the impression of President Obama that such feelings empowered his lead was correct.

At the beginning of August, only 38 per cent of Americans surveyed said that the United States had a responsibility to get involved in Iraq.[78] A later survey just after the assassination of James Foley shows that 45 per cent of polled Americans now argued that 'the U.S. must destroy ISIS', a higher number despite the much more demanding framing of the survey question. In the UK, data from *YouGov* shows that public approval for air strikes went from 37 per cent in August to 57 per cent at the end of September when the British Prime Minister announced his country's participation in the strikes.[79]

Another element of the US strategy was to leave a wide margin to other states to decide what their own contributions would be, when they would join, while keeping them constantly informed about their own actions. The US team let France claim leadership and organize a summit in Paris on 15 September. French leaders would be the first core Western allies to announce that they would join the US air campaign three days later, on 18 September. It was important for French policymakers to organize this summit so that they could argue that they had taken the initiative, and not merely followed the US lead. As first followers, French policymakers became champions who strongly defended the leader's stance in the transatlantic security community.

British leaders joined the US effort later at the end of September, most likely because their attention was focused at the time on another emotional issue: the referendum on Scotland's independence. American diplomats refrained from public pressure or shaming on the issue of tackling ISIS, arguing instead that allies were free to contribute in any way that they wanted. At a round table during the Paris summit, Kerry declared, 'We don't want every country to play a military role.'[80] The Secretary of State sent the message that any contribution would be helpful, and that he was not going to ask military action from all his partners. This flexibility made it easier for countries more reluctant to conduct air strikes to support the US stance while participating in different ways.

German policymakers went beyond what their public wanted by sending weapons to support the Kurds, although they declined to join in the air strikes.

German policymakers and their broader public have strong negative emotional memories associated with bombardments and understand these means as illegitimate.[81] Emotions resonated differently for German leaders, who avoided direct intervention while still making their own contribution. German leaders retained their agency in this process. A poll in mid-September revealed that 54 per cent of Germans opposed the participation of their country in military operations while only 34 per cent supported it.[82] These numbers are consistent with the diverging culture and different emotional resonance in Germany regarding the issue of air strikes.

From hesitation to action: Why now?

In 2011, regarding the crisis in Libya, Obama had been reluctant to intervene, in the end following a French and British diplomatic lead for NATO to impose a no-fly zone over the country. In 2013, despite videos of gruesome chemical attacks on civilians, Obama stepped back from striking key infrastructure of the Assad government. He did so despite the fact that French allies were ready to follow his lead in an air campaign. Why was ISIS in 2014 different?

Emotional mechanisms are always part of a broader causal complex that includes other factors. I do not claim that emotions explain everything, nor are they the only factor that structure international cooperation. Nonetheless, emotion mechanisms have a role to explain why the fight against ISIS was different.

In line with SIT, a deep emotional drive should be stronger when intense emotions are associated with the fate of one's group. The campaign against ISIS is the only case when videos of Western citizens' assassination circulated broadly. Furthermore, the initial trigger for the strikes involved the important objective of protecting American personnel in Erbil, now endangered by the advance of ISIS. The ingroup was directly threatened. There was no such threat in Libya and Syria.

Both the emotions of fear and the strategic consequences of not intervening were amplified by the emotional memory of the events of Benghazi in 2012. Four Americans, including the US Ambassador to Libya, died on 11 and 12 September when the US compound in Libya was overrun by militants. In the following months, Republicans in Congress and right-wing media saw an opportunity to criticize and vilify the Administration over the events. When ISIS came close to Erbil, US officials explained, 'We didn't want another Benghazi.'[83]

The initial intervention was triggered when Americans were in danger, and brought forth emotional memories of the attack on Benghazi. The push to broaden action to a broad campaign stemmed from Western journalists' murder. Later during the crisis, French and German leaders intensified their involvement in response to another emotionally resonant trigger: the terrorist attack in Paris in November 2015.

Conclusion

International leaders attempt to embody the ideal of their community, empower followers to take action and relate to their partners and their various audiences when they resonate with shared emotions. They work themselves up to feel certain emotions perceived as appropriate in the context, which in turn amplify their own emotions and the emotions of the targets they seek to influence. These emotions and the actions taken may elicit further emotions, transform the situation, which in turn inspire new policies. Further events may emotionally resonate as policymakers constantly try to adjust, through emotions labour, to what is seen as representative of the group. New events create new emotional memories and beliefs; it reconfigures the groups' emotional norms and ties, influencing future prospects for cooperation.

These dynamics raise important moral questions, such as the danger of playing ISIS's own game by making them look fearsome, reinforcing the postcolonial stereotype of a threatening oriental 'other', and policymakers instrumentalizing women's suffering to strengthen their case. In any case, emotional mechanisms of the leadership process are crucial to understand international cooperation.

Notes

1. Ben Rhodes, *The World as It Is: A Memoir of the Obama White House* (New York: Random House, 2018), 343.
2. Samantha Power, *A Problem from Hell: America and the Age of Genocide* (New York: Basic Books, 2002), XVIII.
3. Todd H. Hall, 'On Provocation: Outrage, International Relations, and the Franco-Prussian War', *Security Studies*, Vol. 26, No. 1 (2017), 1–19.
4. Todd H. Hall, *Emotional Diplomacy: Official Emotion on the International Stage* (Ithaca, London: Cornell University Press, 2015).
5. Naomi Head, 'A Politics of Empathy: Encounters with Empathy in Israel and Palestine', *Review of International Studies*, Vol. 42, No. 1 (2016), 95–113.

6   Joshua Baker, 'The Empathic Foundations of Security Dilemma De-Escalation', *Political Psychology*, Vol. 40, No. 6 (2019), 1251–66.
7   Marcus Holmes and Keren Yarhi-Milo, 'The Psychological Logic of Peace Summits: How Empathy Shapes Outcomes of Diplomatic Negotiations', *International Studies Quarterly*, Vol. 61, No. 1 (2017), 107–22.
8   Seanon S. Wong, 'Emotions and the Communication of Intentions in Face-to-Face Diplomacy', *European Journal of International Relations*, Vol. 22, No. 1 (2016), 144–76.
9   Jonathan Mercer, 'Emotion and Strategy in the Korean War', *International Organization*, Vol. 67, No. 2 (2013), 221–52; Jonathan Mercer, *Reputation and International Politics* (Ithaca, NY: Cornell University Press, 1996).
10 Lucile Eznack, *Crisis in the Atlantic Alliance: Affect and Relations among NATO Members* (New York: Palgrave Macmillan, 2012).
11 Emma Hutchison, *Affective Communities in World Politics: Collective Emotions after Trauma* (Cambridge: Cambridge University Press, 2016).
12 Robin Markwica, *Emotional Choices: How the Logic of Affect Shapes Coercive Diplomacy* (Oxford: Oxford University Press, 2018).
13 Mercer, 'Emotion and Strategy'; K. M. Fierke, 'Emotion and Intentionality', *International Theory*, Vol. 6, No. 3 (2014), 563–7.
14 Simon Koschut, 'Appropriately Upset? A Methodological Framework for Tracing the Emotion Norms of the Transatlantic Security Community', *Politics and Governance*, Vol. 6, No. 4 (2018), 125–35; Simon Koschut, 'Emotion (Security) Communities: The Significance of Emotion Norms in Inter-Allied Conflict Management', *Review of International Studies*, Vol. 40, No. 3 (2014), 533–58.
15 Andrew A. G. Ross, *Mixed Emotions: Beyond Fear and Hatred in International Conflict* (Chicago: The University of Chicago Press, 2014); Sara Ahmed, *The Cultural Politics of Emotion* (Edinburgh: Edinburgh University Press, 2004).
16 William I. Hitchcook, 'The Ghost of Crises Past: The Troubled Alliance in Historical Perspective', in Jeffrey Anderson, G. John Ikenberry and Thomas Risse (eds), *The End of the West? Crisis and Change in the Atlantic Order* (Ithaca, NY: Cornell University Press, 2008), 53–81.
17 Jonathan Paquin and Philippe Beauregard, 'U.S. Transatlantic Leadership after Iraq', *Cooperation and Conflict*, Vol. 50, No. 4 (2015), 510–30; Rebecca Adler-Nissen and Vincent Pouliot, 'Power in Practice: Negotiating the International Intervention in Libya', *European Journal of International Relations*, Vol. 20, No. 4 (2014), 889–911.
18 Peter Hedström and Petri Ylikoski, 'Causal Mechanism in the Social Sciences', *Annual Review of Sociology*, Vol. 36 (2010), 50–4; James Mahoney, 'Review: Beyond Correlational Analysis: Recent Innovations in Theory and Method', *Sociological Forum*, Vol. 16, No. 3 (2001), 578–81; Roy Bhaskar, *A Realist Theory of Science* (Leeds: Leeds Books, 1975), 12, 51.

19 Patrick Thaddeus Jackson and Daniel H. Nexon, 'Relations before States: Substance, Process and the Study of World Politics', *European Journal of International Relations*, Vol. 5, No. 3 (1999), 302.
20 Michael Barnett and Raymond Duvall, 'Power in International Politics', *International Organization*, Vol. 59, No. 1 (2005), 45.
21 Adler-Nissen and Pouliot, 'Power in Practice', 894.
22 Ibid., 895.
23 See Raymond D. Duvall and Arjun Chowdhury, 'Practices of Theory', in Emmanuel Adler and Vincent Pouliot (eds), *International Practices* (Cambridge: Cambridge University Press, 2011), 341–2.
24 See Florian Böller, 'A Breakdown of Trust: Trump, Europe and the Transatlantic Security Community', in Michael T. Oswald (ed.), *Mobilization, Representation, and Responsiveness in the American Democracy* (Cham: Springer International, 2020), 301–19.
25 Alexander Wendt, *Social Theory of International Politics* (Cambridge: Cambridge University Press, 1999).
26 Jeffrey Lantis, 'Agentic Constructivism and the Proliferation Security Initiative: Modeling Norm Change', *Cooperation and Conflict*, Vol. 51, No. 3 (2016), 384–400; Alexandra Gheciu, *NATO in the 'New Europe': The Politics of International Socialization after the Cold War* (Stanford: Stanford University Press, 2005).
27 Jeffrey T. Checkel, 'International Institutions and Socialization in Europe: Introduction and Framework', *International Organization*, Vol. 59, No. 4 (2005), 801–26; Jeffrey Lewis, 'The Janus Face of Brussels: Socialization and Everyday Decision Making in the European Union', *International Organization*, Vol. 59, No. 4 (2005), 937–71.
28 See Ole Jacob Sending, 'Constitution, Choice and Change: Problems with the "Logic of Appropriateness" and Its Use in Constructivist Theory', *European Journal of International Relations*, Vol. 8, No. 4 (2002), 443–70; Vaughn P. Shannon, 'Norms Are What States Make of Them: The Political Psychology of Norm Violation', *International Studies Quarterly*, Vol. 44, No. 2 (2000), 293–316.
29 See Ole Elgström, 'Norm Negotiations. The Construction of New Norms Regarding Gender and Development in EU Foreign Aid Policy', *Journal of European Public Policy*, Vol. 7, No. 3 (2000), 457–76.
30 Hutchison, *Affective Communities in World Politics*, 106.
31 Eznack, *Crisis in the Atlantic Alliance*, 65–6.
32 Koschut, 'Emotion (Security) Communities', 536–7.
33 Neta C. Crawford, 'Institutionalizing Passion in World Politics: Fear and Empathy', *International Theory*, Vol. 6, No. 3 (2014), 535–57.
34 Emmanuel Adler and Michael Barnett, *Security Communities* (Cambridge: Cambridge University Press, 1998), 39.
35 Hall, *Emotional Diplomacy*, 3.

36 Brent E. Sasley, 'Theorizing States' Emotions', *International Studies Review,* Vol. 13, No. 3 (2011), 452–76.
37 Hall, 'On Provocation'.
38 Hall, *Emotional Diplomacy*, 21.
39 Neta C. Crawford, 'The Passion of World Politics: Propositions on Emotion and Emotional Relationships', *International Security,* Vol. 24, No. 4 (2000), 155.
40 Thomas M. Dolan, 'Emotion and Strategic Learning in War', *Foreign Policy Analysis,* Vol. 12, No. 4 (2016), 571–90.
41 Markwica, *Emotional Choices*, 68–9.
42 For example, see Mercer, 'Emotion and Strategy', 225.
43 Todd H. Hall and Andrew A. G. Ross, 'Affective Politics after 9/11', *International Organization,* Vol. 69, No. 4 (2015), 857–61.
44 Ross, *Mixed Emotions*, 18–20; Ahmed, *Cultural Politics of Emotion*.
45 Kennet Lynggaard, 'Methodological Challenges in the Study of Emotions in Politics and How to Deal with Them', *Political Psychology,* Vol. 40, No. 6 (2019), 1201–15.
46 Barbara Keys and Claire Yorke, 'Personal and Political Emotions in the Mind of the Diplomat', *Political Psychology,* Vol. 40, No. 6 (2019), 1235–49.
47 Sarah C. Hains, Michael A. Hogg and Julie M. Duck, 'Self-Categorization and Leadership: Effect of Group Prototypicality and Leader Stereotypicality', *Personality and Social Psychology Bulletin,* Vol. 23, No. 1 (1997), 1087–99; Alexander S. Haslam and Michael J. Platow, 'The Link between Leadership and Followership: How Affirming Social Identity Translates Vision into Action', *Personality and Social Psychology Bulletin,* Vol. 27, No. 11 (2001), 1469–79; Michael A. Hogg, 'A Social Identity Theory of Leadership', *Personality and Social Psychology Review,* Vol. 5, No. 3 (2001), 184–200.
48 Stephen Reicher and Nicolas Hopkins, 'Self-Category Constructions in Political Rhetoric: An Analysis of Thatcher's and Kinnock's Speeches Concerning the British Miners' Strike (1984-5)', *European Journal of Social Psychology,* Vol. 26, No. 3 (1996), 355.
49 Alexander S. Haslam, *Psychology in Organizations: The Social Identity Approach*, 2nd ed. (London: Sage, 2004), 47.
50 Thomas Kessler and Susan Hollbach, 'Group-Based Emotions as Determinants of Ingroup Identification', *Journal of Experimental Social Psychology,* Vol. 41, No. 6 (2005), 677–85.
51 Haslam and Platow, 'Link Between Leadership and Followership', 1471.
52 Janaki Gooty et al., 'Leadership, Affect and Emotions: A State of the Science Review', *The Leadership Quarterly*, Vol. 21, No. 6 (2010), 991–3.
53 Marion B. Eberly and Christina T. Fong, 'Leading via the Heart and Mind: The Roles of Leader and Follower Emotions, Attribution and Interdependence', *The Leadership Quarterly,* Vol. 24, No. 5 (2013), 696–711.
54 Barack Obama, 'Statement by the President', *The White House*, 7 August 2014.

55   Obama, 'Statement by the President'.
56   Mark Mazetti, Eric Schmitt and Mark Landler, 'Struggling to Gauge Threat, Even as U.S. Prepare to Act', *The New York Times*, 11 September 2014.
57   John Kerry, 'Remarks at Syria Ministerial', *US Department of State*, 24 September 2014.
58   Barack Obama, 'Remarks by President Obama in Address to the United Nations General Assembly', *The White House*, 24 September 2014.
59   John Kerry, 'Secretary Meets with Staff and Families at Embassy London', *US Department of State*, 13 June 2014.
60   Arlie Russel Hochschild, *The Managed Heart: Commercialization of Human Feeling* (Berkeley: University of California Press, 2003), 7.
61   Hochschild, *Managed Heart,* 90.
62   Alicia A. Grandey, 'When "The Show Must Go On": Surface Acting and Deep Acting as Determinants of Emotional Exhaustion and Peer-Rated Service Delivery', *The Academy of Management Journal,* Vol. 46, No. 1 (2003), 86–96; John D. Kammeyer-Mueller et al., 'A Meta-Analytical Structural Model of Dispositional Affectivity and Emotional Labor', *Personnel Psychology,* Vol. 66, No. 1 (2013), 47–90.
63   Gerald F. Burch, Ronald H. Humphrey and John H. Batchelor, 'How Great Leaders Use Emotional Labor: Insights from Seven Corporate Executives', *Organizational Dynamics,* Vol. 42, No. 2 (2013), 119–25.
64   See James D. Laird, *Feelings: The Perception of Self* (Oxford: Oxford University Press, 2007) for a summary of how behaviour influences emotions.
65   Helene Cooper, Michael D. Shear and Rod Nordland, 'U.S. Pulls Back on Plans for a Mountain Rescue', *The New York Times*, 15 August 2014; Rhodes, *World as It Is,* 292.
66   Susan Rice, *Tough Love: My Story of the Things Worth Fighting For* (New York: Simon & Schuster, 2019), 420–1.
67   Peter Baker, 'Paths to War, Then and Now, Haunt Obama', *The New York Times,* 14 September 2014.
68   Rhodes, *World as It Is,* 312.
69   Jeffrey Goldberg, 'The Obama Doctrine', *The Atlantic,* April 2016, https://www.theatlantic.com/magazine/archive/2016/04/the-obama-doctrine/471525/.
70   Jonathan Mercer, 'Feeling Like a State', *International Theory,* Vol. 6, No. 3 (2014), 524; Ross, *Mixed Emotions*, 22.
71   For example, David A. Snow et al., 'Frame Alignment Processes, Micromobilization, and Movement Participation', *American Sociological Review,* Vol. 51, No. 4 (1986), 474–81.
72   Vittorio Gallese and George Lakoff, 'The Brain's Concepts: The Role of the Sensory-Motor System in Conceptual Knowledge', *Cognitive Neuropsychology,* Vol. 22,

No. 3/4 (2005), 455–79; Paula M. Niedenthal, 'Embodying Emotion', *Science*, Vol. 316, No. 5827 (2007), 1002–5.
73 Kimberly Gross and Lisa D'Ambrosio, 'Framing Emotional Response', *Political Psychology*, Vol. 25, No. 1 (2004), 1–29.
74 Hall and Ross, 'Affective Politics after 9/11', 859.
75 Quote from an interview with a US Department of State official, conducted on 22 May 2018.
76 Helene Cooper, 'Obama Recruits 9 Allied Nations to Combat ISIS', *The New York Times*, 6 September 2014.
77 Michael R. Gordon, 'Arab Nations Vow Help "as Appropriate" to Fight ISIS', *The New York Times*, 12 September 2014.
78 The Economic/ YouGov, 'The Economist/YouGov Poll', *YouGov*, 9 August 2014, https://d25d2506sfb94s.cloudfront.net/cumulus_uploads/document/kpttc84jke/econToplines.pdf.
79 Will Dahlgreen, 'ISIS: How 57 % Came to Favour Air Strikes', *YouGov*, 26 September 2014, https://yougov.co.uk/news/2014/09/26/isis-how-majority-came-favour-air-strikes/.
80 John Kerry, 'Roundtable Discussion with Press in Paris', *US Department of State*, 15 September 2014.
81 Douglas Peifer, 'Why Germany Won't Be Dropping Bombs on Syria, Iraq or Mali', *Orbis,* Vol. 60, No. 2 (2016), 276.
82 Mathias Schmidt, 'Luftschläge Gegen Den IS: Bevölkerung Gegen Deutsche Beteiligung', *YouGov*, 16 September 2014, https://yougov.de/news/2015/09/16/luftschlage-gegen-den-bevolkerung-gegen-deutsche-b/.
83 Mark Landler, Alissa J. Rubin, Mark Mazetti and Helene Cooper, 'White House Saw "Another Benghazi" Looming', *The New York Times*, 9 August 2014.

10

Gender and diversity in diplomacy

Ambassador Dr Bonnie Jenkins

Diplomacy encompasses how representatives from a country, generally through dialogue, promote that country's policies abroad. The process can be conducted in different channels of communication, including bilateral or multilateral negotiations. Those individuals who are engaged in diplomacy are the face of America in these diplomatic settings. Unfortunately, the faces have traditionally not reflected the country's diversity. Diplomats and other representatives have instead showcased the power held by those with the most privilege in our society.

Making our diplomatic corps more diverse is not an easy task. It requires recognition and understanding of the diversity issue. It involves the acceptance that a lack of diversity is a problem as well as action to make a change. It also demands an adjustment in culture and a commitment to go against the status quo.

Recognizing the need for women and diversity in diplomacy and making the argument for change is only one part of the effort. One must also understand the barriers to entry, or else one may successfully shed light on the problem but never truly fix it. In that respect, the challenges to increasing diversity in diplomacy are not just about why it is important to have gender and other differences in the diplomatic corps. It is about what it means to be one of the diverse people in those circles and the barriers in our society that prevent change. This chapter will touch on these points.

Why is diversity important?

The global community is facing several extremely challenging threats today. We are still trying to understand the near and long-term ramifications of COVID-19. There remains a lack of confidence about going back to normal life and whether another wave of the disease will be back in the fall and winter seasons. However, other threats of a global scale also exist that will continue to grow if there is a lack of attention on them. These challenges include climate change, food and water security, and other environmental concerns regarding our oceans and biodiversity. Other threats, also from greed and insensitivity, stem from illegal trafficking of humans, animals, drugs and arms. All of these are threats that are not the traditional challenges that will respond immediately to a strong military or weapons of mass destruction. They require other tools at our disposal, including better foreign policies and diplomacy.

These are challenges that will impact us and require a response that, in many ways, might be like what we are experiencing in the reaction to COVID-19. Some of these threats, like climate change, will be global in scale, while some like food and water security can affect countries or regions. However, regardless of the origin of any such challenge, these issues do not respect borders, or the people affected. Also, the repercussions of these concerns will affect more aspects of our society and lives than we may envision.

We need to prepare. We need to start discussing how we are going to prevent, mitigate and respond to these issues. A fundamental aspect of finding our way forward is to seek input from a more diverse community. We need ideas that challenge our processes and to find ways to think outside the box, and that goes in the opposite of status quo approaches. We need creative thinking. In other words, we need to shake up how we do things and the people who are in the discussions and making final policy choices.

The status of diversity today

'The count of women ambassadors in Washington has never budged past 30, out of roughly 177 posts. It reached a high when Hillary Clinton was U.S. secretary of state but has since dropped to the usual figure – roughly two dozen.'[1]

Women were not allowed to join the diplomatic corps until 1922. Women make up over 50 per cent of the US population, which is not reflected in our diplomacy. What does this mean? The United States is, therefore, engaging other countries on issues that impact over 50 per cent of Americans and many women abroad yet women are not adequately providing input on those engagements. The lack of representation also means that there is not enough of a gender lens in how policies will impact such a large portion of the population.

Women bring an individual style to the negotiation table that complements the very process of negotiations itself. Madeleine Albright, Secretary of State under President William Clinton, stated in 2018 that 'women are particularly good at diplomacy ... It does require the human touch ... women are much better at having a peripheral vision and also multitasking and having the capability of telling it like it is. Many of the best diplomats are women, although there are men who can do it.'[2]

Women can incorporate many aspects of leadership that are not only focused on power. They can recognize that success in negotiations should be measured in not just what is agreed but the effects of that outcome on many other aspects of life and well-being to the community, issues that are not about power but the human factor. Women recognize more so the costs of conflict and the need to find ways to seek resolution, knowing that conflict is a last resort. We value relationships in a different way and pursue partnerships as paramount in our diplomatic relations. Ambassador Wendy Sherman, the lead negotiator in the US nuclear negotiations with Iran, stated, 'So you have to build alliances. You have to understand other people's interests.'[3]

Women should also be part of diplomacy because of the impact of US foreign policies directly on their lives. In 2019, I wrote an article titled 'Global Treats Imperil Women of Color' that discusses the effects of peace and security challenges on women of colour. In that article, I note that 'I find the need to make my case particularly crucial for communities of colour. Why? Because whether the global issue is climate change, infectious disease, food and water security, migration, peacekeeping, or weapons of mass destruction, people of colour – particularly women of colour – are more seriously affected.'[4]

Women of colour are impacted most heavily on threats to their peace and security. However, they are not represented in the policymaking circles regarding how the United States engages on these issues. Women of colour are not leading the diplomatic negotiations on issues that impact them. There is again a disconnect between those affected and those making the decisions for those impacted. We need to do whatever is possible to increase the representation of those making those policies as doing so will also increase the chances of policy effectiveness.

Diversity in foreign policy is also essential because such policies should reflect the culture of those who are will be impacted. A lack of understanding about culture can lead to others ignoring or devaluing such things as foreign assistance. We need people in the diplomatic corps who understand these different cultures to help ensure the success of efforts in the long term. It is a statement of who the government sees as representing the United States.

Diplomacy is about engaging other countries and working with them, or in some cases, challenging them, to promote US policies. When the United States engages in diplomacy, the people who represent it reflect the trust that the US government has in those leading diplomatic efforts. When a country sends its diplomats overseas for negotiations, and when those individuals sit across the table from officials who represent the United States, that person or persons must include women and other vulnerable communities. The United States must make a statement in that way about the value of diversity in its government.

Since I started working in diplomatic settings and representing the United States in international negotiations, I recognized that I was, for the majority of the time, not only the only person of colour or black woman or woman in the US delegation. I was sometimes the only person with those backgrounds in the room of global officials from other countries. There is a 'burden' one carries in those situations, when one feels one is automatically representing an entire race or gender to individuals who may have their own prejudices or stereotypes and bring those attitudes into these negotiations. So, one does not know what that person or persons may say or do based on those biases.

Depending upon those discussions, one may therefore need to work in a situation where there is prejudice. Dealing with being professional, doing one's job to represent the United States, while talking to someone who has his or her issues of discrimination is certainly extra work. However, women or people from other vulnerable communities must be at that table despite the difficulty. Just being there in itself is a statement that the United States sees that person as capable of representing the United States. That is something those with attitudes of discrimination cannot take away from that person or the US government.

There is a different dynamic as a woman or person of colour in these situations. Ann Townes notes this well when she says, 'You approach a group of fellow diplomats at a reception, each holding a cocktail, and notice how they huddle together with their backs to you so they can continue their conversation in peace. This happens not just once, but several times. It then becomes clear that you are not merely an ambassador, but a *female* ambassador.'[5]

The other challenges of culture

The effort to increase the presence of women and people of colour in diplomacy is a goal that must confront the history and culture of both the entities we want to change and the culture of America itself. While a valid argument can be made about the vital role of women and diversity in our international relations, we also need to address the barriers that exist to bringing in these individuals.

Organizations must confront the culture within itself to determine whether that organization is one that is open to people of different backgrounds and variety of opinions. Whether the government or another type of entity, an organization will not attract diverse candidates or keep them if that organization is not diverse itself or is not inclusive of those who are different. There are many ways that an organization can become diverse, but it must have the commitment of its leadership. The need for diversity must start at the top, with the Secretary of State. That effort must be pushed downwards to all the various bureaus and offices within the Department. There should be a strategy for such an initiative that is sustained and regularly tested to determine if there are positive results.

Unfortunately, right now, the number of people representing diversity at the Department is not positive overall. The recent Government Accountability Office (GAO) report was an eye opener in many respects. However, the results should not be a complete surprise. The GAO reached several conclusions in its February 2020 report on diversity at the Department, which reflect a Department of State (DOS) that has many challenges regarding diversity. For example, the GAO found that though State's workforce has grown more diverse, racial or ethnic minorities are still underrepresented, particularly in the senior ranks.[6] Racial or ethnic minorities in the State's Civil Service were 4 per cent to 29 per cent less likely to be promoted than their white coworkers with similar education, occupation or years of federal service. The direction of change for specific groups varied. For instance, the proportion of Hispanics increased from 5 per cent to 7 per cent, while the percentage of African Americans decreased from17 per cent to 15 per cent.[7] Also, the proportion of racial or ethnic minorities and women was lowest at management and executive levels.[8] GAO recommended that State take additional steps to identify diversity issues that could indicate potential barriers to equal opportunity in its workforce.[9]

Fortunately, there are several programmes that are bringing women and other diverse voices into the Department of State as well as the US Agency for International Development (USAID) diplomatic corps.

The Thomas R. Pickering Fellowship Program has as its focus bringing into the State Department minority groups historically underrepresented at the Department, women and those who have financial need. It states that it is based 'on the fundamental principle that diversity is a strength in our diplomatic efforts, the program values varied backgrounds, including ethnic, racial, social, and geographic diversity'.[10] Each fellow serves for two years, and when they complete these fellowships, including completing a master's degree and Foreign

Service entry requirements, the Fellows can become Foreign Service Officers. This programme will 'promote positive change in the world'.[11]

Another programme that is a direct pathway to increasing women and diversity at the Department is the Charles Rangel International Affairs Program. The programme seeks to 'promoting a positive U.S. presence in the world that reflects and respects the strength and diversity of America'. Like the Pickering Program, the Rangel programme also seeks applicants from minority groups, women and those with financial need. The fellows also complete a two-year master's programme that leads to an appointment in the foreign service.

The other programme that focuses on the increasing diversity in the diplomatic corps is the Charles Payne Fellowship Program. This programme, like those above, seeks applicants who are from historically underrepresented groups in the Foreign Service as well as those with financial need.[12] After the fellowship, the fellows receive an appointment into the USAID Foreign Service upon also completing requirements.

In addition to these official programmes, the US Department of State has a Diplomat-in-Residence programme. This programme includes sixteen foreign service officers who visit various universities to recruit for international service. They also make visits to historically black colleges and universities and Hispanic-serving institutions as well as institutions with significant minority enrollment.[13]

These programmes are significant pathways to bringing more diversity into the foreign service and the diplomatic corps. They all remain as relevant today as when they were first envisioned, particularly as we see that there is still more work to be done. These programmes will help to prepare America for the future to address global threats as they help to diversify foreign policy institutions and the voices at the table. However, there remains an issue with retention of these fellows and other qualified diverse individuals, which the GAO report highlights. The lack of women and people of colour at the higher levels at State speaks for itself. The GAO report noted discrepancies in midcareer promotion of racial or ethnic minorities relative to whites.

Another culture that one must recognize when working to increase diversity is the culture of America itself. There are many barriers that women and other vulnerable communities face all their lives. These racial, gender and other obstacles serve to make it challenging to achieve the diversity that organizations wish to gain. The point here is not that an organization can take on the sizeable cultural aspect of racism in America. However, it is essential to take these other cultural barriers into consideration when promoting diversity and inclusion in the programmes that State engages to ensure inclusivity. For example, role models are essential, but particularly for a community that does not see itself in diplomatic circles. Young people need to be able to envision themselves in these communities. When women and people of colour see people speaking on foreign policy issues, they do not see enough or, in some cases, any diversity. There need to be role models for women and people of colour to empower them to pursue a career in diplomacy, who can assist them in excelling in their careers.

In the recently released 'Feminist Foreign Policy Report', it was noted that it is essential to empower young girls and women into the field of diplomacy. 'Improved political, security, and socio-economic outcomes when girls and women are healthy, educated, and able to enjoy equal opportunities and access to their human rights.'[14] Part of ensuring we have women and other diverse communities playing a role in international relations and diplomacy is do what is possible to provide the tools so they can continue to be in these roles in the future.

UNSCR 1325 (2000)

Gender and diversity in diplomacy can be viewed from another, related lens as well, and one we want to build on in the future. UNSCR 1325, adopted in 2000, recognizes the critical role that women play in promoting peace and in peace negotiations. Specifically, UNSCR 1325 'urges all actors to increase the participation of women and incorporate gender perspectives in all United Nations peace and security efforts. It also calls on all parties to conflict to take special measures to protect women and girls from gender-based violence'.[15] This resolution has brought increased attention to the critical role that women play in conflict resolution, peacebuilding and peacekeeping, and that despite that fact, women are again seldom included. This is problematic not only because a large part of society is not involved in the aspects of peace, but because, as noted earlier, women are so much more impacted by wars and conflicts. It is only logical that they be included in discussions about peace, of which they have such a keen interest in maintaining. It has also been shown that when women are included in peace negotiations, it is more likely that such peace will remain. According to the Council on Foreign Relations, the participation of civil society groups, including women's organizations, makes a peace agreement 64 per cent less likely to fail.[16] Also, when women participate in peace processes, the resulting agreement is 35 per cent more likely to last at least fifteen years.[17] Higher levels of gender equality are associated with a lower propensity for conflict, both between and within states.[18]

In this respect, there has been new energy by the United States on the implementation of UNSCR 1325 that we must continue. This year is the twentieth anniversary of the resolution. The United States has sought to incorporate UNSCR 1325 through its US National Action Plan (NAP) on Women, Peace and Security. This action plan was launched in 2011 and then again in 2016. The United States went on to pass in 2017 the Women, Peace, and Security Act and the National Strategy on Women, Peace and Security of 2019.[19] These domestic actions to help implement UNSCR 1325 should be part of any policy development in the United States regarding the role of women in peacebuilding and reflected in our own concepts of diplomacy, both at the United States and other levels of representation around the world. This lens of empowerment of women and diverse communities should permeate all our thinking on the way forward.

Conclusion

The United States should increase the diversity of people in the diplomatic corps to better prepare for the challenges facing the United States and global community. As noted earlier, we need to include more diverse and wide-ranging viewpoints and opinions into our discussions on how to deal with today's and future challenges. We can no longer afford to have discussions within a small group of select people, nor can we sit back and watch group thinks by people who all see the world the same way. We need to include voices that are not at the table yet are most impacted by these challenges. COVID-19 is a wake-up call to the global community for many reasons. It should also be a time for the State Department to make changes to have a more inclusive diplomatic corp.

Therefore, it would make sense that the US government, including the Department of State, combined with the findings from the GAO report, take an active role in bringing more diverse voices into their ranks. There is no excuse at this moment in time not to do so and, in fact, it can even be argued to be inexcusable not to seek a change for the betterment of our diplomatic efforts. Any process dedicated to increase diversity must also consider the cultural challenges that exist within organizations and society. Programmes to promote diversity should incorporate this knowledge into their processes and must include efforts that will promote inclusion.

Finally, noted in this article are some of the findings from the GAO report on the Department of State. We as a country need to improve on the numbers reflecting diversity at the Department. We just need to do it. We have the study, and we have the evidence. Now we need to make something happen. When there is no change, that reflects a lack of understanding, appreciation or interest in improving the situation. Change can happen if there is a commitment to do so.

Notes

1. 'Female Ambassadors to U.S. Make Strides, although Progress Uneven', *The Washington Diplomat*, March 2019, https://washdiplomat.com/index.php?option=com_content&view=article&id=19366:female-ambassadors-to-us-make-strides-although-progress-uneven&catid=1582&Itemid=428
2. 'Madeleine Albright: "Many of the Best Diplomats,"' *The World*, January 2018, https://www.pri.org/stories/2018-01-25/madeleine-albright-many-best-diplomats-are-women
3. Ibid.
4. 'Global Threats Imperil Women of Color', *Outrider Foundation*, 2019, https://outrider.org/climate-change/articles/global-threats-imperil-women-color/
5. 'Female Diplomats Clash with Male Norms', *Wallenberg Foundation*, https://kaw.wallenberg.org/en/research/female-diplomats-clash-male-norms
6. 'GAO Report: State Department Report', February 2020, https://www.gao.gov/products/GAO-20-237
7. Ibid.
8. Ibid.
9. https://www.gao.gov/assets/710/704050.pdf
10. 'Pickering Foreign Affairs Program', https://pickeringfellowship.org/
11. Ibid.
12. 'Payne International Development Fellowship', https://www.paynefellows.org/
13. 'GAO Report: State Department', https://www.gao.gov/assets/710/704049.pdf
14. The White House, 'Women's Global Development and Prosperity Initiative', *The White House*, 2019, https://www.whitehouse.gov/wgdp/
15. 'Landmark Resolution on Women, Peace and Security', https://www.un.org/womenwatch/osagi/wps/
16. 'Women's Participation in Peace Processes', January 2019, https://www.cfr.org/interactive/womens-participation-in-peace-processes
17. Ibid.
18. Ibid.
19. The White House, 'United States Strategy on Women, Peace, and Security', *The White House*, 2019, https://www.whitehouse.gov/wp-content/uploads/2019/06/WPS-Strategy-FINAL-PDF-6.11.19.pd

Conclusion

Professor Jack Spence, Dr Claire Yorke and Dr Alastair Masser

Diplomacy has an expansive reach. As the chapters in these two volumes demonstrate, diplomacy touches many parts of our lives and encompasses a wide array of actors and issues. Despite their focus on new perspectives, these volumes show that diplomacy has not fundamentally changed, nor are we facing something entirely new. Instead, these chapters illustrate that diplomacy is a constant process of continuity and evolution. The central tenets of diplomacy remain integral to its function – the art of exercising different forms of power and influence, dialogue, communication, negotiation, the management of order and the pursuit of interests. Yet these are shaped by changes to the nature of power, shifts in technology, the need to incorporate a wider range of voices in the international space, the nature of political leadership and public will, and the power of identities. Critical to effective diplomacy, therefore is the ability and willingness to adapt to, and manage, change.

These volumes were not designed to showcase any one point of view. All contributors were asked to look at the future of diplomacy and share their expertise and offer perspectives on what is new, or what should be seen in a different light. The result is a mixture of theoretical and methodological chapters, and an innovative and engaging array of approaches to traditional topics of study. What emerge in the process are certain common themes.

Although diplomacy is often seen through great power relations, these chapters have shown how power is shifting. We are in a more multi-lateral age, with the power of the United States in question, and the prospect of a rise of China. China has already tried to step in where the United States has stepped back, and this has been reinforced most recently with its attempts to deliver aid to countries struggling with the pandemic.

Beyond the great power focus, we need to look more at the space between them, and how smaller states leverage their own power to achieve strategic objectives or gain influence in international relations. Under President Trump, some small states have turned away from American guarantees of aid or security, and only time will tell if these shifts are enduring. Under the Trump administration, and with the progression of Brexit, transatlantic and European alliances have been strained. The pandemic has revealed divides in how countries respond to crises and seek to protect their citizens, either alone or in concert with others.

Samir Puri reveals the limitations of US power in his chapter where he details how proxy wars in Ukraine and Syria are being used to expand the influence of other states. More needs to be done to understand why states such as Russia seek to use proxy wars, not just operationally, but as diplomatic and political tools with far-reaching implications for international relations.

This speaks, to how 'Western' approaches to war and diplomacy are too restrictive. As Ofer Fridman articulates, with a Western-centric focus, academics and practitioners can fail to understand how different actors view the international space and operate from diverse base assumptions. Whether it is information war, or power, or success, how we define these concepts needs to account for other states' different definitions and meanings as they have implications for its conduct and its aim.

Alliances are strategic pillars that aid the process of diplomacy, facilitate the resolution of disputes and help countries adapt to the certainty of change. As Alastair Masser argues, today's new strategic threat environment has created an imperative for cooperation among nations states. Nations have been forced to engineer a faster and more nuanced response to the insecurity that confronts them, ensuring that a greater degree of security cooperation between nations is now not just desirable but essential. Threats are simply too numerous, concealed and disparate to be monitored and countered effectively by a single state, regardless of the scale of their resources. This also leads to greater cooperation with non-state actors and organizations who are powerful actors in their own right, and able to reach different audiences or coordinate responses.

Although diplomacy is led by diplomats, political leaders are integral to diplomatic initiatives. Whether leading summits and building personal relationships with foreign counterparts, setting the foreign policy agenda, or gaining popular support for their policies, there have been shifts in political leadership, and in the values associated with efficacy and diplomatic success. The 'strongman' style of politics that has accompanied a rise in populism has proved less effective at managing a global health crisis, and forms of leadership rooted in emotional intelligence and cooperation have come to the fore.

Philippe Beauregard demonstrates how leaders use emotions, and *emotional labour*, in the construction and response to diplomatic challenges. Leaders are able to connect to their allies, and their publics through the mechanisms of emotions and the responses and attachments they provoke, such as anger, moral outrage or compassion. The study of emotions is an important element in revealing some of the motivating forces at play in why some initiatives succeed in gaining support while others fail. This connects to the recurrent themes throughout these two volumes of identity and foreign policy values.

Identities go beyond the traditional idea of the nation state. Harris Kuemmerle examines how leaders harness environmental identities as a part of diplomatic initiatives. These identities are both domestic and international, aligning with political parties and global ideas of community. Although the emergence of identities can take time, they can shape political will, and influence policy priorities. It will be interesting to see what new identities emerge as the world recovers from the pandemic. Will there be new forms of collective identity? And what will it mean for international approaches to diplomatic cooperation and global health? As well as for the pressing concerns of climate change?

Given the power of identity, we need to stop looking at other countries through a Western lens, but understand other countries as they understand themselves in order to cultivate more responsive and country-specific policies. Embracing plurality and tolerating difference are key to good diplomacy. At a national level, such an approach has powerful implications for diplomacy's practice and conduct. As Bonnie Jenkins demonstrates, more needs to be done to increase diversity and representation among the diplomatic cadre to be more reflective of the societies they serve and bring new ways of thinking into the service

At an international level, as many of the chapters in these two volumes demonstrate, there is a wider array of actors than ever before. They offer new channels and domains for diplomatic encounters, and can use their networks to champion certain issues: whether that is human rights, or climate change, or restrictions on movement. The power of these groups to affect change is in part to do with whom the public trust, and why certain messages resonate with the public more than others. This is especially relevant given concerns over the spread of disinformation, misinformation and fake news, and its ability to undermine social cohesion, disrupt elections or democratic processes. Greater focus on where trust lies, and the power it holds, can help understand the future course of diplomacy. It poses questions for the role of social media companies, who have growing power in this space, and who moderate content, and provide a platform for disparate groups to disseminate their messages and reach international audiences. Moreover, it forces governments and those in power to reflect on how they can better engage with publics and cultivate trust. What does this mean for transparency, communications and the nature of open diplomacy?

As has been illustrated repeatedly, technology has further democratized diplomacy and expanded the reach of official figures. Twitter connects President Trump to statesmen and supporters alike, or enables people to highlight the plight of refugees or seek support after a disaster. Although the reach of communications has expanded and time and distance between people around the world has shrunk, this is not entirely new. The public have long been a part of diplomacy and the politics that surrounds it. What is often not examined is how public narratives and perceptions of diplomacy differ to the official line. Thomas Colley's investigation of the British public's understanding of British diplomacy reveals how many in the public still view diplomacy as an elite, private and secret domain. Their perceptions of British foreign policy can often be rooted in myths that no longer reflect reality. This can have a detrimental impact on the conduct of diplomacy and the legitimacy accorded to diplomatic initiatives. It can also enable certain groups to exploit or take advantage of powerful stories for their own political ends.

For diplomats and practitioners, engagement with citizens is critical to aiding the democratization of diplomacy. As Negah Angah and Inga Trauthig make clear, the Arab Spring revealed the power of social media and the corresponding importance of enhancing public diplomacy and engagement. Yet the advent of social media and its widespread popularity have also highlighted the rigidity of traditional structures of diplomacy, which have make it slow to react in a timely manner to events that that unfold rapidly and, increasingly, publicly.

However, it means more needs to be done to understand the different ways people view diplomacy and their role in it – how it has an impact on their lives, and what stories, assumptions and myths give meaning to the actions of the state. Such understanding will help governments to gain greater legitimacy in their foreign policy and help publics make more informed decision, which facilitates accountability and fosters more active and engaged societies.

For scholars and practitioners alike, our understanding of diplomacy is enhanced by learning from the past. Not for concrete lessons or definitive analogies, but for different ways of viewing the world around us. Historical analogies inform many approaches to diplomacy. Yet by looking beyond the traditional stories we tell, such as that appeasement is bad because we have learnt Neville Chamberlain's lesson, we might find different cases and examples that shine new light on contemporary problems, as Andrew Ehrhardt's chapter reveals. His account of Lord Lansdowne details the power of diplomats and individuals to change the direction of diplomacy and create a different vision for a country's role in the world. In part, this involves looking to how other countries manage change, while recognizing a country's own relative weaknesses and shortcomings. In addition, it reinforces ideas about the proper conduct of diplomacy that involves a certain level of formality, decency and norms of proper behaviour, even as diplomacy embraces informality in the process of becoming more accessible.

Diplomacy is more relevant now than ever. Given the scale of challenges we face, and their transnational nature – climate change, pandemics, cyber, terrorism, migration etc. – we need continued engagement between states and the many actors in the diplomatic space to be able to anticipate threats, to be adaptable to the new risks that destabilize society, and to have in place the relations that enable us to weather the storms and collaborate.

Crises, as the infamous maxim goes, offers unique opportunities. In light of recent events and developments in diplomacy, there is a need for new ways to adapt to change. Scholars and practitioners alike have opportunities to be innovative, to think creatively about strategy and find new approaches to address contemporary challenges, while also anchoring ourselves in something practical and real. We also have to accept that such change takes time and innovation is a long-term commitment rather than a short-term solution.

Change is constant, and progress is possible. We cannot go back, nor reclaim a lost age. New perspectives encourage us to look ahead, to widen the aperture of what we see as real, and what we imagine is possible.

Select bibliography

Abrahamsen, R. and Michael Williams, 'Security beyond the State: Global Security Assemblages in International Politics', *International Political Sociology* 3 (2009): 1–17.

Adelmann, M., 'Quiet Diplomacy: The Reasons behind Mbeki's Zimbabwe Policy', *Africa Spectrum* 39, no. 2 (2004): 249–76.

Adler, E. and V. Pouliot (eds), *International Practices* (Cambridge: Cambridge University Press, 2011).

Adler-Nissen, R. and V. Pouliot, 'Power in Practice: Negotiating the International Intervention in Libya', *European Journal of International Relations* 20, no. 4 (2014): 889–911.

Baram, A., 'Deterrence Lessons from Iraq', *Foreign Affairs* 91, no. 4 (July/August 2012): 76–90.

Barnett, B. and R. Duvall, 'Power in International Politics', *International Organization* 59, no. 1 (2005): 39–75.

Barston, R., *Modern Diplomacy*, 4th ed. (Oxon: Routledge, 2019).

Bellamy, Alex J., 'The Humanisation of Security? Towards an International Human Protection Regime', *European Journal of International Security* 1, no. 1 (2016): 112–33.

Bergman, R., *Rise and Kill First: The Secret History of Israel's Targeted Assassinations* (London: John Murray, 2019).

Berridge, G. R., *Diplomacy: Theory and Practice* (New York City: Springer, 2015).

Berridge, G. R., H. M. A. Keens-Soper and T. G. Otte, *Diplomatic Theory from Machiavelli to Kissinger* (Basingstoke, UK: Palgrave Macmillan, 2001).

Bjola, C., *Digital Diplomacy: Theory and Practice* (London: Routledge, 2015).

Blight, J. G. and J. M Lang, *The Fog of War: Lessons from the Life of Robert S. Mcnamara* (Maryland, United States: Rowman & Littlefield, 2005).

Booth, K. and N. Wheeler, *The Security Dilemma: Fear, Cooperation, and Trust in World Politics* (New York City: Palgrave Macmillan, 2008).

Braithwaite, R., *Armageddon and Paranoia: The Nuclear Confrontation* (London: Profile Books, 2017).

Bull, H., *The Anarchical Society – A Study of Order in World Politics*, 4th ed. (Basingstoke: Palgrave Macmillan, 2012)

Campbell, D., *Writing Security: United States Foreign Policy and the Politics of Identity* 2nd revised ed. 1998 (Manchester: Manchester University Press, 1992).

Von Clausewitz, C., *On War*, ed and trans. Michael Howard and Peter Paret (Oxford: Oxford University Press, 2008).

Cogan, C., 'Hunters Not Gatherers: Intelligence in the Twenty-First Century', *Intelligence & National Security* 19, no. 2 (2004): 304–21.
Coker, C., *Globalisation and Insecurity in the Twenty-First Century: NATO and the Management of Risk* (Oxford: Oxford University Press, 2004).
Colley, T., *Always at War: British Public Narratives of War* (Ann Arbor: University of Michigan Press, 2019).
Connolly, W. E., 'Identity and Difference in Global Politics', in *International/Intertextual Relations: Postmodern Readings of World Politics*, edited by James Der Derian, Michael J. Shapiro (Lexington, MA: Lexington Books, 1989), 323–43, https://discover.libraryhub.jisc.ac.uk/search?ti=International%2FIntertextual%20Relations&rn=1.
Constantinou, C., P. Kerr and P. Sharp (eds), *The SAGE Handbook of Diplomacy* (London: Sage, 2016).
Cooper, A. F., J. Heine and R. Thakur (eds), *Oxford Handbook of Modern Diplomacy* (Oxford: Oxford University Press, 2013).
Costigliola, F., '"Unceasing Pressure for Penetration": Gender, Pathology, and Emotion in George Kennan's Formation of the Cold War', *The Journal of American History* 83, no. 4 (1997): 1309–39.
Crowards, T., 'Defining the Category of Small States', *Journal of International Development* 14, no. 2 (2002): 143–79.
Daalder, I., 'Responding to Russia's Resurgence: Not Quiet on the Eastern Front', *Foreign Affairs* 96, no. 6 (November/December 2017): 29–38.
Darst, R., *Smokestack Diplomacy* (Cambridge: MIT Press, 2001).
Davis, P. K. and B. M. Jenkins, *Deterrence and Influence in Counterterrorism: A Component in the War on al Qaeda* (Santa Monica, CA: Rand Corporation, 2002).
De Waal, A., *The Real Politics of the Horn of Africa. Money, War and the Business of Power* (Cambridge: Polity Press, 2015).
Der Derian, J., *Antidiplomacy: Spies, Terror, Speed, and War* (Cambridge, MA: Blackwell, 1992).
Der Derian, J., 'Mediating Estrangement: A Theory for Diplomacy', *Review of International Studies* 13, no. 2 (1987a): 91–110.
Der Derian, J., *On Diplomacy: A Genealogy of Western Estrangement* (Oxford: Oxford University Press, 1987b).
Duncombe, C., *Representation, Recognition and Respect in World Politics: The Case of Iran-US relations* (Manchester: Manchester University Press, 2019).
Duncombe, C., 'Twitter and the Challenges of Digital Diplomacy', *SAIS Review of International Affairs* 38, no. 2 (2018): 91–100.
Duncombe, C., 'Twitter and Transformative Diplomacy: Social Media and Iran-US Relations', *International Affairs* 93 (2017): 546.
Farrow, R., *War on Peace: The End of Diplomacy and the Decline of American Influence* (New York City: W. W. Norton, 2018).
Ferris, J., *Intelligence and Strategy: Selected Essays* (Oxon: Routledge, 2005).

Fletcher, T., *The Naked Diplomat: Understanding Power and Politics in the Digital Age* (London: HarperCollins UK, 2016).

Freedman, L., *Strategy: A History* (Oxford: Oxford University Press, 2013).

Fridman, O., *Russian 'Hybrid Warfare': Resurgence and Politicisation* (New York: Oxford University Press, 2018).

Frost, M., 'Putting the World to Rights: Britain's Ethical Foreign Policy', *Cambridge Review of International Affairs* 12, no. 2 (1999): 80–89.

Fukuyama, F., *The End of History and the Last Man* (New York: Free Press, 1992).

Gaddis, J. L., *The Cold War* (New York: Penguin, 2006).

Galeotti, M., 'Hybrid, Ambiguous, and Non-Linear? How New Is Russia's "New Way of War"', *Small Wars & Insurgencies* 27, no. 2 (2016): 282–301.

Gheciu, A., *NATO in the 'New Europe': The Politics of International Socialization after the Cold War* (Stanford: Stanford University Press, 2005).

Gilboa, E., 'Searching for a Theory of Public Diplomacy', *Annals of the American Academy of Political and Social Science* 616 (2008): 393–415.

Gow, J. and Cathie Carmichael, *Slovenia and the Slovenes: A Small State in the New Europe*, 2nd ed. (London: Hurst and Co., 2010).

Granelli, F., *Trust, Politics and Revolution: A European History* (London: I.B. Tauris, 2019).

Haas, R. N., 'Supporting US Foreign Policy in the Post-9/11 World', *Studies in Intelligence* 46, no. 3 (2002). https://www.cia.gov/library/center-for-the-study-of-intelligence/csi-publications/csi-studies/studies/vol46no3.

Hall, T. H., *Emotional Diplomacy: Official Emotion on the International Stage* (Ithaca, NY: Cornell University Press, 2015).

Hamilton, K. and Richard Langhorne, *The Practice of Diplomacy: Its Evolution, Theory, and Administration* (London: Taylor & Francis, 2011).

Hansen, L., *Security as Practice: Discourse Analysis and the Bosnian War* (London: Routledge, 2006), 18–54.

Harding, L., *The Snowden Files* (London: Faber & Faber, 2014).

Harding, L., *Wikileaks: Inside Julian Assange's War on Secrecy* (London: Faber, 2013).

Head, N., 'A Politics of Empathy: Encounters with Empathy in Israel and Palestine', *Review of International Studies* 42, no. 1 (2016): 95–113.

Head, N., 'Transforming Conflict Trust, Empathy, and Dialogue', *International Journal of Peace Studies* 17, no. 2 (2012): 33–55.

Herman, M., 'Diplomacy and Intelligence', *Diplomacy & Statecraft* 9 (1998): 2.

Herman, M., 'Ethics and Intelligence after September 2001', *Intelligence & National Security* 19, no. 2 (2004): 342–358.

Herman, M., *Intelligence Services in the Information Age* (London: Frank Cass, 2005).

Hibbert, R., 'Intelligence and Policy', *Intelligence & National Security* 5, no. 1 (1990): 110–28.

Holmes, M. and K. Yarhi-Milo, 'The Psychological Logic of Peace Summits: How Empathy Shapes Outcomes of Diplomatic Negotiations', *International Studies Quarterly* 61, no. 1 (2016): 107–22.

Holsti, O. R., *Public Opinion and American Foreign Policy* (Ann Arbor: University of Michigan Press, 2004).

Howard, M., 'Reassurance and Deterrence: Western Defense in the 1980s', *Foreign Affairs* 61, no. 2 (1982): 309.

Jabri, V., *Discourses on Violence: Conflict Analysis Reconsidered* (Manchester: Manchester University Press, 1996).

Janis, Irving L., *Victims of Groupthink; a Psychological Study of Foreign-Policy Decisions and Fiascoes* (Boston: Houghton, 1972).

Jeffery, K., *MI6: The History of the Secret Intelligence Service, 1909–1949* (London: Bloomsbury, 2010).

Jervis, R., 'Cooperation under the Security Dilemma', *World Politics* 30, no. 2 (January 1978): 167–214.

Jervis, R., 'Deterrence Theory Revisited', *World Politics* 31, no. 2 (January 1979): 289–324.

Jervis, R., *The Meaning of the Nuclear Revolution: Statecraft and the Prospect of Armageddon* (Ithaca, NY: Cornell University Press, 1989).

Johansen, Robert C., 'The Impact of US Policy toward the International Criminal Court on the Prevention of Genocide, War Crimes, and Crimes against Humanity', *Human Rights Quarterly* 2, no. 28 (2006): 301–31.

Jonsson, O., *The Russian Understanding of War: Blurring the Lines between War and Peace* (Washington, DC: Georgetown University Press, 2019).

Keens-Soper, M., 'Abraham De Wicquefort and Diplomatic Theory', *Diplomacy and Statecraft* 8, no. 2 (1997): 16–30.

Kennedy, G. C. and K. Neilson (eds), *Incidents and International Relations: People, Power, and Personalities* (Westport: Praeger, 2002).

Kennedy, P., *The Realities behind Diplomacy: The Background Influences on British External Policy, 1865–1980* (London: Fontana Press, 1989).

Kennedy, P., *The Rise and Fall of the Great Powers: Economic Change and Military Conflict from 1500 to 2000* (London: Unwin Hyman, 1988).

Keys, B., 'Henry Kissinger: The Emotional Statesman', *Diplomatic History* 35, no. 4 (2011): 587–609.

Keys, B., and Claire Yorke, 'Personal and Political Emotions in the Mind of the Diplomat', *Political Psychology* 40, no. 6 (2019): 1235–49.

Kissinger, H., *Diplomacy* (London: Simon and Schuster, 1994).

Kissinger, H., *World Order* (London: Penguin, 2014).

Koschut, S., 'Emotion (Security) Communities: The Significance of Emotion Norms in Inter-Allied Conflict Management', *Review of International Studies* 40, no. 3 (2014): 533–58.

Kurtz, G. and P. Rotmann, 'The Evolution of Norms of Protection: Major Powers Debate the Responsibility to Protect', *Global Society* 1, no. 30 (2015): 3–20.

Landsberg, C., 'African Solutions for African Problems: Quiet Diplomacy and South Africa's Diplomatic Strategy towards Zimbabwe', *Journal for Contemporary History* 41 (2016): 1.

Langhorne, R., 'The Diplomacy of Non-State Actors', *Diplomacy and Statecraft* 16 (2006): 331–9.

Lechner, S. and Mervyn Frost, *Practice Theory and International Relations*, Cambridge Studies in International Relations (Cambridge: Cambridge University Press, 2018).

Lomas, D. and Christopher Murphy, *Intelligence & Espionage: Secrets and Spies* (Oxon: Routledge, 2019), 94.

Markwica, R., *Emotional Choices: How the Logic of Affect Shapes Coercive Diplomacy* (Oxford: Oxford University Press, 2018).

Martin, C. and L. Jagla, *Integrating Diplomacy and Social Media* (Washington, DC: The Aspen Institute, 2013).

Martin, P., 'Yoga Diplomacy: Narendra Modi's Soft Power Strategy', *Foreign Affairs* 25 (2015): 25.

McDermott G., *The New Diplomacy and Its Apparatus* (London: Plume Press, 1973).

Melissen, J. (ed.), *Innovation in Diplomatic Practice* (Basingstoke: Springer, 2016).

Melissen, J. (ed.), *The New Public Diplomacy: Soft Power in International Relations* (Basingstoke: Palgrave, 2005).

Mercer, J., 'Emotion and Strategy in the Korean War', *International Organization* 67, no. 2 (2013): 221–52.

Mercer, J., *Reputation and International Politics* (Ithaca, NY: Cornell University Press, 1996).

Mitzen, J., 'Ontological Security in World Politics: State Identity and the Security Dilemma', *European Journal of International Relations* 12, no. 3 (2006): 341–70.

Mohamed, A. N., *The Diplomacy of Micro-States*, Discussion Papers in International Diplomacy, no. 78, The Hague: The Netherlands Institute of International Relations, Clingendael, 2002.

Morgenthau, H. J., *Politics among Nations: The Struggle for Power and Peace* (New York: Knopf, 1966).

Mueller, R. S., *Report on the Investigation into Russian Interference in the 2016 Presidential Election*, US Department of Justice, Washington, DC (2019).

Murray, C., *Dirty Diplomacy* (New York: Scribner, 2007).

Murray, W., R. Hart Sinnreich and J. Lacey (eds), *The Shaping of Grand Strategy: Policy, Diplomacy, and War* (Cambridge: Cambridge University Press, 2011).

Nicolson, H., *Diplomacy* (London; Oxford; New York: Oxford University Press, 1969).

Nicolson, H., 'Diplomacy Then and Now', *Foreign Affairs* 40 (1961): 39.

Nye, J. Jr., *Soft Power: The Means to Success in World Politics* (New York: Public Affairs, 2005).

Nye, J. S., *The Paradox of American Power* (Oxford: Oxford University Press, 2002).

O'Shaughnessy, N., *Politics and Propaganda: Weapons of Mass Seduction* (Manchester: Manchester University Press, 2000).

Pahlavi, P., 'Evaluating Public Diplomacy Programs', *Hague Journal of Diplomacy* 3 (2007): 255–81.

Pamment, J., *New Public Diplomacy in the 21st Century: A Comparative Study of Policy and Practice* (London: Routledge, 2012).

Pedwell, C., *Affective Relations: The Transnational Politics of Empathy* (Basingstoke: Palgrave Macmillan, 2014).
Pouliot, V., *International Pecking Orders: The Politics and Practice of Multilateral Diplomacy* (New York: Cambridge University Press, 2016).
Puri, S., *The Great Imperial Hangover* (London: Atlantic, 2020).
Putnam, R. D., *Bowling Alone: The Collapse and Revival of American Community* (London: Simon & Schuster, 2000).
Putnam, R. D., 'Diplomacy and Domestic Politics: The Logic of Two-Level Games', *International Organization* 42, no. 3 (1988): 427–60.
Rachman, G., *Zero Sum World* (London: Atlantic, 2010).
Regan, R. J., *Just War: Principles and Cases* (Washington, DC: The Catholic University of America Press, 1996).
Rice, C., *No Higher Honor: A Memoir of My Years in Washington* (New York: Crown, 2011).
Rifkin, J., *The Age of Access: The New Culture of Hypercapitalism* (New York: Penguin Random House, 2001).
Risse-Kappen, T., 'Public Opinion, Domestic Structure, and Foreign Policy in Liberal Democracies', *World Politics* 43, no. 4 (1991): 479–512.
Ross, A. G., *Mixed Emotions: Beyond Fear and Hatred in International Conflict* (Chicago: The University of Chicago Press, 2014).
Rubin, M., 'The Temptation of Intelligence Politicisation to Support Diplomacy', *International Journal of Intelligence and CounterIntelligence* 29, no. 1 (2016): 1–25.
Sagan, S. D., 'Why Do States Build Nuclear Weapons? Three Models in Search of a Bomb', *International Security* 21, no. 3 (1997): 54–86.
Sandre, A., *Digital Diplomacy: Conversations on Innovation in Foreign Policy* (Lanham, MD: Rowman & Littlefield, 2015).
Satow, E. M., *Satow's Guide to Diplomatic Practice* (London: Longman, 1979).
Schake, K., *Safe Passage: The Transition from British to American Hegemony* (Cambridge, MA: Harvard University Press, 2017).
Schelling, T. C., *Arms and Influence* (New Haven, CT: Yale University Press, 2008).
Schelling, T. C., *The Strategy of Conflict* (Cambridge: Harvard University Press, 1960).
Schmidt, E., *Foreign intervention in Africa: From the Cold War to the War on Terror* (Cambridge: Cambridge University Press, 2013).
Scott, L., 'Secret Intelligence, Covert Action and Clandestine Diplomacy', *Intelligence & National Security* 2, no. 19: 322–41.
Seib, P. M., *Real-Time Diplomacy: Politics in the Social Media Era* (Malden, MA: Polity Press, 2012).
Sevin, E., and D. Ingenhoff, 'Public Diplomacy on Social Media: Analyzing Networks and Content', *International Journal of Communication* 12 (2018): 1–23.
Siko, J., *Inside South Africa's Foreign Policy: Diplomacy in Africa from Smuts to Mbeki* (London: I.B. Tauris, 2014).
Slaughter, A. M., 'America's Edge', *Foreign Affairs* no. 88, Issue 1 (2009): 94–113.

Sobelman, D., 'Learning to Deter: Deterrence Failure and Success in the Israel-Hezbollah Conflict, 2006–16', *International Security* 41, no. 3 (January 2017): 151–96.
Sofer, S., 'The Diplomat as a Stranger', *Diplomacy and Statecraft* 8, no. 3 (1997): 179–86.
Soroka, S. N., 'Media, Public Opinion, and Foreign Policy', *Harvard International Journal of Press/Politics* 8, no. 1 (2003): 27–48.
Srinivasan, K., James Mayall and Sanjay Pulipaka, *Values in Foreign Policy* (London: Rowman and Littlefield, 2019).
Steiner, Z., *The Foreign Office and Foreign Policy, 1898–1914* (Cambridge: Cambridge University Press, 1969).
Surowiec, P. and Ilan Manor, *Public Diplomacy and the Politics of Uncertainty* (Switzerland: Palgrave, 2021).
Susskind. L. E., *Environmental Diplomacy: Negotiating More Effective Global Agreements* (Oxford: Oxford University Press, 1994).
Talbott, S., 'Globalization and Diplomacy: A Practitioner's Perspective', *Foreign Policy* 108 (1997): 69–83.
Tolba, M. K. and I. Rummel-Bulska, *Global Environmental Diplomacy: Negotiating Environmental Agreements for the World, 1973–1992* (Cambridge: MIT Press, 1998).
Trager, R. F. and Dessislava P. Zagorcheva, 'Deterring Terrorism: It Can Be Done', *International Security* 30, no. 3 (Winter/2006 2005): 87–123.
Trenin, D., *Should We Fear Russia?* (Cambridge: Polity Press, 2016).
United Nations, Vienna Convention on Diplomatic Relations 1961, Done at Vienna on 18 April 1961. Entered into force on 24 April 1964. United Nations, Treaty Series, Vol. 500.
Watson, A., *Diplomacy: The Dialogue between States* (London: Eyre Methuen, 1982).
Watts, J.F. and Fred L. Israel (eds), *Presidential Documents: The Speeches, Proclamations, and Policies That Have Shaped the Nation from Washington to Clinton* (New York: Routledge, 2000).
Weldon, L., *When Protest Makes Policy: How Social Movements Represent Disadvantaged Groups* (Ann Arbour: University of Michigan Press, 2011).
Wendt, A., *Social Theory of International Politics* (Cambridge: Cambridge University Press, 1999).
Wenger, A. (ed.), *Deterring Terrorism: Theory and Practice* (Stanford: Stanford University Press, 2012).
Wheeler, N. J., 'Investigating Diplomatic Transformations', *International Affairs* 89, no. 2 (2013): 477–96.
White, R. K., 'Misperception and the Vietnam War', *Journal of Social Issues* 22, no. 3 (1966): 1–164.
Williams, P., *War and Conflict in Africa*, 2nd ed. (Cambridge: Polity, 2016).
Wilner, A. S., *Deterring Rational Fanatics* (Philadelphia: University of Pennsylvania Press, 2015).

Wilner, A. S., 'Deterring the Undeterrable: Coercion, Denial, and Delegitimization in Counterterrorism', *Journal of Strategic Studies* 34, no. 1 (February 2011): 3–37.

Wong, S. S., 'Emotions and the Communication of Intentions in Face-to-Face Diplomacy', *European Journal of International Relations* 22, no. 1 (2016): 144–67.

Wong, S. S., 'Stoics and Hotheads: Leaders' Temperament, Anger, and the Expression of Resolve in Face-to-Face Diplomacy', *Journal of Global Security Studies* 4, no. 2 (2019): 190–208.

Xia, Y., *Negotiating with the Enemy: Us-China Talks during the Cold War, 1949–1972* (Bloomington: Indiana University Press, 2006).

Zagare F. C. and D. Marc Kilgour, *Perfect Deterrence* (New York: Cambridge University Press, 2000).

Index

9/11 terrorist attacks 1, 3, 17, 18, 20, 24, 31, 32, 195

Acheson, Dean 13
Aegis 22
Afghan National Army 18
Afghanistan 5, 20, 23, 30, 31, 32, 58, 60, 61
African Standby Force 18
AFRICOM 18
Agreement Concerning Cooperation in the Quarantine of Plants and Their Protection against Pests and Diseases 103
Ahrar al- Sham 46
Ahtisaari, Martti 44
al Qaeda 19
Al-Arabiya 84
Albright, Madeline 5, 210
Algeria 55, 84, 86
Al-Jazeera 85, 86
American Revolution 158
Amin, Idi 20
Anglo-Japanese Alliance 54, 61, 64, 65
Anglosphere 124
Annan, Kofi 43
Ansar al-Sharia 5
Antarctic Treaty System 104
anti-austerity 165, 170, 172
Apartheid 23
Arab League 43
Arab Spring 14, 8, 19, 29, 43, 77, 78, 79, 86, 87, 165, 170, 172, 176, 177, 222
article 5 13, 20
Asian Financial Crisis 1
Assad, Bashar al- 29, 42, 43, 44, 45, 46, 47, 48, 154, 155, 156, 157, 201

Bahrain 81
balance of power 3, 12, 57, 148
Barston, Ronald 4
Bataclan terrorist attack 20
Battle of Britain 128

Bay of Pigs operation 30
BBC 84, 85, 126
Belarus 37, 78
Ben Ali, Zine El Abidine 172
Benghazi 5, 87, 201
Berlin Wall 13, 11
Berridge, Geoffrey 3
bin Salman, Mohammed 19, 81
Bismarck, Otto von 55, 192
Boko Haram 18
Bouazizi, Mohammed 78
Boxer Rebellion 55, 60
Brahimi, Lakhdar 45
Brazil 14
Bretton Woods 13
Brexit 8, 123, 124, 125, 127, 128, 130, 131, 132, 133, 134, 135, 136, 165, 167, 169, 170, 178, 220
British Empire 53, 55, 57, 58, 59, 63, 64, 128, 129, 131
Bull, Hedley 10
Bush, George W. 32, 110
Butt, Khruam 19
Byrd–Hagel Resolution 109, 112

Cambodia 102
Cambridge Analytica 176
Cameron, David 19, 45
capitalism 1
Castro, Cipriano 63
Castro, Fidel 30
Catalonia 170
Chamberlain, Joseph 57
Chamberlain, Neville 222
chemical weapons 45
Chernysh, Vadym 40
China 14, 15, 23, 32, 55, 56, 59, 60, 61, 64, 66, 67, 81, 137, 167, 168, 219
CIA 30, 31
CIS 156
citizen diplomacy 135
civil service 124, 134

Clausewitz, Carl von 36, 143, 144, 151
Clicktivism 175
climate change 14, 4, 5, 8, 99, 100, 108, 112, 114, 165, 170, 172, 175, 179, 210, 211, 221, 223
Clinton, Bill 108, 211
Clinton, Hillary 5, 44, 210
CNN 85
Coca-Cola Company 169
cocaine 15
Cold War 1, 2, 3, 4, 12, 13, 15, 20, 22, 23, 24, 29, 30, 31, 37, 50, 103, 104, 108, 110, 146, 154, 155, 158, 168
collectivism 166
Colour Revolutions 170
Commonwealth 124, 127, 133
compound warfare 31
Comprehensive Test Ban Treaty 102
Conference on Security in Europe 37
conflict dynamics 193
Congress 4, 19, 110, 111, 201
Constitution of the European Commission for the Control of Foot and Mouth Disease 103
Convention on Biological Diversity 102
Convention on Civil Liability for Nuclear Damage 102
Convention on International Trade in Endangered Species of Wild Fauna and Fauna 103
Convention on Long Range Transboundary Air Pollution 104
Convention on the Conservation of Migratory Species of Wild Animals 104
Convention on the Law of the Sea 102
corruption 6, 85, 165, 170
Council on Foreign Relations 215
COVID-19 11, 3, 114, 209, 210, 216
Crimea 29, 33, 35, 42, 149, 151
Critical National Infrastructure 15
cultural influence 17, 127
cyber agents 89
cybersecurity 23

Daesh 177
Davis, David 124, 134
D-Day landings 36
de Mistura, Steffan 45

Democratic Party 108
Denmark 92, 97, 199
Department of Defense 18, 22
Dick, Cressida 17
digital age 121, 137
digital diplomacy 121, 129, 135
digital revolution 2, 5, 8, 92
diplomatic corps 79, 209, 210, 211, 213, 214, 216
diplomatic superiority 8, 123, 133
Disraeli, Benjamin 57
diversity 9, 34, 125, 170, 209, 212, 213, 214, 215, 216, 217, 221
Dnipro-1 35
Donbas rebel republics 41
Donetsk Airport 38
drones 177
Dual Alliance 55, 57, 65
Dubs amendment 171
Dugin, Aleksandr 149, 153

emotion 190, 191, 193
emotional labour 188, 194, 196, 197, 221
English language 126
Entente Cordiale 65
environmentalism 108, 113
Esper, Mark 30
Espionage 15
European Union 2, 8, 54, 66, 68, 151, 175
Eurosceptic 126
exceptionalism 124, 125, 126, 128, 129, 131, 132, 133, 134, 135, 137
Extinction Rebellion 7, 8, 114, 115

Facebook 2, 78, 86, 87, 89, 165, 175, 176
fake news 122, 221
Family Guy 132
Fashoda Incident 55
Female Genital Mutilation 171
Feminist Foreign Policy Report 215
financial crash 14
First World War 10, 13, 36, 178
Fletcher, Tom 91, 92, 122
Foley, James 198, 200
Foreign Office 6, 8, 58, 59, 62, 64, 66, 67
Foreign Policy Concepts 154
fourth estate 178
Fox, Liam 124

Framework Convention on Climate Change 102, 109
Free Syrian Army 43, 46
Freedom of Justice Party 91
Fusion Doctrine 17

G7 14
G8 14, 42
G20 14
Gaddafi, Muammar al- 20, 22, 31, 86, 189
Gambia 65
Gareev, General Makhmut 150, 158
gender 6, 9, 88, 125, 172, 209, 210, 212, 214, 215
Geneva Conferences 157
Geneva II 45
Geneva Process 44
geopolitics 100, 105, 106, 107, 113
Germany 38, 53, 55, 56, 57, 59, 60, 61, 66, 199, 201
Global Britain 127, 128
Global Coalition to Defeat ISIS 83
globalization 13, 2, 7, 11, 12, 14, 15, 16, 20, 24, 92, 167, 176
Good Friday Agreement 17
Gorbachev, Mikhail 153
Gore, Al 109
Government Accountability Office 213
great power 53
Great Recession 1
green revolution 87
Grey zone war 32
Grey, Sir Edward 66
Gulf Cooperation Council 81
Gulf States 44, 48

Hagel, Chuck 199
Hague, William 129
Hayashi, Baron 60
Hezbollah 29, 43, 44, 45, 48
High Negotiating Committee 18, 46
Hitler, Adolf 124, 153
HIV/AIDS 15, 114
Holbrooke, Richard 5
House of Commons Foreign Affairs Committee 18
House of Lords 61, 63
human rights 13, 17, 172, 177, 215, 221
humanitarian diplomacy 172

Hungary 14, 57
Hussein, Saddam 85
hydropolitics 7, 99, 100

Ilovaisk, Battle of 35
Ilyin, Ivan 145
India 14, 21, 53, 55, 58, 60, 61, 64, 133
Information War 8, 144, 146, 147, 148, 149, 150, 151, 153, 155, 157, 158
Informational Revolution 146
intelligence 6, 10, 14, 15, 16, 19, 23, 31, 33, 35, 81, 89, 151, 196, 220
International Atomic Energy Agency 20
International Campaign to Ban Landmines 171
International Security Assistance Force 20
International Syria Support Group 18, 45
international trade 13, 14
internationalism 14, 15
Invasion of Iraq 20, 86
Iran 23, 30, 32, 33, 44, 45, 46, 48, 77, 78, 81, 82, 87, 88, 89, 92, 155, 157, 167, 211
Iraq War 198
ISIL 31, 32, 43, 47, 48, 187, 188
ISIS 7, 9, 18, 83, 188, 194, 195, 196, 198, 199, 200, 201, 202
Islamic State 31, 155, 156, 188
Islamism 5, 17, 18, 195
Israel 71, 157, 226
Israeli-Palestinian war 86
Italy 57, 71, 99, 199

Jabhat al-Nusra 47
Jihadist 47
Johnson, Boris 134
Joint Centre for Control and Coordination 39
Joint Comprehensive Plan of Action 33

Kerry, John 196
KGB 35
Khashoggi, Jamal 19
Kim Jong-Il 20
kinetic military force 147
Kissinger, Henry 4
Kokoshin, Andrey 144
Kolomoyskyi, Ihor 35
Kosovo 31

Kremlin 8, 34, 144, 145, 151, 152, 153, 154, 155, 156, 157, 158
Kuchma, Leonid 37
Kyoto Climate Change Agreement 8, 108, 109, 110, 111, 112, 115

Laos 102
Lavrov, Sergei 44
leave campaign 124
Lebanese Broadcasting Corporation 85
Lebanon 33, 44, 84, 86
Leer, Genrikh 144
LGBTQ+ 9, 172
liberal democracy 130, 169
Libya 4, 22, 31, 44, 77, 78, 84, 86, 87, 90, 189, 190, 201
Lidington, David 128
Logan Act 170
London Bridge terror attack 19

Malaysian Flight MH-17 36
Mali 22, 31
Manchuria 55, 60, 64
Mandela, Nelson 3
Martynov, Evgeny 146
May, Theresa 17, 134
McGurk, Brett 83
Mekong River Commission 102
MENA region 78, 79, 80, 83, 84, 85, 86, 90, 93
Mercenaries 22, 23, 34, 37
Metropolitan Police 17
Middle East 8, 43, 44, 77, 78, 79, 81, 83, 85, 87, 89, 91, 93, 95, 155, 156, 195
Mikryukov, Vasilii 144
militarism 4
military strength 1, 127
Mine Ban Convention 171
Minsk Protocol 37, 38
Minsk II agreement 38
Minutemen 132
Mitchell, George 5
Mobutu, Sese Seko 23
Monroe Doctrine 63
Montreal Agreement 102
Mordaunt, Penny 127
Morsi, Mohammed 91
Mubarak, Hosni 172
multilateralism 4, 6, 8, 14, 15

Munich Security Conference 154
Muslim Brotherhood 44, 91, 177

national identity 123, 128, 137, 167
National Security Concept 150
National Strategy on Women, Peace and Security 216
NATO 2, 13, 14, 20, 31, 42, 44, 67, 189, 199, 201
network diplomacy 9, 179
New Capitalism 176
Nigeria 65
Normandy Format 36
North Korea 4, 23
Northern Alliance 31
Northern Ireland 5, 17
Novichok nerve agent 135
nuclear waste 102

Obama, Barack 9, 32, 44, 45, 110, 176, 187, 188, 195, 197, 198, 200, 201
Occupy Wall Street 170
Operation Overlord 36
Organisation for Security and cooperation in Europe 37
Organisation for the Prohibition of chemical weapons 45

P5+1 nuclear negotiations 82
Pakistan 4, 5, 23, 30, 110, 111, 114
Paris Agreement 100, 108, 110, 111, 112, 114, 115
parliamentary democracy 86, 126
Partial Test Ban Treaty 103
peacebuilding 6, 215, 216
people of colour 211, 212, 214, 215
Philippines 78
Poland 42, 185, 199
political discourse 14, 111, 144, 149, 150
political elites 127, 128, 132, 193
Pompeo, Mike 19
populism 2, 4, 6, 92, 170, 220
Poroshenko, Petro 40, 41
Power, Samantha 187
Private Military Security Companies 21
PSYOPs 148
public diplomacy 78, 79, 80, 82, 88, 89, 90, 94, 97, 121, 137, 169, 175, 176, 178, 179, 222

public-private partnership 90
Putin, Vladimir 34, 35, 36, 137, 149, 151, 153, 154, 155, 156

Qatar 84, 86, 157

racism 214
Reconstruction Security Support Services Iraq (RSSS-I) 22
referendum on Scottish independence 200
Remain campaign 124
Republican Party 101, 108, 109, 110
Resolution 2254 45
responsibility to protect 15
Rhodes, Ben 198
Rice, Condoleezza 5, 187
Rice, Susan 198
Roosevelt, Theodore 63
Royal Navy 56, 61
Russia 14, 5, 8, 9, 29, 30, 31, 32, 33, 34, 35, 36, 37, 39, 40, 41, 42, 44, 45, 46, 47, 48, 49, 53, 55, 56, 57, 58, 60, 61, 64, 65, 66, 79, 81, 144, 145, 146, 148, 149, 150, 151, 152, 153, 154, 155, 156, 157, 158, 159, 220
Rwandan genocide 20

Salafism 46
Salisbury attack 127, 135
sanctions 6, 8, 33, 42, 144, 151, 152, 153, 154, 158, 173, 174
Saudi Arabia 18, 19, 44, 45, 48, 81, 84, 86, 157, 199
Sawt al-Arab 84
Second World War 13, 38, 68, 124
Security Council 17, 43, 45, 47, 126, 154, 155
Security Sector Reform 18
Security Service (MI5) 19
Senate Intelligence Committee 5
Separatism 34, 35, 38
Sharia law 177
Sherman, Wendy 211
Silicon Valley 81, 92
Skripal, Sergei 135
social capital 166, 174
Social identity theory 194
social media 11, 2, 5, 8, 77, 78, 79, 80, 81, 82, 83, 84, 85, 86, 87, 88, 89, 90, 91, 93, 121, 135, 165, 172, 175, 177, 221, 222
Soft power 129
Solonevich, Ivan 145, 148
South Africa 23, 54, 55
Soviet Union 4, 24, 30, 104, 146, 155
Spanish Armada 128
Spanish-American War 55, 62
Spartacus Effect 176
special forces 15
State Department 4, 5, 46, 88, 89, 92, 178, 213, 216
statecraft 6, 33, 49, 54, 68, 69, 79, 105, 192
Stevens, Christopher 4, 5
Stewart, John 91
Strategic Defence and Security Review 16
Sun Tzu 158
Sustainable Development Goals 15
Syria 7, 29, 30, 33, 42, 43, 44, 45, 46, 47, 48, 49, 77, 81, 84, 90, 153, 154, 155, 156, 157, 158, 188, 196, 201, 220
Syrian conflict 8, 45, 48, 144, 155
Syrian crisis 153

Taliban 31, 32
techplomacy 8, 92
Tennessee Valley Authority 103
terrorism 14, 1, 7, 11, 15, 17, 18, 19, 24, 31, 42, 47, 167, 168, 175, 223
Thailand 78, 102
The People's Vote 178
Thunberg, Greta 114, 169
Tiananmen Square massacre 23
trafficking 210
Transitional National Coalition 44
Transnistria 39
Trump, Donald 2, 8, 19, 32, 47, 67, 68, 82, 83, 100, 110, 114, 115, 126, 137, 167, 169, 170, 171, 172, 179, 190, 220, 222
Tsar Nikolas II 153
Turkey 19, 44, 45, 46, 47, 48, 157, 199
Twitter 2, 78, 81, 82, 86, 87, 89, 90, 91, 92, 165, 190, 222
two power standard 56

Ukraine 7, 29, 30, 31, 33, 34, 36, 37, 39, 40, 41, 42, 46, 48, 49, 220
Ukrainian Crisis 151
UN Climate Change Conference 169

UNICEF 19, 171
unipolarity 7, 30, 32, 49
United Kingdom 15, 2, 14, 16, 17, 18, 19, 21, 44, 45, 54, 55, 56, 68, 81, 92, 125, 127, 169, 171, 199, 200
United Nations 13, 2, 20, 92, 102, 109, 187, 215
United States 14, 1, 2, 4, 5, 7, 8, 9, 15, 18, 19, 21, 22, 24, 29, 30, 31, 32, 33, 43, 44, 45, 47, 48, 49, 53, 54, 55, 56, 62, 63, 64, 68, 81, 82, 88, 89, 90, 100, 101, 103, 108, 109, 110, 112, 114, 115, 137, 151, 176, 195, 196, 198, 200, 210, 211, 212, 216, 219
Universal Declaration of Human Rights 13
UNSCR 1325 215, 216
US Agency for International Development 213
US Army 31

Venezuela 62, 63, 156
Venezuela Crisis 62
Verkhovna Rada 41
Vernon-Harcourt, William 57

Vietnam 30, 102
Virtual Embassy 88
virtual exchange programs 90
Vladimirov, Alexander 144, 145

War on Terror 3, 18, 20
water security 102, 210, 211
weapons of mass destruction 11, 14, 195, 210, 211
Weltpolitik 55
White House 110, 119, 198
Wikileaks 5, 178
Wilson, Woodrow 10, 178
women 5, 9, 177, 195, 196, 202, 209, 210, 211, 212, 213, 214, 215, 216
Women, Peace, and Security Act 216

Yanukovych, Viktor 34
Yemen 19, 33, 84
Yezidis 195, 198
Youssef, Bassem 91

Zelenski, Volodymyr 41

www.ingramcontent.com/pod-product-compliance
Ingram Content Group UK Ltd.
Pitfield, Milton Keynes, MK11 3LW, UK
UKHW021906220326
469204UK00008B/217